Praise for *Relationship Economics*, Revised and Updated Edition

"In today's networked world, relationships are everything. David shows you how to build lasting, mutually beneficial relationships. Read this book—build your network!"

—**Marshall Goldsmith,**
New York Times best-selling author of
What Got You Here Won't Get You There and
Mojo; executive coach to global CEOs

"*Relationship Economics* is a terrific guide, filled with good, practical advice for building valuable, lasting relationships that can help you and your organization succeed. "

—**Richard Girgenti,**
National Practice Leader, KPMG

"*Relationship Economics* is about so much more than networking—it's a systematic approach to building and nurturing relationships to get things done."

—**William L. Koleszar,**
Senior Vice President and
Group Marketing Officer, BBVA Compass

"Social capital is essential for success, and *Relationship Economics* provides an approach to enhancing its value. "

—**Terry C. Blum,**
Director, Institute for Leadership
and Entrepreneurship,
Georgia Tech College of Management

"In any industry, strategic relationships are instrumental to your success to drive profitable, long-term growth. David Nour has captured that essence in *Relationship Economics.*"

—**Randy Martinez,**
Colonel, USAF (Ret.) and Group Vice President,
Government and Defense Services, AAR Corporation

relationship economics

Transform Your Most Valuable Business Contacts into Personal and Professional Success

Revised and Updated

David Nour

WILEY

John Wiley & Sons, Inc.

ISBN 978-1-118-05712-4 (pbk)

Printed in the United States of America

10 9 8 7 6 5 4 3 2 1

Contents

Foreword   *The Strategic Value of Business Relationships*
              —Alan Weiss, Ph.D.   *vii*

Preface   *ix*

Acknowledgments   *xv*

1 Why Most "Networking" Doesn't Work!   1

2 The Evolution of Quantifiable Relationships   41

3 Strategic Relationship Planning   87

4 Understanding the Science of Social Network
      Analysis (SNA)   119

5 Relationship-Centric Goals for Revenue Growth   143

6 Pivotal Contacts for Leadership Development   163

7 Relationship Bank for Strategy Execution   187

8 Relationship Currency for Adaptive Innovation   207

9 Transforming *Us* and *Them* into *We*   227

10 Social Media and Business Relationships   251

About the Author   *285*

David Nour Speaking Topics   *287*

Index   *291*

Foreword
The Strategic Value
of Business Relationships

I've long observed that consulting is a relationship business. But then, so are most businesses. Relationships vary in their degree, scope, tenure, and value. Too often, we tend to spend time with people who can't say "yes," but can say "no." So what do they eventually say? "No!"

Yet the true nature of strategic business relationships is win-win. This is not a zero-sum game, or a competition, or a hydraulic system. It is about reciprocating in relationship building while also making sure that you achieve your own best interests.

Organizations move forward by building on strength, not by correcting weakness. Strategic relationship management is an underappreciated, underutilized strength that most firms can begin building on immediately with no capital investment whatsoever.

Relationships have value. If you don't believe that, think about the worth of a referral from a business colleague who sent business your way with no cost of acquisition whatsoever. What if that business renews with you for five years and that relationship provides four more new, analogous business relationships through referrals?

If you think that's far-fetched, talk to any veteran, successful business leader and you'll soon be disabused of the myth. *I can trace more than 90 percent of all my current business in a seven-figure consulting practice to four early relationships.* Most of us who are enjoying great success can cite similar dynamics. I've been in business for 25 years. I haven't made a cold call in 10 years or more.

There is a huge and appropriate emphasis on branding today. But branding is simply a form of creating high-value relationships through the consistent representation of uniform quality. I've long advised consultants and other professional services providers that logic makes people think, but emotion makes them act. Brands form emotional connections. Relationships are the most essential conductors of emotion.

We buy from, hire, employ, heed, support, and are loyal to those we trust, those who take an interest in us, and those who appeal to our own self-interest (which they apparently share). So the question becomes this: Are we identifying, nurturing, and retaining *those relationships that are most important for our business*? Not all customers are created equal. We must differentiate among those relationships which are the most vital for the growth of our enterprise.

David Nour, *the* global thought leader in strategic relationships and a member of my Master Mentor® program, raises this pursuit to an art form. He recognizes the value of differing potential relationships, but he also delves into how to identify, nurture, and capitalize on them.

Where else do you find that kind of potential source of life within your own organization? This book is your divining rod.

—ALAN WEISS, Ph.D.
Author, *Million Dollar Consulting*

Preface

My journey began more than four decades ago, when my dad would walk me through the bazaars of Iran during our Friday errands. I didn't understand the notion of relationship economics then, but I certainly do now. Dad got things done, whether it was getting a plumber to the house that afternoon or gaining access to an influential politician, by leveraging his most valuable relationships in the very real and thriving global *favor economy*.

Within the enterprise, beyond cost-cutting efforts of the past decade, frontline contributors to senior leaders and board members can fuel growth through their portfolio of relationships. This book is a how-to guide. Its applications go beyond just getting and giving business cards, working a room, or getting the most out of a conference. Its focus is how to strategically invest in relationships as your most valuable asset.

In my strategic relationship consulting work with global organizations, having spent thousands of hours with high performers in a broad array of industries, I submit that beyond your technical, product or service, and overall market expertise, your ability to engage and influence others, often without authority, is your unique and sustainable differentiator. Yet most of us don't spend enough time building and nurturing the key relationships that we need to achieve success. That's where relationship economics will create a far greater return on your relationship investments.

The academic notion of relationship economics, inspired by the famous British economist Ronald Coase and Nobel

Prize–winning economist and political philosopher Friedrich Hayek, uses economic tools to study variables traditionally focused on by sociologists. The practical notion of relationship economics isn't about networking. It's about learning how to invest in people for an extraordinary return. It's about exchanging *relationship currency*, accumulating *reputation capital*, and building *professional net worth*. It's about learning the art and *science* of transforming your most valuable relationships into execution, performance, and results.

During my business trips to Barcelona, Amman, and Cape Town, I am often reminded that the rest of the world builds relationships first, *before* they do business. As businesspeople from North America, we're so focused on the business that *if, and only if,* that goes well, we'll think about the relationship part! Even the very language used in other countries highlights the importance that is placed on building these connections.

In Arabic, for example, the literal translation of *bin* is *son of.* One's genealogy, sources of referrals, and collective cultural history carry more weight toward business success in many parts of the world than any product or service you represent, access you desire, or project you're trying to complete. In China, *guanxi* (pronounced *guan-shi*) literally means *relationships* and is understood to be the network of relationships among various parties that cooperate and support one another. Beyond the perceived advantages of an organization's products or services, with the right *guanxi* an organization in China minimizes risks, frustrations, and disappointments when doing business; determines its competitive standing in the long run with the relevant Chinese authorities; and minimizes the inevitable risks, barriers, and setups one will encounter.

In essence, relationships are the gateway to business in the rest of the world, in contrast to the United States, where business is often the gateway to relationships. The world economy does not understand our cart-before-the-horse tactics. In too many global circles, our tactics appear insincere, shortsighted, and even flat-out rude.

By understanding and developing the three types of relationships—*personal, functional,* and *strategic*—you hone critical skills to develop a nose not only for identifying great opportunities but also for determining which relationships to tap for execution, performance, and results. Personal relationships are the easiest for most; they're the ones you build at home, at your kids' soccer games, at school, and with your favorite community friends. These are people who like you for who you are, and your interactions with them take place in a fairly safe environment for exposing personal challenges and seeking insights. The obstacle for many is the inability to bridge relationship *creation* to relationship *capitalization.*

Functional relationships are likewise easily understood. They are those you build at work to perform your daily functions. They're formed with peers, subordinates, and superiors and include your exchanges with customers and suppliers distinctly focused on getting tasks at hand completed. The relationship members are usually mandated by your function, job description, and key corporate initiatives, all of which are typically driven by others. You build functional relationships with those who can support your efforts or help you overcome obstacles. Although they are practical for the time being, this relationship building has little foresight and tends to keep us busy with the urgent tasks on our respective to-do lists.

The transactional collaborations simply won't enable you to see over the corporate horizon or around corporate corners for what's next. They will not allow you to see faint emerging trends before your competition or alert you to early warning signals that may threaten your market positions.

Unfortunately, strategic relationships are the ones most often underdeveloped. Strategic relationships elevate your efforts and thinking beyond your current realm of responsibilities and push you to think about new business opportunities and key stakeholders you'll need to succeed. Strategic relationships transcend time, function, and geographic limitations. They create accelerated access, long-term personal and professional growth opportunities, and new market insights, and they shed light on *return on influence* versus concerns about corporate politics.

As a first-generation immigrant, I came to this country with $100, a suitcase, and no fluency in the English language. Over the past three decades, I've developed personal, functional, and strategic relationships to build and enhance my career, obtain a top 10 MBA program education, find valuable suppliers and customers, and complete challenging projects. As an entrepreneur, I've leveraged relationships to raise institutional capital, proactively participate in various mergers and acquisitions, attract and retain global talent, build a multitude of brands, and consult with *Fortune* 100 clients, including KPMG, Hewlett-Packard (HP), and Siemens.

	Personal	Functional	Strategic
Purpose	Enhancing personal and professional development; referral to useful information and contacts	Creating efficiency Maintaining capacity and functions required of the group	Uncovering future challenges and priorities; garnering support of diverse and influential stakeholders
Location and temporal orientation	Mostly externally focused Current and future potential	Mostly internally focused Current demand orientation interests	Internal and externally oriented toward the future
Players and recruitment	Key contacts are mostly discretionary Not always clear who is relevant	Key contacts are relatively nondiscretionary; prescribed by task and organizational structure Very clear on who is relevant	Key contacts flow from strategic context and the organizational environment; specific membership is discretionary Not always clear who is relevant
Network attributes and key behaviors	Breadth by reaching out to contacts who can make referrals	Depth focused on building working relationships	Leverage by creating hybrid of internal-external connections

I know how to strategically quantify business relationships, and so can readers of this pragmatic how-to book of global best practices. But it is critical to point out what this book is *not* about. It's not about networking, using people, learning how to become more manipulative, keeping score, or doing for others only if they do for you. It's not about schmoozing, working a room, or using others in general to get what you want. I'm also strenuously against special favoritism, nepotism, cliques, secret societies, and in particular, any efforts perceived as antidiversity or anti-inclusion. On the contrary, I strongly believe that diversity is more than affirmative action. It is the inclusion of all unique walks of life and experiences, which ultimately delivers a broad-based perspective.

We are all products of the advice we take. I don't want anything from you. Rather, what I want *for* you in reading this book is a fresh perspective on the relationships you have today and the ones you should invest in nurturing for a brighter tomorrow. As you read these chapters, I hope you'll develop the mind-set, the tool set, and the road map to fuel your personal and professional growth through a better understanding of strategic relationships. Here's to your strategic relationship success!

Acknowledgments

As I approach the tenth anniversary of The Nour Group, Inc., I am indebted to the many clients of the past and present who have allowed me to become a student of how relationships work and to hone an evolutionary understanding of their impact in global organizations. Their trust continues to fuel my aspirations.

If we are all products of the advice we take, I would be remiss not to mention my past mentors, such as Bill Neill, Lee Nicholson, Ken Marcks, Bruce Kasanoff, and Christian Gheorghe; over the past three decades they, along with countless others, have provided invaluable investments and insights into my personal and professional development.

My thanks go to Alan Weiss, one of the best minds in the relationship business, who has helped me realize that wealth is discretionary time; Andy Stanley, Charlie Paparelli, Dan Brown, Dale Jones, and Paul Young for the purity of their faith in refilling my cup; Veronica Tompkins for her branding brilliance and infectious kindness; Ali Kafashzadeh for his friendship, unwavering support, and sharp mind in the research and development of my most recent work for this updated edition; Matt Rosenhaft and the Social Gastronomy team for their insights into social market leadership; Chris Kopp and Jennifer Whitt for their "content curator" skills; and Shannon Vargo and Matt Holt at John Wiley & Sons for their continued support of this endeavor.

My deepest gratitude to my parents, Manouchehr and Nayareh, in Iran, who so unselfishly gave up their son to live the

American dream; to Uncle Ken, Aunt Jan, Uncle Taghi, Aunt Badry, and Brother Brian for opening their lives and encouraging the passion to dream with the discipline to execute; to my sister Hanieh—I miss you every day and see your zest for life and kind soul in Grayson's eyes; I know you're looking down on our family with love and pride.

Finally, I dedicate this book to Wendy, Grayson, and Justus. Thank you for your continued and unconditional love and support.

1

Why Most "Networking" Doesn't Work!

Today, we are more likely to *call* a colleague who works three offices down the hall from us—or worse yet, send a *text* or post a note on the person's Facebook wall—rather than make the short trip for a face-to-face visit. After having spent the past several months on conference calls, exchanging voice mails and e-mails on key projects, and even attending the same company meetings, we pass key team members in our corporate hallways and have no idea who they are. Whom are you e-mailing? Whom are you asking for resources? Whom are you selling to? Whom are you listening to? Whom are you asking for help?

When technology, even with its vast operational effectiveness and efficient capabilities, determines the nature of our human interactions, is it any surprise that many believe there has been a dramatic erosion of our sense of community and our ability to touch people? Have we gone so far that we need "No E-Mail Fridays" and have to have corporate access to various social networking sites blocked?

In 1916, L. J. Hanifan, practical reformer of the Progressive Era and state supervisor of rural schools in West Virginia, described *social capital* as "those tangible substances [that] count for most in the daily lives of people: namely good will, fellowship, sympathy, and social intercourse among the individuals and families who make up a social unit" (quoted by Robert D. Putnam in *Bowling Alone*, p. 19).

Isn't it interesting that Hanifan's account of social capital anticipated virtually all of the crucial elements in later interpretations of what is essentially the lubricant of our day-to-day interactions as human beings? Unlike the generation before mine, which was proactively involved in various lodges, parent-teacher associations (PTAs), churches, and political parties, I submit that we are becoming increasingly disconnected as a society in many ways, and even more so in business, where many of us spend the majority of our waking hours.

My intent in the next several chapters is not only to illustrate a practical and applicable process for identifying, building, nurturing, and leveraging relationships instrumental to your personal and professional success, but also to help *quantify* the economic value of your most valuable and often *strategic* relationships. In short, relationship *creation* alone won't suffice—regardless of how many cups of coffee or lunch visits you schedule. Savvy professionals find opportunities to monetize their business relationships by bridging relationship *creation* with relationship *capitalization*.

There are three fundamental attributes of growth—the gradient or slope of growth, the torque or speed of growth, and the fuel efficiency or profitability of growth. I'll elaborate on each in the next chapter. We have proved that enterprises can fuel their growth, through a unique return on their strategic relationships. In developing a broad array of value-based relationships, two schools of thought are prevalent. On one end of the spectrum is the *art* of building relationships. For many, this is the ability to *engage* others through the exchange of business cards and the building of transactional relationships. There is little or no shortage of resources in the marketplace today to help train and develop those who seem otherwise introverted and must adapt to a social network. I'm intrigued by recent developments in this area, such as 118 in *The Mirror Test* (the 21st-century version of the elevator pitch), created by Jeffrey Hayzlett, former Kodak chief marketing officer (CMO), and Steve W. Martin's work in *Heavy Hitter Selling: How Successful Salespeople Use Language and Intuition to Persuade Customers to Buy*. On the other end of the spectrum is the world of social network analysis (SNA). You may be surprised to know that it has very little to do with Facebook, Twitter, or YouTube. What began as the study of patterns of human interaction in the 1930s has evolved into a fascinating discipline, although often very dry and rather academic.

Relationship Economics—*the art and science of relationships*—is the balanced, hybrid approach necessary for anyone who needs to build and leverage relationships to get things done. Effectiveness and productivity are both measures of outputs, but efficiency also includes the amount of *input* required. Let's start by looking at why most people are inefficient when it comes to business networking and building long-term, value-based relationships.

Top 10 Reasons Why Networking Doesn't Work

I deliver 50 to 80 global keynote speeches along with consulting on a dozen or so projects annually, and I have found that one of the consistent reasons many people become frustrated with networking is that they don't believe it produces any quantifiable results. Simply put, they don't think much of their effort really works. Whether we are talking about senior executives, business unit leaders, project managers, or salespeople new to a territory, it's amazing to me how many undervalue their portfolio of relationships.

Beyond your educational foundation, professional experience, industry wisdom, and all of the skills and talents you have acquired over the years, your portfolio of relationships transcends geography, function, company, and often any particular point in time.

When I simplify business networking into the three stages of preparation, interaction, and follow-through, I have identified the top 10 culprits that render traditional networking ineffective. They include a lack of purpose or planning, engagement of the wrong people or the inability to disengage when necessary, and the absent notion of triangulation.

Let's take a quick look at each.

Preparation Phase

In the *preparation* phase, your goals, strategies, and tactics will drive efficiency.

1. Lack of Purpose

Most people network without a purpose. When they come to me and ask, "Do you know this executive at XYZ company?" My first question in response is, "What is your intent or purpose for networking? *Why* do you feel like you need to get to know this person?"

Typically, they don't have a well-thought-out answer, or what they do say is often very transactional and based on an immediate need, such as job transition or a prospective client.

Relationship-Centric Best Practice: Purpose

Purpose, by the way, has nothing to do with what you do for a living. It is your guiding light, and it starts with a healthy self. If you're not centered—if you don't know who you are, what you stand for, and your true intent for building relationships—how can you genuinely articulate the same to someone else or make course corrections in your efforts along the way? There is no right or wrong answer here, but it is critical that you start your relationship-building path with an overarching purpose. For example, there is the paternal purpose: *I want to pave an easier path for my children. If I build and nurture key relationships now, it will make it easier for them to get into better schools, land more promising jobs, and have access to a greater wealth of time and opportunities than I did growing up.* This is a purpose that is clearly independent of any particular point in time, geography, or specific functional job.

Others have defined their purpose as personal and professional growth: *By getting to know others, I get to know myself better and can build on my strengths.*

> By starting with a succinct purpose of personal and professional development, building and nurturing productive relationships becomes your compass rather than your stopwatch.

2. Fuzzy Goals

There is no shortage of relationship *formulation*—many can identify great contacts—but we often struggle with consistent relationship development *execution*. Goals are the fundamental link to how you translate great ideas into actionable impacts in your life and in your personal and professional relationships.

The notion of business relationships is not a stand-alone concept. It's an enabler toward achieving business goals and maximizing an individual's, team's, and organization's performance, execution, and results. Without succinct, measurable, and success-proof goals, many of your investments in relationship creation will be lost in the nurturing, development, and ultimate capitalization of those relationships. Said another way, you'll spend a lot of time and effort on unproductive coffee shop or lunch visits and have little to show for that investment of time, effort, or resources.

Are you new to a project team, sales territory, divisional, or leadership role? How will networking help you succeed given the dynamics of your new role? Which relationships will help you enable, accelerate, or maximize your ability to achieve your goals?

By succinctly crafting three to five specific and measurable goals—not just simply self-directed ones such as "becoming a better person," but those that will require collaboration with or cooperation from others, what we refer to as relationship-centric goals—you develop a crystal-clear destination for this desired journey. Many business goals, such as attracting and retaining top talent, growing profitable revenues, improving cost performance, and maintaining lasting behavioral changes, cannot be achieved in isolation. They require value-based relationships to be accomplished. This is a critical point, because quantifiable relationships must have a barometer against which you can measure your efforts.

3. Lack of a Relationship Development Plan

The bulk of my strategic advisory services is focused on helping clients link their strategic direction with personal action, that is, how to execute great ideas by leveraging not just the *what* and *how* but also the *with* and *through whom*—in essence, collecting, connecting, and capitalizing the dots. Your approach to building and nurturing key relationships must be agile, similar to a speedboat, so that if you are not headed in the right direction, you can expeditiously make course corrections.

You simply can't improve what you don't measure. So, if you keep going out and getting involved with organizations and attending networking functions, how are you measuring the results of that attendance? You constantly meet with the same group of individuals, either inside or outside the organization. Are those investments really producing any meaningful results in your efforts toward reaching your goals and objectives?

One of the fundamental reasons networking doesn't work is that most people network without a plan. They are not methodical, systematic, or disciplined about *which* events they attend, *why* they attend them, *what* they are trying to achieve while there, and *how* they will follow through after the event.

To quickly review, the critical first three areas in which networking fails are *purpose*, *goals*, and *plan*—PGP. This is a great mechanism to consistently think about not only *why* you are building relationships but also *how* you will drive results well beyond any single interaction.

Relationship-Centric Best Practice: Vibration versus Forward Motion

It is critical not to confuse vibration with forward motion. Many people equate busy work in networking with progress in relationship creation and capitalization, when, in fact, it's just that—vibration. Countless meals and coffee visits will seldom turn into newly acquired customers, great employees, or the execution of critical milestones. The results you seek will come from a changed behavior. Get in the habit of sitting down in a quiet place 15 minutes in advance of the next networking event or coffee shop meeting and really think through your relationship development continuum. What has to happen for you to get to know them and give them a chance to get to know the *real* you? Open, candid discussions regarding respective interests, agendas, and success criteria move discussions and relationships forward at an accelerated pace. Consistently thought-of and executed PGP can help you realize the desired forward motion in achieving critical business goals and objectives through your portfolio of relationships.

Interaction Phase

In the *interaction* phase, different situations mandate unique rules of behavior, which will deliver relationship development effectiveness. Networking is not simply a noble cause but rather an endeavor to create preferential advantage. It cannot be left to chance. Here are some common culprits in this phase.

4. Haphazard and Reactive Efforts

The process of identifying, building, and nurturing relationships requires disciplined thought and action. In essence, this needs to become the dye in the fabric—not a patch. The dye permeates throughout the fabric. In many ways, the dye *defines* the fabric. A patch is just that—a bandage, a fix, a transaction. If building relationships becomes what you do every day, as opposed to something you feel like you have to do to get by, it tends to become less of an afterthought.

Let me tell you about my first encounter with Joan. It was 6:00 A.M. on a Saturday in May and I was standing in line at a local YMCA, registering my children for upcoming summer programs. Next to me stood an unassuming, five-foot-tall, middle-aged woman (as she later described herself) wearing no makeup, a T-shirt that should have been donated years ago, and black Spandex, with shuffled registration paperwork spilling from her arms. Curious, I simply began by asking about her children and which programs she was registering them for. As she reciprocated and we got to know each other, I met a giant personality beneath this unpretentious exterior.

Want to know what Joan does for a living? She orchestrates global events for some of the biggest multinational organizations, private conglomerates, industry associations, and non-profit causes—often in the 15,000-attendee range. Her broad sphere of influence extends beyond business leaders to include numerous policy makers and serial entrepreneurs. My question to you is: How many Joans are you walking by every day? How many prospective employees, clients, suppliers, worthy causes, and investors are you choosing to ignore simply because you perceive the circumstances to be inopportune?

Relationship-Centric Best Practice: An Opportunity Every Minute of Every Day

You have an opportunity to build relationships every minute of every day, both within your organization and outside of it. Unfortunately, people go through most days with their heads buried in their respective checklists, running from one meeting or conference call to the next. I equate this to having a lot of machetes, making sure that they are all freshly sharpened, and chopping down a lot of trees without ever stopping to ask if you are in the right jungle! "Let's set aside two hours a day to network" is a patch. "I will make time to meet and really get to know a broad array of diverse, interesting people at every opportunity" is the dye. You never know whom you are going to meet at the grocery store or church or while standing in line registering your kids for summer camp. These are but a few opportunities missed every single day by those who either lack the skills, willingness, or humbleness to engage or are simply oblivious to the fact that our lives are all inherently intertwined in a bizarre way. Forget the six-degrees-of-separation cliché; with the advent of social networks, now three degrees of separation is very real.

Think of the last networking event you attended. Most people often have no real resolution or intent as to why they were there. The organization was getting together, so they thought that they should probably show up. (By the way, there is nothing wrong with the innate need to belong. In time, your involvement will provide a multitude of benefits.) Furthermore, most had no idea who else would be at the event and tended to migrate to attendees they already knew versus extending or expanding their reach to a broader contact base. And, most were running late from all of the different *have-to* events in their lives, so they could only grab a quick drink before the program started. They didn't really give themselves an opportunity to engage current and prospective relationships and then ended up leaving immediately afterward to attend yet another commitment.

Sound familiar? If this describes you, then why did you pay the entrance fee and set aside the time to attend the event if you weren't going to be more systematic and disciplined? Are you really starving for more small talk?

Now, consider a different approach to the same networking scenario: First, you prioritize the organizations most relevant to your personal and professional goals and objectives. Many groups plan and publicize their events well in advance, so you aggregate a master list of upcoming events and prioritize your attendance based on those most strategic to your predetermined set of goals, objectives, and action items. You pay and register in advance and place a solid date on your calendar to avoid possible conflicts. Two weeks to a month in advance, you invite a handful of others who you think would also appreciate attending this event. You go online, and with the use of Google and various social media sites, you research the speaker's point of view, subject matter of the presentation, or panel discussion so you can arm yourself with insightful perspectives. Most events actually have the attendees' name badges at the registration table, so you arrive early so that you have an opportunity to browse the attendees. You identify three to five people you would like to get to know better and give yourself plenty of time to meet and greet a broad spectrum of attendees. When you meet someone who may not be as engaging or relevant to what you do, you politely disengage—something most people I've met can't do politely or very effectively!

Time and intellect are your two most valuable assets; you can't afford to waste either. If a conversation is not interesting or productive, you simply must be disciplined enough to move on. Most people get little or no value out of small talk. Instead, ask a poignant question to engage, often a unique and highly differentiated strategy. I'd much rather attend an event and really get to know four or five dynamic, intelligent, interesting, quality people with whom I can follow up after the event instead of going to an event, "working the room," and collecting a handful of often useless or irrelevant business cards. Let me save you the time and aggravation: there is something called the Yellow Pages, and it provides the exact same value as the stack of business cards you collected. But if you engage others in meaningful discussions, proactively listen to the content presented, and then have a systematic process to follow through with them afterward, you will have used your time much more fruitfully. Attending events becomes a great deal more relevant if you have thought about your goals, strategies, and tactics in advance.

The other fundamental challenge here is the very reactive nature of most networkers. An example of this is when people are in job transition. What do they do? They network like there is no tomorrow. Their job becomes finding the next job. They ask everyone they meet, "Do you have a job opening? Do you know someone who has a job opening?" What typically happens when they find a job? I think we've all seen it. Most stop building those relationships and, worse yet, forget everyone who helped them get there until three years from now, when they start calling or e-mailing again. And what do they want? That's right—the next job! By establishing this pattern, they build a reputation that says that the only time they call is when they want something, versus proactively staying in touch and truly nurturing critical relationships along the way.

Recommended Readings on Value-Based Relationships

Years ago, my dad, an avid reader himself, told me, "Leaders are readers, and readers are leaders." I had no fluency in English when I first came to this country, and to this day, I still go through the process of looking up definitions and synonyms to grasp a contextual understanding of the

(continued)

Recommended Readings on Value-Based Relationships
(Continued)

broader content. Through this practice, I have managed to develop a passion for not only absorbing interesting content but also really thinking through its applications in my work.

In my keynote speeches as well as in this book, I highlight many influential works. At any given time, I am often reading four or five books on a variety of topics. Instead of aimless music or obnoxious radio talk shows, I prefer books on CDs or insightful podcasts from a dozen or so mentors on my iPod. I have read 100-plus books on the topic of business relationships, and my suggested reading lists follow. Most are available on the authors' respective web sites.

- Baker, Wayne
  - *Achieving Success Through Social Capital: Tapping Hidden Resources in Your Personal and Business Networks*
  - *Social Networks and Loss of Capital*
  - *Positive Organizational Network Analysis and Energizing Relationships*
  - *Enabling Positive Social Capital in Organizations*
- Brafman, Ori, and Beckstrom, Rod
  - *The Starfish and the Spider: The Unstoppable Power of Leaderless Organizations*
- Burt, Ron
  - *Brokerage and Closure*
  - *Teaching Executives to See Social Capital: Results from a Field Experiment*
  - *Network Duality of Social Capital*
  - *Gossip and Reputation*
- Cialdini, Robert
  - *Influence: The Psychology of Persuasion*

- *The Practice of Social Influence in Multiple Cultures*
- *Training in Ethical Influence*
- Cohen, Don, and Prusak, Laurence
  - *In Good Company: How Social Capital Makes Organizations Work*
- Covey, Stephen M. R.
  - *The Speed of Trust: The One Thing That Changes Everything*
- Gladwell, Malcolm
  - *Blink: The Power of Thinking Without Thinking*
  - *The Tipping Point: How Little Things Can Make a Big Difference*
- Putnam, Robert D.
  - *Bowling Alone: The Collapse and Revival of American Community*
- Rosen, Emanuel
  - *Buzz: Accelerating Natural Contagion*
  - *The Anatomy of Buzz: How to Create Word-of-Mouth Marketing*
- Watts, Duncan
  - *Six Degrees: The Science of a Connected Age*
  - *Small Worlds: The Dynamics of Networks Between Order and Randomness*

I'm often reminded of Harvey Mackay's book *Dig Your Well Before You're Thirsty*. You have to build and nurture these relationships well before you need them. People are a lot less likely to respond and react if you call only when you want something; you should also get in touch to find out how they are doing and how you can become an asset to them. (See the section on relationship givers, takers, and investors later in this chapter.)

When I hear someone say, "I *need* to network," it sounds desperate to me. That's *reactive*. They are looking for a job, they are behind in their sales quota and are scrambling to find prospects, or they are in trouble with their project deliverables. Success comes from being much more proactive.

I liken proactive and consistent networking to playing a game of chess. What I love about playing chess is that to be successful, you must proactively think a number of moves ahead. Similar to what I understand of military situations, it also challenges you to constantly conduct situational analysis. Where am I today, what am I trying to achieve, what happens if I make these efforts, and what's next? Investing in your relationships is also a constant situational analysis. It's critical to think about relationships as investments, and like any other investment, it's imperative to evaluate your return on that investment. When it comes to relationships, ROI needs to be reinvented. Think about this in regard to your *return on involvement*. You belong to all of these different organizations and attend all of these functions. What do you have to show for it? Later in this book, we'll discuss return on integration, return on impact, return on influence, and return on image—all quantifiable perspectives on investments in a critical soft asset: your relationships.

5. What's in It for Them?

You have to find ways to invest in others—or make *relationship currency deposits*—as I cover in later chapters. Find ways to become an asset to others and link your quantifiable value added to their efforts. Those who understand the true value of a relationship will find a way to reciprocate—maybe not today, tomorrow, or this year, but reciprocity is a natural and undisputable law in the *favor economy*.

Unfortunately, many people overlook the critical nature of such reciprocity in favor of focusing solely on their own situation. Another observation that I've made in working with a broad array of functional teams in various organizations has been the perpetual nature of many who think, "What's in it for me?" In essence, when they meet others, both within and external to their organizations, they have their hands out. To recipients of this posture, the interaction becomes a complete turnoff, being perceived as insincere and entirely self-serving. Questions that should be conversational come across as an interrogation, and the person probing often asks intimate questions about information most people are not comfortable sharing with someone they don't know well (read "like or trust"). Their comments come across as scripted or somehow manufactured. They are, in essence, *harvesting conversations.*

Compare and contrast this approach with the one that we teach to frontline contributors and to executives alike, which involves investing most effort in engaging the other person to really understand what that person is about. Take the time to understand the other person's issues and challenges, and give him or her a reason to want to get to know you better. If you add value to every conversation with a unique perspective, the comment you most often tend to hear is, "Wow, I never thought of it that way." And the perception becomes one of continued interest for a follow-up dialogue.

Relationship-Centric Best Practice: Ask Better Questions

If you want better answers, start by asking better questions! Alan Weiss often comments: "Ask engaging questions and you'll influence the conversation. Influence the conversation and you'll influence the relationship. Influence the relationship and you'll influence the outcome you desire." What engaging questions are *you* asking to influence your conversations and key relationships?

(*continued*)

Relationship-Centric Best Practice: Ask Better Questions ***(Continued)***	
INSTEAD OF ASKING:	**TRY ASKING:**
What do you do?	How are you measured?
Are people *really* your biggest asset?	Where would developing intracompany relationships rank in your performance evaluation plan?
Do your people know how to collaborate?	Do you have teams or committees?
How effective is your formal mentoring program?	How is reverse mentoring keeping your company on the leading edge of innovation?
Tell me about your talent acquisition efforts.	Tell me about your fear of flight risk.
What keeps you up at night?	What frustrates you the most about your role? Or What takes you and your team entirely too long to accomplish?

When I meet an executive or individual for the first time, I'm not gauging whether we can do business together, whether we can do a project together, or whether that person can help me. Instead, I'm asking myself, "Does this person understand and value relationships? And if I start by making a deposit—by finding a way to become an asset in solving his or her challenges—will this individual find a way to reciprocate?" It is important to point out that I am not talking about doing only for others who are going to do for you, but as we all know, it is a lot easier to ask for a withdrawal *after* you have made a deposit.

According to the psychological perspective of former PepsiCo, Lucent, and Hewlett-Packard (HP) human resources executive Pat Dailey, Ph.D., a friend of mine, "establishing relationships is a process of successive disclosures. You give me a little of you, I take it and make a judgment. I give you a little of me, you absorb it and make a judgment." This evolutionary process comes to fruition faster for those with the DNA to process the give-and-take more quickly and naturally. However, you certainly don't have to be slick and quick to become an efficient relationship builder. In our experience, everyone has a unique pace in mastering these skills and behaviors, and it is critical to clearly understand the line of too much, too fast in the early stages of relationship formation.

Every job has its issues and challenges. At the next internal or external networking function, start by asking people you meet about their roles and realm of responsibilities and how you can become an asset to their personal or professional efforts. Think about who you know that can help them and how you can make an impactful deposit for this person. Share a contrarian perspective they may not have previously considered, and aim to add value to every interaction.

I have a personal three-touch rule that I follow. I will make three investments without expecting anything in return. As I meet individuals who are looking for knowledge, talent, or an introduction to an influential relationship, I'll go out of my way to somehow become an asset to them. But the fundamental challenge is that you simply don't have enough bandwidth to invest in all of your relationships equally. How you prioritize which relationships you invest in has to be congruent with your relationship-centric goals and objectives and your individual definition for a return on your relationship investments.

Everyone is tuned in to the same FM station—WIIFM: What's in It for Me? The next time you meet someone, instead of having your hand out and wondering what this person can do for you, *lend* a hand by asking yourself, "How can I *really* get to know this person and find ways to become an asset to *him or her*? How can I find ways to create *quantifiable value* for this person?"

Relationship Economics @ Work:
Bob McIntosh at RockTenn Company

When Bob McIntosh, senior vice president and general counsel for RockTenn Company, is evaluating potential service providers, at the top of his evaluation list are competency, service level, and expense. But relationships are also an important factor.

"Performance comes first," he said. "But relationships absolutely come into play. Take investment bankers, for example. These are very large firms that often service a particular industry. They are in the business. They are selling their services, but as a potential buyer, you also want an investment banker who will bring you deal flow when they come across an opportunity."

RockTenn's corporate strategy includes organic growth plans, as well as some inorganic opportunities, according to Bob. These strategies are transparent to bankers, who are aware of the kinds of acquisitions the firm is interested in. Investment banking firms that want to do business with RockTenn will regularly visit and share ideas about potential transactions that might interest the firm. This includes companies (or divisions of companies) that may be available for purchase.

"They may bring it up to gauge our interest," said Bob. "Of course, the hope is that they build a relationship with us so that when a deal comes up that we're interested in because it is a quality deal that fits within our growth strategy, we'll choose them as the investment bank that assists us with the deal."

6. Engagement of the Wrong People

Two of the best opportunities to expand your portfolio of relationships are internal company meetings (particularly if you work for a midsize or large organization) and industry conferences. In both examples, two aspects motivate most attendees: content and community. That is, what insightful information can I get exposed to, learn, or otherwise gather, and who else will be there of particular interest and value?

In the internal company meeting example—think of an annual sales kick-off meeting—the attendees are from the far corners of the organization. Field sales professionals meet to review the previous year's results, get updates on new products or services, and understand expectations of them in the coming year. Corporate marketing people, product or service line leaders, key people from finance, technology representatives, and even a number of international or cross-brand attendees are also there. I've spoken at several global meetings where new acquisition team members are there for the first time, or it's the merger of two entities that are coming together as a new team. Needless to say, it's an environment rich in relationship development.

At many industry conferences, you have the opportunity to explore the latest market trends and the competitive landscape and to hear from thought leaders. Likewise, it's a fertile environment to extend and expand the diversity and quality of your business relationships. Even at events with great opportunities such as these, you tend to have those in attendance who are not relevant to your current role, realm of responsibilities, or aspirations. The number one mistake most people make when they walk into events like these is that they spend an inordinate amount of time and effort talking to someone who is not relevant to what they are doing, and they get sidetracked from their relationship development playbook. When I refer to the "wrong people," it is not intended to mean that some people have less value than others. I am simply trying to get you focused on *relevancy*. How relevant is this individual to the goals and objectives that you are trying to achieve? Please understand that this comment is not to be construed as manipulative. It's not about an elegant way of using people, but about becoming smarter in how you invest your valuable time, efforts, and resources. You simply cannot afford to invest in every interaction equally. (More about how to leverage technology to help you do some of this in later chapters.)

One of the best practices in this section is to identify what we call influential hubs. These are subject matter experts or those naturally highly connected who are consistently able to engage and influence others over a certain period of time. If you think of the classic bike wheel, they represent the hub in the middle with the many spokes fanning out from that position.

Certain functional roles lend themselves naturally well to this concept. The best commercial real estate agents I know are very well connected in their communities to a multitude of possible direct client or referral sources. The best attorneys, accountants, insurance agents, recruiters, nonprofit fundraisers, lobbyists, and industry consultants are often very good hubs because of the diversity of friendships that they build over the years. It is critical to your relationship-building approach to identify those hubs and find ways to become an asset to them.

Relationship Economics @ Work:
Dan Brown and Heavy Hitters at Various Functions

According to Dan Brown, a personal friend and former executive at SunTrust Bank, "It all starts with relationship building. You have to find some common ground with whomever you are dealing with. You can't be too needy—it has to be a relationship of equals. This begins with a centered self. If I am at an interesting function and there are some heavy hitters there, I don't necessarily have to approach them. If I am there having conversations with a group of people, some of these heavy hitters might come up to me and introduce themselves."

So I asked Dan, how does he characterize a *heavy hitter*? "This is someone in a relationship-type area who deals with a lot of people, travels globally; they're often an expert in their respective field—someone who if you are in that function, is deemed very influential."

What makes some of these hubs more attractive than others? "It largely depends on the function and the person. There is the internal persona and then the role that they play. Some people are heavy hitters internally—no matter where they are, they are people you want to know. Others have a heavy hitting function, but they are not necessarily someone you care to spend any time with. Others, no matter what position they are in, they are an interesting person to get to know.

"Where do I spend my time? Sometimes you just spend time with people whom you find interesting, not necessarily someone whose role can benefit you."

Dan and I have been involved in the High Tech Ministries Prayer Breakfast for years, thanks to another personal friend and mentor, Charlie Paparelli. In many ways, Dan was instrumental in helping me focus my avocation as my vocation. Eight years ago, over a cup of coffee, he mentioned that I networked better than anyone else he had ever met and wondered if I would come to his church and speak about my approach to building and nurturing relationships.

Assuming there would be a dozen or so attendees, I prepared a few remarks only to find myself in an auditorium in front of 250-plus audience members. After a 45-minute speech, I stayed for 90 minutes afterward to

(continued)

Relationship Economics @ Work:
Dan Brown and Heavy Hitters at Various Functions (Continued)

answer individual questions and share best practices. From that one session, I was invited to speak to 30 other similar gatherings of church, Rotary, and academic groups. This led to consulting and speaking engagements with global corporations, which then led to the industry associations and academic forums today. Dan remains a great personal friend and is now an interim executive on various operations and strategic technology assignments.

Remember that one of the fastest ways to turn off a hub is to go to that person and say, "What can you do for me?" Although these hubs are typically genuine and go out of their way to help people, you will quickly brand yourself a taker by approaching them in this way. What is critical to hubs, or to any relationship development effort, is that you truly invest time, effort, and resources in advancing the achievements of others.

Follow-Through Phase

During the *follow-through* phase, systematic, disciplined thought and action will drive recognition. If you believe in the premise that most people genuinely want to help, then it becomes incumbent upon you to not just follow up (transactional) but follow through (transformational) the initial success in meeting and engaging interesting, relevant contacts.

7. Failure to Arm Others with the Right Ammunition

When people say that networking doesn't work, they usually cite as evidence the fact that they have invested in others in the past without any reciprocity from the other side. When I inquire specifically, "How did you arm them with the appropriate context to introduce or recommend you?" the answer is often a blank stare.

Business Relationship Don'ts: "John Nobody Sent Me!"

I recently received a voice mail to the effect of: "David, this is Steve Blank, friend of John Nobody (*whose name I honestly did not recognize at first and later recalled that I didn't care for him at all*). I was wondering if you could meet me on XYZ dates and times and let me pick your brain to become a consultant, an author, or a professional speaker. John says you've become an overnight success." You can't make this stuff up.

I continue to wonder what he was thinking. What in that voice mail could possibly propel me to take action? Nonetheless, acting on a favorite grandmother's advice to always be nice, I returned Steve Blank's call to inquire about his background. "Well, I was most recently a VP of sales," he declared. "I have been selling for 40-plus years and can't possibly imagine a company out there that I couldn't help."

I asked him about possible target industries, size, or types of companies, or relevant background and applicable strengths. With each of these inquiries, I consistently felt that he was making me draw this information out of him.

Because Steve Blank was not forthcoming in discussing his situation, I wasn't able to help him in the manner that he had hoped. He essentially wanted the return on his investment—without having to make any investment.

We can easily distinguish between the "Steve Blank" approach of looking for a handout versus Keith Conley's style of trying to figure out a way to become an asset in the best practice that follows. In this process, if you can get to know me, understand my business, and learn what my challenges are, you can uncover ways to help me. And when you do, my next logical question will be: How can *I* help *you*? That's when you can tell me that you are in transition and looking for a VP of sales position.

Relationship Economics @ Work: Stephen Ebbett and ProtectYourBubble.com

In my two decades of consulting experience, I've found that every organization reaches an inflection point—think of it as a fork in the road to continue down the status quo path to "commodity town," or pave a new road to "margin-ville," as I once heard it described. This new path is often the vision of someone in the most unlikely of places who find themselves in an opportune environment to shine—with an undervalued client, unique product or service launch, or simply an interesting perspective in how to look at a mature business. The relationships they build and the manner in which they engage and influence those relationships to further their mission or vision are often the differentiating factors between just another interesting idea and a fundamentally different path for the organization.

Stephen Ebbett, head of global direct distribution for Assurant Solutions is one such client. Although in his early to midthirties, Stephen comes across as sharp and very knowledgeable about the e-commerce world. His first hand experience in getting a dozen or so previous e-commerce sites live has served him well—particularly when trying to replicate that past success in a conservative organization.

Stephen was recruited to Assurant Solutions UK three years ago to launch a direct to consumer web site selling tangential insurance policies online, in order to reach a customer base outside of the reach of the organization's existing B2B distributors. Since then, he has not only executed on the business goals and objectives set out for Protect YourBubble.com in the UK, but has more recently been promoted to lead a broader direct distribution effort for Assurant Solutions.

One of Stephen's biggest assets is his ability to communicate his progress, with a broad array of constituents—*consistently, intently, and strategically*. By arming his portfolio of internal and external relationships with ammunition to see his progress, and believe-in (as well as buy-in) on his efforts, he has managed to raise the awareness, interest, and the company's investment in his vision of an "e-commerce site that sells insurance, versus an insurance company that sells policies online."

It's a strong new path for the organization, and a considerably broader realm of responsibilities—as well as a personal and professional growth opportunity for Stephen. Did I mention that he reports directly to the CEO now?

Arm people with the appropriate information they need to help you. It is critical not to leave this to chance. Come to the table prepared with a systematic game plan that explains how you can become an asset to their efforts.

Personal and highly informative e-mails such as the one in Figure 1.1 from Stephen Ebbett elevate you above the market noise.

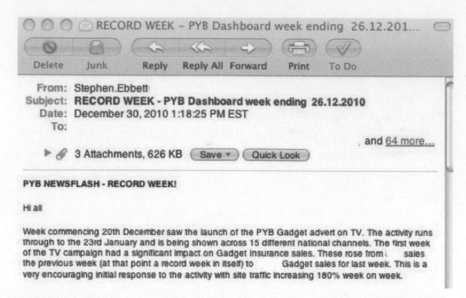

FIGURE 1.1   Consistent E-Mails Updating the Team on PYB's Progress

Relationship Economics @ Work: Pat Dailey on Becoming an Asset and Arming with Success-Proof Information

I met Pat Dailey several years ago when he was in career transition. Pat is a global human resources (HR) leader who is passionate in the recruitment and integration of senior teams around the globe. As I got to know him, I learned that he is fundamentally an architect of employer-of-choice practices that attract top-tier talent. With each interaction, he clearly demonstrates deep expertise in transforming organizations challenged by strategic repositioning, globalization, turnarounds, SG&A (selling, general, and administrative) cost reductions, and reengineering. Working in a function that many believe is focused purely on the tactical aspects of the role, Pat is a clear-thinking business leader with a proven ability to upgrade both the credibility and the quantifiable contribution of the HR team.

His background includes chief administrative officer at Herbalife International, VP of global workforce management at HP, VP of HR for the network products group of Alcatel-Lucent, VP of HR for Banc One Services Corp. (now a division of JPMorgan Chase), and a partner at Korn/Ferry International. Performance clearly trumps all, but beyond that, as we got to know each other, Pat has always offered to be an asset. In an effort to reciprocate his kindness, I offered to introduce him to a number of private equity relationships. What follows is an example of the information with which he armed me, not only to make that offer more successful (after all, who best to present your credentials than you?), but to mitigate the risk of me formulating his credentials to chance.

Subject: Virtual Intro: Pat Dailey—PepsiCo-trained Senior HR Executive

Neal—I had a good lunch visit with David today and he asked about the progress of our discussions, so I wanted to touch base to see if you've thought any further about getting the portfolio execs together in 2012. I will also call you early next week to follow up.

Separately, I want to introduce you and Steve to Patrick Dailey. Pat is targeting his search for a number one HR role—most likely with a company navigating business transformation and proactively upgrading its competitive capability. His geography is wide open and his hands-on expertise includes best practices at companies such as PepsiCo, Hewlett-Packard, and the U.K.-based BOC Group.

Pat is a leader with distinctive experience including:

Chief Talent Scout. Recruiting, assessing talent, and assembling senior leadership teams, globally

Changing the DNA. Leading and partnering a range of organizational transformation and performance initiatives

(continued)

> **Relationship Economics @ Work: Pat Dailey on Becoming an Asset and Arming with Success-Proof Information** *(Continued)*
>
> *Succession Planning.* Developing the leadership pipeline and orchestrating leadership change with continuity
>
> *Board of Director Experience.* BOD selection. Installing *performance-based* executive compensation plans
>
> *High-Performance Culture.* Building sustainable cultures and reward systems that guide and retain great talent
>
> *Protecting the Corporation.* Managing and monitoring Sarbanes-Oxley (SOX) and Code of Conduct compliance
>
> *Global HR Leadership.* Inspiring and coaching a lean, global HR team within a highly matrixed organization
>
> I can answer questions you might have about Pat but please feel free to contact him directly at XXX. His CV is also attached.
>
> Best,
>
> David Nour

8. Less Than Ideal Relationship Profiles

There are many social networking tools on the market today to help you find specific contacts. Some of the better ones I've found include LinkedIn, ZoomInfo, Spoke, and Jigsaw. All of these tools enable you to identify contacts. The web site TheyRule.net, for example, will show you who is on whose board and profiles these key individuals.

Type "Equifax," one of the credit-reporting companies, based in Atlanta, into ZoomInfo and you will see that Rick Smith, the current CEO, came to the company following 22 years at GE. ZoomInfo not only shows you Rick's background and tells you that he is on the board of directors of the Commerce Club, attended Purdue University, and held previous roles at GE, but also shows you a picture of the Equifax board and provides you with their respective profiles. (See Chapter 10 for an in-depth review of the most prevalent social networking technologies on the market today.) Figure 1.2 is one of the best concepts I've seen from TheyRule.net.

There is a plethora of publicly available information out there to help you profile key individuals who could be instrumental to your success. This independent due diligence prepares you for an insightful interaction, with intelligent remarks about the company or its leadership, and greater opportunities to work with Rick and his team in addressing critical company challenges and opportunities.

Other popular tools here include Hoovers, OneSource, Factiva, and Leadership Library. There is certainly no shortage of resources for exceptional due diligence information to profile key individuals who are instrumental to your success. Most of these sites are limited to the more visible roles—mainly executives—but with Google, it is difficult for any of us to hide. So if the individual you are trying to meet has ever written an article, been published, or spoken at an event, chances are that his or her profile, background, and points of interest are going to be online. I have also found *McKinsey Quarterly*, Booz Allen's *strategy + business*, and CEOExpress.com to be invaluable tools.

9. Lacking Relationship Insight Validation

Another common mistake in most people's relationship-building efforts is that they do not verify, validate, or void the critical assumptions that they make about key pieces of information or individuals critical to their success. You don't want to walk into a meeting, or any situation, with incorrect or outdated information.

Years ago I created a process I refer to as strategic relationship triangulation (Figure 1.3).

Let me explain. For any person or piece of information critical to your relationship development success, you need to

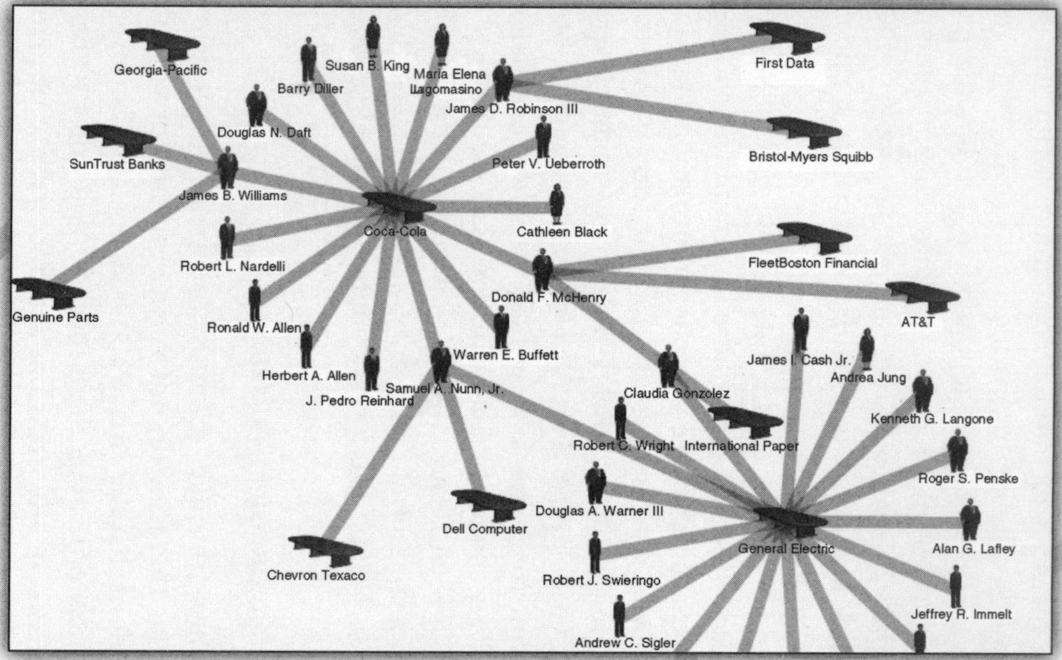

FIGURE 1.2 TheyRule.net Board-Level Social Network

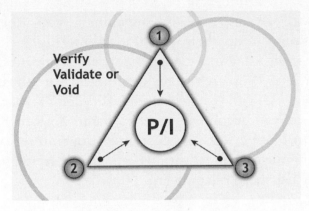

FIGURE 1.3 Strategic Relationship Triangulation

find three independent sources to verify, validate, or void the critical assumptions you're making about that person or information. Is this person still in charge of this project? Is this person responsible for this engagement? Is this person physically based out of this office? I have heard nightmare stories of people getting on a plane for a meeting in New York only to find that the person they are meeting with changed jobs recently and is completely irrelevant to the critical opportunities at hand.

Relationships triangulate a key individual's realms of responsibility. What is this person's real clout? What projects is this person involved in? How many people are on this person's team? If this relationship is important to you, it is critical to do some research in advance to find other trusted sources that this individual works with.

A recent survey polled 100,000 executives about the best way to create access both inside and outside the organization. The overwhelming response—more than 85 percent—was "through a trusted source." That source was further described as an internal lieutenant who works with the individual and knows you and can recommend you, or an outside adviser such as an accountant, lawyer, or consultant whom this individual has worked with who can likewise recommend you. Relationship triangulation can also help you understand highly influential sources within a team, a department, an organization, or an entire industry. Who are the key organization or industry advisers? Who works with real decision makers and in what capacity, and how can you become an asset to them? Knowing this enables you to more effectively customize your presentation and add value to the individual with whom you are trying to develop a mutually beneficial relationship.

10. Givers, Takers, and Investors

In my experience, there are three types of networkers: givers (God bless Mother Teresa), takers (we've all known some), and investors. Which one are you? If I asked your colleagues, customers, suppliers, superiors, subordinates, and industry contacts, which would *they* say that you are?

As I have mentioned before, some people reach out only when they want something. I call those people *takers*. They have a very "me-centric" approach to their networking. I am not sure I would even call what they form *relationships* because their transactional network and contacts are made solely for their benefit—and only *their* benefit. They call you for an urgent task and expect you to drop everything else you're doing to serve their immediate needs. They see you periodically in the market, exchange less than genuine pleasantries, and reiterate "Let's catch up," often meaning "Let me suck out of you all the information I need about what you're doing and what I can replicate from your efforts to improve my situation, and offer no value in return." You must deal with these people cordially but at a distance. Be polite, but guard your valuable assets—knowledge, talent, insights, and, most important, other valuable relationships. Unfortunately this type of behavior seldom improves.

Business Relationship Don'ts: "Drive-By Greetings"

I'm an adviser to the DBM International Center for Executive Options (ICEO). Here in Atlanta, Bob Chaet and team do a great job coaching senior executives in transition to appropriately aim their compass toward an opportunity they'd be most passionate about in the next chapter of their careers. Unfortunately, having had the rug pulled out from under them (often through no fault of their own), most of these execs typically network like mad to uncover that next job. They fill their calendars with endless coffee meetings, countless e-mail touches, and a myriad of "networking events." They proactively reach out to everyone they used to live next to, go to school with, work with, or play with, and even parents of their kids' soccer teammates. They really work it . . . until they find a job.

Then, not only do many stop the activity and tend to go dark under the new rug (which will get pulled out from under them in another few years), but much more detrimentally, they forget the amazing alumni of friends and colleagues, advisers, and hubs who helped them in the process. Other colleagues who are likewise in search of their next opportunity are suddenly forgotten. Favors promised are ignored. And catch-up visits with those still in the market become less important than that corporate visit.

Instead of embracing the very portfolio of relationships that enabled their success, many of these executives further distance themselves. Until three years down the road . . . when they come looking for another job. How likely are you to help them? Most are not. I actually ask them, "When was the last time you called to see how *I* was doing and how *my* business has been since your last search?"

However, the altruistic givers are just as challenged. Don't get me wrong; there is certain nobility in being the Mother Teresa of relationship giving. All this crowd does is give. Constantly doing for others drives them, but they become sheepish when *they* need help. They go out of their way to help people with important projects, often neglecting their own needs, desires, or deadlines. They're often perceived to be incredibly sweet, kind, and giving. There is absolutely nothing wrong with any of these attributes. They simply become an open door for many to take advantage of this kindness. When engaging a giver, you must ensure that you don't become a taker! Always be gracious, thank them for their generosity, and consistently offer to add value to their efforts; for example, constantly ask, "What can I do to help you?" They may never accept your offer, but it's incumbent upon you to keep the balance in a giver relationship.

Patricia, a good friend of mine, is directly responsible for a great number of chief information officers (CIOs) having found their current roles. Yet, when she could have used their help for a charity fundraising event, an incredibly worthy cause, she was reluctant to seek their support.

What Patricia and all the other givers must realize is that when you give, you are making deposits—by doing for others—and those investments are perishable. You will lose the opportunity to leverage those relationships and therefore will have zero to show for all of that generosity, other than self-gratification. It is critical to point out here that we are not talking about keeping score or doing for others only who do for you. But as with most things in life, too much of either of these—taking or giving—will fail to produce the desired outcomes. You must find an appropriate middle ground on which to form personal connections.

The professional balance is a *relationship investor*. This type of person understands that you have to start by giving. You have to make an investment to get a return on that investment.

Long before a need to capitalize or monetize relationships, an investor has accumulated a great deal of social capital through the development of a strong *relationship bank*. This person's name alone creates a sense of obligation to deliver value. Said another way, these are the people you would bend over backward to help, not only because they have gone out of their way to help you in the past, but because whenever you need help, they embrace you with open arms.

Similar to any other investments, relationship investors read their prospectuses. They truly consider their portfolio of relationships to be their biggest asset and constantly aim to analyze and enhance their return on relationship investments. In Chapter 3, I discuss strategic relationship planning best practices.

No one has enough resources to invest in every relationship equally, so you must prioritize your relationships and decide which to invest in more. This is not to say that you should be anything less than cordial and gracious in meeting and engaging others. But you also have to make sure they understand that true relationships are reciprocal in nature and investments made in building and nurturing relationships must be realized as a value-added item at some future time.

Corporate Relationship Deficit Disorder

Business relationships are formed in a variety of contexts. One of the misconceptions of business relationships is that they are purely an external asset or liability. But a great deal of our work over the past several years has been focused on *intracompany* relationships.

Companies, regardless of size or industry, and despite efforts to the contrary by their leadership, tend to build geographic, functional, and project-based silos. Have you ever heard the ongoing disputes between the Los Angeles and New York offices, for example? By definition, those geographies will compete for mind share and wallet share of the corporate headquarters and often create geographic silos.

Likewise, when most organizations are structured by functional capabilities—whether they are practice groups in a law firm or finance, engineering, marketing, and legal departments within most corporations—they are forced to compete for resources. Doesn't that create functional silos?

Last, if key initiatives tend to be organized by cross-geography and cross-functional projects, isn't each project team often competing for access, influence, and resources? As such, aren't project-based silos not only created but often nurtured in time? Many corporations, because of their sheer structure, performance expectations, measurements, and rewards, are not conducive to collaboration and not constructed for communication, and what suffers most are the intracompany relationships. And just like a family, when it is broken on the inside, guess who sees it.

Cultural Divide

An obsession with transactions first and relationships later often tends to distance us from other people instrumental to our personal and professional success. Many have heard of the socioeconomic divide. In more recent years, we have also heard of the digital divide. But I would submit that the cultural divide in our global economy is the biggest culprit in hindering the development and nurturing of both internally focused and externally focused relationships.

Travel to the kingdom of Bahrain and you'll see that a business transaction often includes not only personal embraces but a predominant focus on character—in essence, more emphasis on the DNA of the individual and considerably less on the transaction. On a recent trip to the Middle East, I met Basim Al-Saie, managing director of Installux Gulf, and Fasil Ali Reza, managing director of Ali Reza and Sons. They represent an infectious level of patriotism and all that is right and good about the Arab world. These highly U.S.-educated (both went to school in Boston), affluent, family-centric business executives see more in an individual's character than they do the value of a transaction. As a matter of fact, much of the world comes to the United States and is surprised, if not offended, by our unquenchable thirst for transaction success before we show any signs of a personal connection.

Relationship-Centric Best Practice: Welcoming More Than Just the Employee

Think about it: The last time Michael and his entire family were transferred from San Diego to Chicago, his new immediate manager barely got out an e-mail on the Friday afternoon before that Michael would be joining the team the next Monday. Why not organize a small reception at the manager's home, invite key employees and their spouses along with Michael and his wife, Lori, and make it a personal mission to make sure they feel comfortable in their new personal and professional surroundings? Because despite popular belief, I would submit that (1) what Michael does for a living isn't who Michael is, and (2) if Lori doesn't feel at home in Chicago, the stay for the job will be a short-term transaction rather than a long-term investment in the position of the company.

One of our clients has created a "family buddy system," where they introduce a recently relocated family to several other families and help them adjust. From neighborhoods with great schools, to places of worship, to places to shop for groceries and find activities for the kids, they have determined that the level of engagement in the new community by the entire family directly correlates with the level of satisfaction and comfort by the employee in the new assignment.

2

The Evolution of Quantifiable Relationships

It has been said that knowledgeable people know a lot of facts; they know a lot of information. Successful and prosperous people know a lot of other people. They realize that relationships are their most valuable asset and they consistently, intentionally, systematically, and thus strategically nurture those relationships. Ask yourself how many respected, trusted, influential executives with decision-making ability and real access to power from your list of contacts would return your calls and e-mails within 24 hours. How many would come to your support when called upon in a time of need? In short, do you have *contacts*, or do you have *relationships*?

Many organizations have become fairly astute in the measurement and analysis of their hard assets such as inventory, cost of goods sold, and return on equity (ROE). The next evolution is measuring, analyzing, and capitalizing on their soft assets, including brands, people, and relationships. This chapter highlights the quantifiable value of each of these soft assets and challenges—perhaps even reinvents—the traditional understanding of ROI (return on investment) with that of return on influence, return on involvement, return on integration, return on impact, and return on image.

Product of the Advice We Take

If I were to ask you to map your success to date for me, what would that graph look like? Let's use the horizontal *x*-axis to track time—your teens, twenties, thirties, and so on—and the vertical *y*-axis to plot your definition of success, however you define it.

Figure 2.1 is what mine looks like. Hoping yours will look different, let me ask you a few questions:

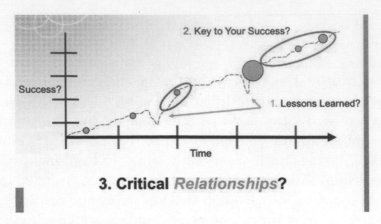

FIGURE 2.1 Sample Success Map

First, how did you define success? For many, it's graduating from college, accepting a first job, being promoted for the first time, getting married, having children, and so forth. They subconsciously categorize key milestones as buckets in their lives—you made more money with this job or you moved to where you live now some 15 years ago or you had children. I submit that it's our personal and professional growth. Graduation, new jobs, career progressions, even the experiences of watching children develop are often incredible sources of joy—but they're also amazing lessons in shaping who we become—the good, the bad, and the ugly!

Second, if you haven't had any dips in your life, what lessons have you really learned? What was the impact of the decisions you made in creating those low points? Did you take a job for the financial gains alone, only to have the company go out of business six months later? Did you volunteer to lead a project, which failed and painted you as the source of that failure? Did you follow a dream only to realize it as an inescapable nightmare?

Much more important than the mistakes we've all made over the years, what lessons did you learn that became keys to your success after a low point? How did you recover from an apparent abyss? What strategies or tactics did you apply to overcome insurmountable debt, the loss of a loved one, or termination from that last job? In my experience, if you can understand what makes you successful after a low point in your life, it helps develop your resiliency as well as foresight in the challenges—and opportunities—ahead.

Most important, what were the critical relationships along the way that facilitated your personal or professional growth? Who was the first manager who took you under his or her wing and taught you this business? Who was that sales or project manager who really took an interest in your development and growth? Who were the formal and often informal mentors who helped you navigate the unforgiving sea of corporate politics, bureaucracy, and constant merry-go-rounds of strategies, tactics, business unit structures, new leadership, and organizational changes?

I believe we're all products of the advice we take! Which strategic relationships have been instrumental in shaping the person you are today? Which strategic relationships had the biggest impact on your graph? Whose graph are you impacting for years to come?

Three Attributes of Organizational Growth

The same idea applies to an organization. Many have cut expenses, staff, and overall resources as much as possible—after all, you can't cut your way to growth. Many board members and senior leadership teams have also shifted their focus on profitable growth strategies.

There are three fundamental attributes of organizational growth: the gradient or slope of growth, the torque or speed of growth, and the fuel efficiency or profitability of growth. Strategic relationships—often thought of as a soft asset—affect each of these attributes and thus the organization's overall growth strategies.

Most organizations clearly understand hard assets such as inventory and real estate and often characterize them as a barometer by which the company's financial stability and capacity for leverage are measured.

Soft assets are characterized as intangible and tend to be more nebulous. In recent years savvy organizations have identified and accounted for their unique and inherent value. They include such line items as brand equity, human capital, and strategic relationships, perhaps identified as alliances, joint ventures, or long-term customer or supplier contracts. Although they may not appear in most financial reports, they are proving to be unique, sustainable competitive differentiators and a certain barrier to entry for others.

Let's take a closer look at each of the three attributes.

Slope of Growth

Have you ever tried riding a bicycle uphill? Did you sit down and peddle intently, or did you stand up and just try to survive? Were you on a casual cruiser or a road bike with multiple gears to support your efforts? How long did it take, and how did you feel at the top of the hill? Did you or would you do it again?

The difference between feeling like Lance Armstrong sprinting uphill or Dom DeLuise riding a unicycle is a combination of the intensity and consistency of your training, your nutritional discipline, your competitive nature, and perhaps the experience and tenacity of your coach.

Figure 2.2 charts an example of biking up that hill; the typical linear growth is shown in line 1 (this is your "steady as she goes" nice little hill), cubic growth is shown in line 2 (this is some of the hills in the north Georgia mountains), and

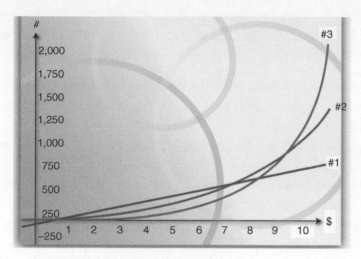

FIGURE 2.2 The Slope or Gradient of Growth

exponential growth is shown in line 3 (think cycling in down-town San Francisco).

Examples of exponential growth include multilevel marketing, where each member recruits multiple others; Moore's law, whereby the maximum number of transistors that can be put on a microprocessor chip inexpensively doubles every 18 months; and compound interest, which increases principal exponentially.

The same idea applied to your organization's gradient or slope of growth means that revenue depends exponentially on time when your current revenue results, multiplied by some growth factor, would create a future revenue target.

What if we applied the same idea to your view of a strategic relationship? Start by succinctly understanding and focusing your efforts on building relationships with specific and highly relevant individuals. Next, educate your team, organization, or the market at large about the unique value you add. Then by demonstrating successful outputs (results) for others you engage, allow prospective relationships to reach out to you with their specific interests.

Relationship-Centric Best Practice: Centers of Influence

An amazing illustration of quantifiable relationships fueling the slope or gradient of an organization's growth is what an individual sales rep at one of our client companies has achieved in the past year. Sandy, starting as a brand-new sales rep a year ago in the Dallas/Fort Worth area, was handed 10 named accounts that had fallen off of the corporate radar and had collectively produced $2M in revenue all of the preceding year. In the current fiscal year, exactly 11 months after she joined the company, she has produced in excess of $30M from the same set of accounts! That's what we call unprecedented growth. And she did it through a unique return on her strategic relationships.

So, how? Well, let me give you a brief backstory: The client is a Fortune 100 company in a very mature business with $100B+ in annual revenues. My client is a new division president brought in to transform the culture. He has replaced 50 percent of the 2,000-person sales force with a newly focused profile of ideal sales professional—one who unequivocally understands and is an advocate of the end client's business. From the outset, he was determined to support his relationship quarterbacks in the field and develop a distribution channel–friendly environment where the most trusted adviser in the field would lead each prospective client engagement.

In the first half of the year, I worked with Sandy, who had been a very successful sales rep and manager in her previous positions, to reinvigorate the 10 accounts she was given. We identified which accounts had a heartbeat—that is, clients who were still speaking with the company but not buying anything—and then we identified where she could get an introduction into the C- or V-suite via some of the former account managers.

What Sandy quickly realized was that the former account managers either were not aware or simply didn't have any relationships in lower levels of the organizations, what we began to define as key centers of influence. To her credit, Sandy invested the first six months of the year gaining village knowledge and mapping relationships of key influencers in various pockets of her client companies.

She methodically used some of our tools and prioritized what I describe in Chapter 6 as pivotal contacts, that is, relationships within her own organization and at her client companies that would be critical to her success. She clearly understood that her prospects were not these neat, segmented buckets, but rather a web of relationships.

In the second half of the year, she identified, prioritized, and invested in these centers of influence—jointly solving problems and identifying distribution channel partners who could add significant value to the equation. She saw that client titles were irrelevant—one of her biggest champions, who doesn't have a title on his business card, happens to report directly to the chief executive officer (CEO)/chairman! Sandy began to win competitive opportunities and marshaled her corporate resources to accelerate her ability to execute.

Want examples of results from investing in strategic relationships? In 11 months, Sandy was able to generate a total of $30M in top-line revenue from 8 of the 10 accounts, $20M coming from one account alone!

When you collaborate in unique ways to create value* for others and empower others to share their experiences, it's amazing how often those people become evangelists and advocates of your brand. In the process, they educate the market for you. Anyone who has ever found a job or closed a sale based on a strong pull through referrals can attest to this. In addition, your advocates create further marketing gravity or pull for a relationship with you.

Which growth curve are you on? Which growth curve should you be on, and how do you know?

Speed of Growth

Torque or speed is the second fundamental attribute of organizational growth. If you've ever used a wrench connected to a nut or bolt, you know that it produces what's referred to as torque, a turning force that loosens or tightens the nut or the bolt.

You see, torque is the tendency of a force to rotate an object about an axis. Just as a force is a push or a pull, a torque can be thought of as a twist. As you can see in Figure 2.3, the magnitude of torque or that force depends on three quantities: (1) the force applied, (2) the length of the lever arm connecting the axis to the point of force application, and (3) the angle between the two.

The torque or speed of growth works very similarly in organizations. The axis, which force is applied to, is your external market opportunity. This may be launching a new product or service launch, trying to penetrate a new account, or perhaps entering a new geographic market.

The force you apply to that market opportunity is a combination of your people, their resources to invest (such as training

---

*Many care a lot less about your input, that is, your methodology, products, and services, and much more about the outcome, that is, how they will benefit from working with you.

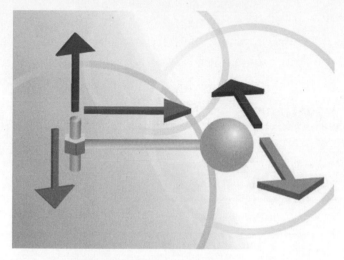

FIGURE 2.3 The Traditional Concept of Torque

and development), a repeatable and predictable sales process, market research, competitive analysis, and marketing communication.

The length of the lever arm connected to the axis is your physical proximity to the market opportunity. This is why it's difficult to parachute into a new geography you're trying to grow and why field-marketing campaigns are seldom effective when they're run from "corporate" 3,000 miles away by people without village knowledge.

The angle between your market opportunity and your force consists of your strategic relationships. Build a robust portfolio of relationships that can provide unique and actionable insights, reciprocate value, and accelerate your ability to get things done, and you'll infinitely enhance your torque or speed of growth. (See Figure 2.4.)

Why does torque or speed of growth matter? It is the difference between having the "first mover" advantage and being a fast follower. In many markets, there is an inherent window of market opportunity and a very real and often substantial opportunity cost of not getting the torque or speed of growth right.

FIGURE 2.4 Speed of Growth in New Market Penetration

Profitability of Growth

You throw enough time and money at it and you can enhance both the slope and the speed of growth in almost any organization. But at what cost? World-class organizations understand the fundamental value of the fuel efficiency or profitability of growth.

Fuel efficiency, in its traditional meaning, is thermal efficiency—of a process that converts chemical potential energy contained in a fuel into kinetic energy or work. In the context of transport, *fuel efficiency* more commonly refers to the energy efficiency of a particular vehicle model, where its total output—in this case, range, or mileage in the United States—is given as a ratio of range units per unit amount of input fuel (miles per gallon of gasoline, or MPG).

So, a logical question would be: What influences that MPG? What gives my car a better MPG versus, say, my wife's sport utility vehicle (SUV)? This ratio is based on a number of factors, such as the engines in our respective vehicles, body drag, weight, and rolling resistance. Her SUV is bigger, is heavier,

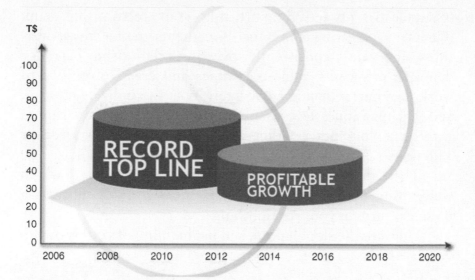

FIGURE 2.5   The Profitability of Growth

and has larger tires. It takes her SUV more power to slow down and stop and to start again from a stop.

Fuel efficiency of growth works very similarly in organizations (see Figure 2.5). The ratio is often measured in terms of profitability of growth—your price minus the costs of bringing your products or services to market: in other words, sales revenues less the cost of goods sold; research and development (R&D); selling, general, and administrative expenses (SG&A); interest expenses; taxes; and extraordinary items.

In my experience, fuel efficiency or profitability of growth is as much a mind-set as it is generally accepted accounting principles. By extending your understanding and acceptance that relationships are important, to the strategic and quantifiable value that makes them significant, you can enhance the fuel efficiency or profitability of your growth.

In the process, the engine, body drag, weight, and resistance load of your organization are translated into ideas such as intently outlining your relationship-centric goals and objectives (Chapter 5); identifying and prioritizing your pivotal contacts

(Chapter 6); proactively nurturing your relationship bank (Chapter 7); creating conceptual agreements on objectives, measures, and value; consistently investing relationship currency deposits; proposing value-based fees and creative options to work together; reducing labor intensity at the individual, team, and organizational levels; enhancing your reputation capital with great work; and building your professional net worth over a lifetime.

These ideas create a strategic relationship scorecard, which we've proved can lead to unprecedented growth through a unique return on your relationships.

How are the slope, speed, and profitability of your growth?

A Relationship-Centric Culture

The challenge with the idea of relationships is that it's seldom a stand-alone concept! Think about it—relationships don't make sense by themselves! They are an application, an enabler, or an enhancer toward getting things done. The impact most of our clients seek in their business, such as improving the attributes of growth mentioned previously, heavily depends on a change in behavior of their people—a fundamental change in how they think about, identify, prioritize, and invest in relationships for an extraordinary return.

Some individuals can make this transition—one of purely transactional interactions to transformational relationships—within and external to the organization. Many others, unfortunately, can't or won't. I can't turn an introvert into an extrovert; what I can do is help key individuals and teams adapt.

The process starts in how your organization attracts, develops, and retains top-notch, relationship-centric talent. Beyond the current global war on terror, there is a global war for talent. This is the reason why sales managers aggressively recruit sales reps with a strong Rolodex, and why acquiring companies are willing to pay handsome multiples for mind share and wallet share growth. A recent Association for Corporate Growth (ACG) Thompson survey attributed the number one reason for the flurry of recent merger and acquisition activity as one of profitable revenue growth—driven by internally as well as externally focused relationships.

As evidenced by popular books such as *Topgrading* by Bradford D. Smart, the war for talent has been defined as a strategic business initiative and critical enabler of corporate execution. It also happens to be the absolute top challenge in hypergrowth markets such as China and the Gulf Cooperation Council (GCC), a trade bloc involving the six Arab states of the Persian Gulf. Every organization has an ongoing need to assess its current, as well as growth-centric, talent requirements. Because of enduring economic and social forces and the struggle to keep top-notch talent in critical roles, this trend is likely to continue for the next several years. A successful campaign in this war requires more than just assertive and creative recruiting. Another critical attribute is a relationship-centric culture with a systematic, disciplined process to retain, develop, and constantly challenge high-performing teams. Countless studies centered on the cost of a bad hire continue to reiterate the critical nature of succinctly identifying this process, as well as executing it with vigor and consistency.

Relationship-Centric Best Practice: Blueprint for High-Performing Teams

According to the *Journal of Applied Psychology*, high-performing employees have a 40 to 80 percent greater positive impact on firm performance than average employees. Based on our research, what follows are the 30 critical

(continued)

Relationship-Centric Best Practice:
Blueprint for High-Performing Teams (Continued)

attributes of highly dynamic, relationship-centric, high-performing teams. There are three categories: individual competencies (self-motivating and self-correcting), team dynamics (competent and credible), and the relationship-centric organization (decentralized and adaptive).

INDIVIDUAL COMPETENCIES	TEAM DYNAMICS	RELATIONSHIP-CENTRIC ORGANIZATION
• *Competitive*—prioritizes external targets and threats, willing and able to compete and win	• *Competent*—very well skilled, well practiced; mastery of communication and inner dependencies	• *Adaptive*—consistently scans the periphery to learn and navigate change with confidence and agility
• *Connected*—proactively creates and capitalizes quantifiable and strategic relationships at the edges of the organization	• *Committed*—emotionally engaged and dedicated to targets and values; very high degree of loyalty	• *Big Thinking*—innovates by doing differently versus incrementally
• *Candid*—exhibits the courage to oppose the status quo	• *Coalition*—builds cross-functional or business influence and respect; collaborates and delivers on commitments; incredibly dependable	• *Emotionally Astute*—deep sense of allegiance with multigenerational workforce
• *Gives Credit*—credits contributions, successes, and ideas of others	• *Conflict as an Asset*—a constructive approach to resolving dysfunctional team dynamics	• *Effective at Execution*—executes with speed, accuracy, and precision; has solid insights

- *Resourceful*—seeks support of others for supplemental, clarifying information

- *Engaged*—uses facts and convictions to persuade with the unique ability to frame, explain, and defend

- *Compliant*—operates within legal and ethical guidelines and allocated resources

- *Focused*—commits to completion while course-correcting or navigating around obstacles and delivers results

- *Clear-Sighted*—is able to boil down any emerging trends or problems early on

- *Intelligent*—is naturally inquisitive; education is a lifelong process

- *Feedback Loop*—high degree of *measure*, *analyze*, and *enhance* processes

- *Peer Discipline*—self-governance of performance expectations

- *Protective*—of each other against outside threats

- *Proud*—deeply believes in "winning is everything"; team success outweighs individual glory

- *Trust-Centered*—has courage to fail and learn

- *Respected*—earned through thought leadership and consistent value-add both within and external to the team

- *Dependable*—follows through; remembers and delivers on commitments made by senior leadership

- *Not Overly Complicated*—consistently transforms metrics and processes into boiled-down, simple, clear, and succinct elements

- *Unbound*—aims high; has workforce on board for the journey ahead

- *Strategic*—early adopter of technology for broad-based functional excellence

- *Magnet for Talent*—home to highly diverse, world-class technical and leadership talent

- *Purposeful*—long-term vision is consistently shared and nurtured

In the McKinsey & Company book *The War for Talent*, the authors describe a pervasive talent mind-set as a deep conviction shared by leaders throughout the company that sustainable competitive advantage in the next two decades can come only from having better talent at all levels. Alarming statistics point to the undisputable fact that emerging markets such as China and India are producing more honor students than we have students, with unprecedented access to evolutionary technology at a drastically reduced acquisition cost. Although I am bullish on the United States' resiliency, I remain skeptical about our ability to win this global war. How long will it take for these countries to outpace the U.S. knowledge economy? How long before we relinquish the intellectual capital advantage?

Greg Alexander, a personal friend and CEO of Sales Benchmarking Index (SBI), has conducted similar market research in partnership with Career Point Consulting. They interviewed 25,000 sales reps and asked for descriptions of their ideal job. Whereas Greg's previous work with Dr. Brad Smart on *Topgrading for Sales* was primarily focused on the buying side, with insights from hiring sales managers, this survey focused on the selling side, looking at what types of companies top-producing sales reps want to work for. The results were shocking; attributes such as a strong compensation plan, competitive territory, and enterprise sales volumes were expected, but the resounding response could be summarized as: *I'm looking for a company to invest in me as an individual and a home where I can build a long-term career.*

"This clearly validates a high interest and value in relationships from the company to these high-performing sales professionals," commented Greg.

Their research also highlighted that during the decade in question (1996 to 2006), sales turnover was estimated to be between 38 and 42 percent in business-to-business (B2B) sales across 19 unique industries. The replacement costs of sales professionals, including recruiting fees, on-boarding, training and development, salary, commission, and benefits, were estimated to be close to $500,000 per rep. With roughly 20 million professionals who classify themselves in B2B sales functions in the United States alone, the sales turnover translates to an estimated 8 million sales reps every year. At $500,000 each, that is a $400 billion problem in the United States every year.

Do you still believe the global war for talent is not a costly one?

The Misperceived Value of a Rolodex

Ask any sales manager what top qualities he or she is looking for in the next great sales hire and I would be surprised if a strong Rolodex wasn't near the top of that list. But if you carefully consider its characteristics, the Rolodex itself is purely transactional. Its perceived or underlying value is desired relationships, which, by definition, lead to accelerated access, enhanced go-to-market, or extended reach at a much more attractive cost of sales.

Unfortunately, like many transactional measures, a Rolodex seldom has the means to represent more than its quantity. Two greater attributes often missed in the analysis of the ultimate value of that Rolodex are the diversity or quality of the individuals it contains. What percentage of that Rolodex includes C- or V-suite executives? How long have those relationships existed? Could you document a natural quality progression of those relationships? How many are invested in daily? What has been the documented repeat or referral business from that Rolodex? Has the inherent built-in trust ever been battle tested?

Greg Alexander, along with Dr. Brad Smart, gathered interesting insights from more than 6,000 interviews with sales professionals over a 20-year period. The research highlighted that many publicly traded companies demanded monthly or quarterly quota performance from their sales organizations, a practice that resulted in a strong shortsighted focus by the individual sales reps. This high-transaction-centric focus versus investment in the longer-term viability of key relationships toward establishing a foundational level of trust was identified as a major mistake.

"I attribute the success of individual reps to three critical areas: 10 percent knowledge, 10 percent luck, 80 percent relationships," commented Greg. "Sales professionals with long-term careers who have succeeded through various economic cycles, selling for multitudes of companies, understand and leverage the transferability of their personal brands."

Relationship Economics @ Work: Greg Alexander at SBI and Transformation Business Development

Greg Alexander called me for this interview from the Accenture Match Play Golf Tournament in beautiful Tucson, Arizona, where he had been requested to give a keynote speech on the strategic value of sales benchmarking to a group of 30 chief sales officers. This exclusive three-day event encompassed educational forums and collaborative discussions, as well as a black-tie gala with significant others.

"We are a small but growing company and simply wouldn't have the resources to put an event of this caliber together for top sales officers at marquee companies such as Sun, BMC, PepsiCo, Best Buy, and Unisys, to name a few," Greg explained. "This opportunity was only possible due to my investment and relationship with Rick Bakosh, managing partner in the Accenture CRM service line with responsibility for Accenture's Sales Transformation solutions."

Greg first met Rick a year ago and resisted the temptation to push for getting into Accenture's accounts and start comparing deal pipelines. He invested the time, effort, and resources to understand Rick's needs and contributed content, introduced him to influential relationships, and helped his staff with different challenges, none as fee work.

"When this opportunity came up, he asked if I wanted to be involved," said Greg. "Conversely, early on in launching our company, I tried to sign regional value-added sales consulting firms that were entrepreneurial with a geographic focus. Because I often went straight to conversations about deals and didn't invest in their business or our relationship, I have zero to show for that investment. I thought, acted, and treated them differently, and as such, I don't have a relationship with any of them and have generated no opportunities from them since."

Greg Alexander is probably one of the sharpest sales executives I know. Yet even for seasoned sales pros, isn't it interesting that many of us often jump right into "the deal conversation" versus investing in the relationship?

Jim Collins of *Good to Great* fame is notorious for highlighting the need for asking the *who* questions and getting the right people on the bus. His research clearly outlines that people can likewise be a quantifiable strategic asset and any investment in an organization's human capital is surely to produce an above-market-rate ROI as the global war for talent continues to strengthen. Beyond the cliché that people are among an organization's greatest assets, they are also quantifiable and strategic soft assets. People are added to an organization because of their promise to deliver quantifiable value. Only through adherence to a systematic process of search for great talent; assessment of their appropriate fit (I'm often amazed at how many nizations "settle"); thorough on-boarding, training, and development of their broad-based business acumen (versus simply their functional expertise); and consistent organizational alignment (for not only what the business needs today, but where the business is headed) and outplacement of a "wrong fit" with the least amount of disruption to the business will an organization be able to fully gain the value of people as a strategic soft asset. That's people promise, value, and equity realized.

Strategic Relationships On-Boarding

Savvy business leaders understand that their greatest strategic value to an organization is proactively investing in their human capital as they aim to align culture with strategy for greater business outcomes. If you look at Figure 2.6, you'll see that as an organization searches for talent, it aims to minimize risk and maximize every individual's impact. The goal is to provide a better result through a better fit by assessing each individual's

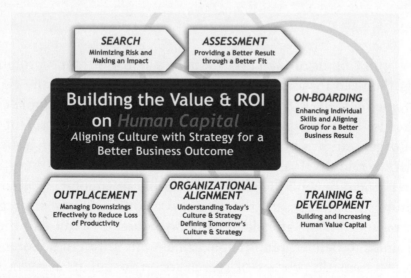

FIGURE 2.6 Return on Human Capital

past performance as well as his or her unique individual characteristics. And as on-boarding continues to be improved, the hope is to also enhance individual skills and align teams for better business outcomes.

Ongoing training and development can strategically build and increase human capital value in a respective organization. But in the aim for organizational alignment, it is critical not only to grasp today's culture and strategy but also to succinctly anticipate and define where the organization is headed in the years to come. And when the fit is simply no longer valid and some of that talent must be displaced, downsizing must be managed to effectively reduce loss of productivity and overall morale of the organization and its presence in the market.

My question to you as a leader is this: Which part of this formula couldn't benefit from stronger relationships? Which individual contributor, team manager, or organizational leader couldn't benefit from stronger intracompany relationships as well as externally focused relationships? From the relationships of frontline sales contributors, with their customers and distribution channels, to those of procurement professionals and their most valuable strategic suppliers, all are substantial, quantifiable, and strategic soft assets in an organization's intracompany relationships. Without them, I struggle to see how any organization, regardless of its size or industry focus, can fully maximize its operational efficiency or effectiveness (not to mention the desire to maintain and ideally gain a competitive market share).

Here is a novel idea: strategic relationship on-boarding. You've heard the adage that people don't leave jobs; they leave managers. I wonder, during their employment, how or what do people learn about how their company builds and values relationships? We teach new hires all about our company, products, services, maybe even competitive landscape and key market trends, yet seldom do we help employees understand how to build strategic relationships within and outside of our company!

I've seen both formal and informal mentoring programs that are world class in every aspect of their design, development, and delivery, yet are missing this crucial component.

Is it because we assume new employees should already have learned this skill? If they came from a Big Name organization, do we assume they learned these skills there? Or do we not think it's an important topic simply because a new hire is outgoing, or the person's specific job doesn't require building relationships?

All three are flawed assumptions. In our consulting work with public and private companies, large and small, we see employees of varying business stature reach a job or a career plateau, get bored, and leave because they lack the willingness and ability to build strategic relationships—in their teams, across departments, across the organization, or externally with key market influencers.

As such, here are 10 best practices for helping new employees—at any level—get a running start at identifying, building, and nurturing strategic relationships to drive performance and results:

1. **Start the learning on day ONE!** The first item on the agenda should be a meeting with a respected executive who clearly helps new hires understand that personal and professional success will not be based on a product or a service, but rather on the manner in which they develop lasting relationships. Share three best practices and ask the new hires about the relationships they want to develop while with the organization, versus what they want to achieve.

2. **Assign peer-level relationship mentors.** Assign new hires to a "relationship colleague" who literally walks them around and introduces them to key influencers and who travels or works on the project with them; this will help provide credibility by association. They need a peer to learn from, bounce ideas off, and relate to without the structural/authoritative pressures and the need to impress.

3. **Help them form "relationship advisory boards."** Particularly at a manager level, help new hires develop a group of subject matter experts and experienced peers, inside and outside the organization, to act as an informal panel of relationship advisers.

4. **Institute and reward relationship coaching by managers.** New hires are often trying to figure out which end is up. Although as a person moves up in the organization, the hand-holding will decrease, ensure that appropriate expectations and a reward system are set up that encourage managers to coach and teach the value of strategic relationships.

5. **Integrate relationship development into your management training.** How do managers learn how to build relationships? Unfortunately, a lot of companies don't provide this training to new managers (kiss of death, by the way!). First-level managers are exactly at the right point in their careers for relationship development training, because they're open to learning. It's ideal to develop a foundation of good habits and skills early.

6. **Raise the bar on human resources' (HR's) strategic relationship value.** HR's role doesn't start or end with getting the candidate hired. HR needs to continue to reach out to employees, introducing insights on the most valuable relationships within the organization. Every new hire should think of HR as a go-to resource and know when to call HR for strategic relationship help.

7. **Provide mandatory relationship compliance training.** Relationships go bad when there are misaligned expectations. If you want to reduce your legal liability, help new hires understand how to more effectively set the right expectations, early and often!

8. **Provide a relationship coach.** Not every company or individual can afford to hire an external coach. But for a high performer who may be rough around the edges, a newly

promoted manager or executive, or a valuable employee or team who works remotely, it's an invaluable asset.

9. **Develop a new-hire relationship integration process.** Cliques exist in many organizations. They develop as a result of the tenured nature of the culture, through various acquisitions and the people who come with them, or as people follow a specific manager. New hires often feel like outsiders, so conduct a new-hire relationship integration process. It's a great way for a team to get to know a new teammate or manager, build early rapport, and establish mutual expectations.

10. **Provide new-hires with one relationship-centric book per month.** Did you know that less than 5 percent of Americans read more than one business book a year? Why not get new employees off to a great start by providing them one relationship-centric book each month and ask them to present a summary at an informal "lunch and learn"?

Maybe, just maybe, we'd lose less incredible talent because employees were able to build lasting, trusting, and candid relationships throughout the organization.

Relationship-Centric Best Practice: Developing an "A-Team"

A client CEO recently asked me how she could more effectively develop her bench of leadership talent. Here are eight best practices I suggest for developing a relationship-centric A-team:

1. **Profile your strongest relationship-developing leaders today.** When looking at your current leadership bench (direct reports as well as perhaps one or

even two tiers down), identify pockets of relationship-development best practices. In our experience, they're seldom exclusive to one individual, so look wide and deep to build an ideal profile for the relationship-centric leader, like you would a puzzle. This will serve as the future state of your bench.

2. **Pick A-players and on-board them to be relationship-centric.** Read the previous section. Use a rigorous and proven process of selection, interviewing, and assessing (*not* an HR role, by the way), followed by an investment in teaching, assimilating, and setting them onto a relationship fail-proof path. Elevate your mind-set to one that sees ROI from all human capital efforts—search, assessment, on-boarding, training and development, strategic alignment, and, when applicable, outplacement. What aspect of this process couldn't benefit from stronger relationships?

3. **Invest in your bench's relationship development.** Leaders who are not willing or able to invest in the development of their bench neglect to do so at their peril. Create the aforementioned profile of a relationship-centric leader, benchmark the team against it, and create individual development pathways for each required role and realm of responsibilities. Remember that relationships are between individuals and people mature in both the art and science of relationships at very different paces. As such, a one-size-fits-all "let's pack everyone in a classroom for a week" approach seldom works.

4. **Be the relationship-centric role model they seek.** Your bench is desperately looking for a role model to emulate. Why not you? Be the leader who walks the

(*continued*)

Relationship-Centric Best Practice: Developing an "A-Team"
(Continued)

relationship development talk. You aim to raise the bar and set a higher standard for the team, but how's the view in the mirror? Are you engaging, centered, and focused? Do you invest strategically, formally and informally, in relationship coaching and mentoring, and are you developing a culture unafraid of retribution and with the courage to fail? Your own relationship development performance, habits, and leadership skills will speak much louder than any memo!

5. **Provide relationship development challenges and opportunities.** When was the last time you had to walk a tightrope between two buildings, or stand behind one of your executives while that person fell backward? So many of our relationship and trust development exercises are ludicrous at best! We go into the woods and do all these goofy things that have absolutely no bearing on the reality of the office. As the leader, you have a fiduciary responsibility to create value-based, real-world scenarios for your bench so that they develop value-based, performance-focused relationships, inside and outside the organization. When the bench has a sense of purpose, meaning, and passion around the relationships they develop every day, they may just surprise you when faced with challenges or opportunities and make the impossible possible. If not, you can always go back to paintball fights and capture the flag!

6. **Develop succinct relationship-centric goals.** At all levels, create goals that individuals, teams, or organizations cannot achieve by themselves—in essence, goals that require leaders to identify, nurture, and in a

win-win manner, leverage relationships. Beyond a clear vision, mission, and strategy (which is often just wall art), help leaders create strategic relationship dashboards, individual relationship initiatives, and personal actions that may or may not call for a change in behavior. This approach tends to have the biggest impact on creating results, as relationship-centric goals drive higher performance. But also keep in mind that relationships go bad when there are misaligned expectations. As such, invest additional time, effort, and resources up front to appropriately align those expectations.

7. **Create a relationship-development learning environment.** Make no mistake about it, performance trumps all. In the end, though, relationships give high performers the extra edge. As such, balance the expectations your bench has of a performing versus learning environment. How?

   - Empower a cascading culture of relationship development; say, "I know you get it; how about the rest of the team?"

   - Remove the unwows! Whatever is unimpressive about how your team identifies, builds, and nurtures relationships—find a way to remove it!

   - Recognize impactful relationships—relationships that are enabling; when they enable success, recognize them openly.

   - Make learning from relationships fun!

   Give me an hour inside any company and I can tell you whether they "get," value, and invest in relationships—and learn a great deal in the process. It's in the air from the minute you walk in. If you can't

   (continued)

Relationship-Centric Best Practice: Developing an "A-Team" (*Continued*)

tell, invite trusted colleagues in who can, and then be open to their input.

8. **Conduct individual and team-based relationship-centric assessments.** Just as fingerprints are unique, we build and nurture relationships in very unique manners based on our past experiences, knowledge, talent, and perceived value for doing so. To understand the team you've assembled, assess them using criteria relating to personality, values, attitudes, interests, or lifestyles—similar to how the popular behavioral assessments such as Myers-Briggs, Hogan, Birkman, DiSC, HBDI, and psychographics have worked. We have developed two: Relationship Signature Index^{TM}, which evaluates individual attributes, and Relationship DNA^{TM}, which takes an empirical look at team attributes.

At the end of the day, a relationship-centric team that is unafraid of retribution and has the courage to fail—fast, forward, and cheap—will learn to perform together and deliver results!

Lack of investment in an organization's human capital and intracompany relationships goes beyond missed opportunities. At the edge of business where each individual's knowledge, talent, time, and critical relationships will translate into the organization's ability (or lack thereof) to attract top performers, repeat customers, crucial alliances, loyal suppliers, and vested shareholders, ignored investments will become cancerous to any organization. Home Depot's diminished customer-centric focus from the days of its founders, Arthur Blank and Bernie Marcus, to that of Bob Nardelli, as well as the often-described dysfunctional and high command-and-control internal interactions, is one such example. By swaying the culture from the original founders' values and people investments—and the relationships each Home Depot associate had developed—the "GE South" model that Nardelli and team brought turned away more engaged clients (internal and external to the organization) than it retained. Comments such as "I can get what I need at Ace Hardware—they're friendlier" from customers or "I'm moving on" from invaluable associates directly affected operating and financial metrics.

ROI Reinvented

It is critical to have a succinct understanding of not only the required business strategies today but what the organization will demand moving forward. This includes appropriately aligning people and strategies, a candid organizational assessment, and the proactive management and agile development of an organization's relationship assets. Only then can an organization move toward improving its peak performance.

Relationship competencies—defined as skills, knowledge, and relationship-centric values—are critical for the reinvention process of ROI and encompass business strategies, an organization's culture, and its leadership requirements. They are meaningful and easily understood, addressing near-term and midterm horizons with a strong future orientation. These competencies have an impact only when fully integrated into the performance evaluation and compensation models across the entire organization—certainly not an easy feat.

Soft assets can directly contribute to the reinvention of ROI. Beyond the traditionally perceived *return on investment*, we have proved the quantifiable and strategic value of relationships in areas such as return on influence, integration, involvement, impact, and image. Let's take a closer look at each.

Return on Influence

In many pockets of our corporate hallways, conference rooms, cafeterias, project meetings, and yes, even off-site strategy sessions, informal networks can sprout in a very spontaneous, ad hoc way. Many times, logical self-interest leads individuals to collaborate (often without directive) around a common goal or shared enemy or threat, for example, research scientists working on a common disease, investment bankers serving the same industry clients, or dissenters of a new proposed government regulation. In situations like these, individuals will openly share their time, knowledge, talent, and influential relationships.

A study of social networks clearly emphasizes an exponentially higher level of diversity and quality of sources and flow of information among these informal networks than does a hierarchical structure (see the section "Return on Integration"). The ability to create value is increasingly driven by the intellectual and social styles of knowledge workers. Their ability to engage and influence others, often without the authority to do so, creates considerably further reaching and faster access to customers, invaluable industry resources, and new untapped markets. They leverage their reputation of trust, which is one of a consistent pattern of predictable behavior.

Corporate leaders who are able to identify and harness key sources of influence in these informal networks can effectively replace traditionally bureaucratic and outdated matrix structures. They can facilitate the creation and socialization of highly unique intellectual capital, as well as further develop and nurture the personal relationships among key members of the talent pool.

Long-term, mutual loyalty between an employee and employer is quickly diminishing (unlike in prior generations). Only by applying the energy and influence of a highly diverse group of professionals can leaders effectively align personal interests with those of the team or the organization's future aspirations.

Relationship Economics @ Work: Mac McClelland, Super Hub

During a trip to Dubai, United Arab Emirates (UAE), I was introduced to Mac McClelland, a retired Marine Corps major. For the past two decades, McClelland has been leveraging his relationships in the Middle East to help companies around the world broker deals in Iraq and beyond. For companies that don't know their way around the Middle East and want to do business there, Mac's your man. He is the classic example of a quantifiable strategic relationship.

"Most of the business we get is referred through colleagues and friends," McClelland said. "It has been very helpful to have deep-rooted, long-term, proven relationships in the Middle East from living and working out here for three decades. I have an expanding address book of contacts and resources that make it much easier for American companies to leverage my relationships into productive business than to start from scratch."

Before going into business for himself, McClelland, who speaks fluent Arabic, served as the political adviser to the admiral who runs the U.S. Navy's Central Command, which oversees naval operations in the Middle East and Central Asia. After retiring in 1996, he worked as a general manager, overseeing Middle East operations for Enron. His trusted relationships with high-positioned local officials in the region have led to engagements with companies to bid on a contract to supply automobiles to the Iraqi police force, a deal with a scrap metal company based in Houston that wants to bid on the remains of Iraqi tanks blown up by U.S. bombs, and various consulting roles to major U.S. companies such as 3M to help them break into

(continued)

Relationship Economics @ Work: Mac McClelland, Super Hub
(Continued)

the Iraq market. He even helped the Saudis develop their marine corps.

In 2003, McClelland leveraged his relationships to put together a team to build a military base in the Middle East for the U.S. Air Force. By the first night, they had 500 airmen in air-conditioned tents. By the next night, they were able to provide hot and cold running water, toilets, and showers. By the third day, hot meals were on hand.

"Not only was it the weekend, but it was an Islamic holiday," McClelland said. "Had we not had the relationships in the region, this would have been an almost impossible task. As it turned out, we exceeded all expectations of the U.S. Air Force and met a service standard they never expected anyone in the region to achieve."

When asked what he thought were the top mistakes U.S. companies make in their attempts to expand in the region, number one on his list was our impatience to make the required investments of time and human capital to build and nurture relationships. Instead, he said, U.S. companies tend to parachute in without spending the time it takes to build relationships.

"Cultures in this part of the world insist on knowing you before they will do business with you," McClelland said. "The relationship is fostered through many meetings where business is not discussed. Instead, they try to gauge you as a person to see how you value family and friends and what your intentions are—both those that are visible and those you don't share. Once you have earned their trust and developed the relationship, only then will business be introduced."

Return on Integration

Corporate executives invest enormous resources in long-range, yet shortsighted, strategic plans, as evidenced by countless initiatives that become obsolete by the sheer dynamics of their markets and competitors. Technological advances, evolving regulations, and social dynamics also affect this obsolescence. Yet many corporate leaders ignore the strategic opportunity to create a truly sustainable competitive differentiation and one of the highest returns with a substantially lower investment of money and risk exposure: creating a highly integrated organization of decentralized relationships.

As succinctly illustrated in Ori Brafman and Rod Beckstrom's book *The Starfish and the Spider*, the massively complex and dynamic ecosystems of today's highly matrixed corporations can more effectively adapt to the market dynamics by way of decentralized competency teams. Substantial organizational inertia creates difficult personality dynamics and also has the potential to bring out highly destructive corporate politics in any effort to drive meaningful change. Our research, coupled with the digitization of social networks, highlights a strategic asset in any manager's, leader's, or executive's investment of time and energy not only in creating decentralized teams but also in nurturing productive relationships in their dynamic environments.

In contrast to the Industrial Age—in which much of the current command-and-control organizational structure was focused on capital as the most valuable resource—the current multigenerational workforce leverages a very different asset for creating shareholder value. The highly integrated business unit, operating company, or division that mobilizes and leverages its broad-based intellectual capital tends to waste fewer cycles in redundant market penetration, talent acquisition, and strategic supplier relationships. Instead, its intracompany as well as external relationship development efforts can translate into not only more rewarding, productive work for its current and future talent but also a greater return on capital at a relatively low risk.

Return on Involvement

Many people believe that the sheer number of extracurricular activities will enhance overall market presence, particularly in professional services, where it is considerably more difficult to elevate your intangible value. But simply joining 15 boards and showing up for meet and greets will not suffice. A much tighter focus on a prioritized select few with a greater impact on execution is the answer to stronger market presence. Your involvement with any intracompany forum to exchange ideas—as well as the more traditional externally focused avenues such as industry associations, professional affiliations, or accreditation bodies—all demand a considerable investment of your limited time, effort, and resources. Although many understand intuitively the potentially influential and certainly the equity value of their involvements, very few measure the actual cost—much less the opportunity cost.

I am involved in well over a dozen industry organizations. In the past, I used to attend their various functions, volunteer for countless causes, and become immersed in each of their respective missions. But when you continue to attend and provide ideas and insights and your time, capital, and introductions to influential relationships, when do you ever get a chance to ascertain a return on your involvement? In my case, I even reached a point of diminishing returns in which critical personal and professional relationships were being neglected at the cost of attending yet another event or function, engaging with people or organizations I didn't much care for. By reducing the sheer *quantity* and focusing on a select few most applicable to your personal and professional goals and objectives, not only do you create more discretionary time, but the investments you choose to make will tend to create a higher return.

Generally, three fundamental functions become the critical arteries of an organization's sustainability: membership, programming, and fundraising. To maximize your return on involvement, take a leadership role in one of these critical functions. Join a few select boards, and through the execution of critical milestones, you'll earn the trust and respect of your peers to exert influence from that active and impactful involvement. Choose fewer organizations with high-quality professional members who are decidedly relevant to your personal or professional endeavors. Aim to attend or help create content-rich events with actionable takeaways, not simply a motivational rah-rah. Recommend or help create multiple revenue streams so that the organization does not rely solely on membership dues or corporate sponsorships of a single annual event. And especially in volunteer-based organizations, become the connector, the collaborator, and the consensus builder with a track record of execution.

As I mentioned previously, people gather for two fundamental reasons: content and community—what can I learn, and who else will be there? A good example of this model is our annual Relationship Economics Retreat. At the end of each summer, I invite an intimate group of noncompeting senior executives and their spouses/significant others to an exclusive resort. During a highly engaging three days, a group of senior leadership peers and thought leaders gather at a magnificent setting to discuss:

- Management of strategic relationships
- Development of a quantifiable return on strategic relationships
- Impact of social media on the enterprise
- Reorientation of the organization
- Growth and competitiveness strategies ahead

These are an intensive three days; we work hard and play hard. But attendees expect the toughest kind of hard work: mental challenge. These events are an intellectually rewarding experience, which is probably rare and perhaps unprecedented in an executive's normal career progression.

Relationship Economics @ Work: Steve McGaw at AT&T and Relationship-Centric Problem Solving

Almost every person's most precious commodity is time. Many business relationships begin to break down when there is a perception that one side is extracting more time than that side is contributing value.

Steve McGaw, senior vice president (SVP) of corporate strategy for AT&T, has been with the company for more than 20 years. He was formerly SVP of Mobility Supply Chain and Fleet Operations, where he managed more than 1,200 full-time employees in addition to some 3,000 contractors. The company usually dealt with partners the managers knew, liked, and trusted, but there were times when the success of the business called for more difficult relationships.

"I once had a project that we were really struggling with as a company," Steve said. "We could not reach an agreement with the data company we were working with at the time and had a number of unsolved issues. Every time we got on the phone with them, they were late. When we would finally reach an agreement, they would draw up the paperwork and it would be totally different than what we were expecting."

"It is unlike me to jump on a plane and spend time with somebody without a clear agenda and purpose, but eventually, I invited them to a golf event in their city and they agreed," he continued. "We spent the weekend together and hardly talked any business. We built a relationship that weekend and two weeks later all of our business issues had been resolved."

Return on Impact

As highlighted by Larry Bossidy in his book *Execution*, when people, processes, and tools converge with a mind-set to execute, you realize return on impact. Those who can consistently deliver performance, execution, and results—despite macroeconomic or microeconomic conditions, setbacks, roadblocks, and challenges—develop a reputation and a quantifiable return on any investment made for their ability to perform. An organization's ability to candidly assess, proactively manage, and develop its high-performing and high-potential talent with a great sense of agility is a fundamental contributor to this return on impact.

High-potential individuals must be systematically measured on current performance and development paths for both breadth and depth of competencies and capabilities, as well as their true potential for not only becoming a leader but also progressing along this continuum (how they react to the good, the bad, and the ugly during this journey). So how do you proactively identify and systematically nurture the breadth and depth of relationship development knowledge, behavior, and skills in an up-and-comer? Fewer organizations, unfortunately, are willing to take risks with high potentials in critical roles—they're demanding high performers and high provens. So how do you assess a high potential's relationship-centric readiness to drive very real impact in the business? Here is a simple formula:

Current state of performance (competencies/skills)
  + *Developmental plan* (good and bad experiences, motivation)
  + *Potential* (readiness traits)
  = *Relationship-centric readiness*

That readiness then has to be questioned in context. Specifically, are they ready *now*? Will they be ready in one to two years with this additional development? In one to two years with a great deal of development? Or should you wait and see

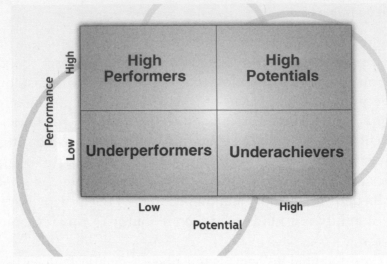

FIGURE 2.7 Return on Impact Matrix

(which is a maintenance mode) and keep them in their current roles to see how well they adapt and respond to challenges?

The result is a return on impact matrix such as that shown in Figure 2.7.

Relationship-Centric Best Practice: At the Table or on the Menu?

News Flash: The only person responsible for your professional growth is you! When you're a candidate for a promotion that ends up going to a peer, are you left wondering, "Why him (or her) and not me? Why was she (or he) promoted to manage or lead a broader realm of responsibilities, but not me? Why, when I am the one who is more consistently and more recently invited to spend time with the boss, is he (or she) the one receiving the promotion?"

If this has happened to you, I recommend you take some time for careful introspection regarding why you didn't receive this growth opportunity. To do this effectively, I offer you a 10-point litmus test. Be candid when considering these points, and take some time for introspection:

1. Have I demonstrated performance under pressure?
2. Have I completed an initiative that clearly demonstrates my core strengths and capabilities?
3. Have I consistently supported my colleagues by taking a genuine interest in their key initiatives and by helping them achieve quantifiable results?
4. Are my communication skills, written and oral, as proficient as they could be?
5. Have I consistently demonstrated the ability to confront others on issues with respect and to problem solve with decisiveness?
6. Have I achieved a high degree of influence to reinforce the ability of proactively engaging others and getting things done?
7. Have I supported my superiors by taking on difficult projects and offering value-based counsel?
8. Have I succinctly defined my long-term goals and objectives, and do I have a road map of how my current and future activities will help me obtain my goals?
9. Have I consistently completed prioritized assignments for others before completing my own? In other words, have I put other people's projects ahead of my own?
10. Have I established a strong personal brand of presence and utmost competence?

If you answered "no" to any of these questions, you may be prohibiting a potential promotion at your current

(continued)

Relationship-Centric Best Practice:
At the Table or on the Menu? *(Continued)*

organization. Sharp A-players realize sooner or later that you either move up or move out, so take steps to move up whether within your current company or into another organization.

Becoming an Object of Interest

"When one comes across as a confident leader, a mover and shaker, they have this sense of destiny about them," commented Jim Boone, a friend and president and CEO of CORESTAFF Services. "They are straightforward in their answers, curious, bright, with a lot of energy and drive." They possess what he referred as the "wow factor"; you get the sense that they have their act together and are going places. "I can't wait for the board to meet him."

A CEO recently asked if I could help his senior leaders build a stronger portfolio of relationships. Although extremely competent in their individual roles and realms of responsibilities, he thought they could become better "connectors." After evaluating each executive's relationship development efforts, my goal in coaching them was to see them become more intentional about their investment efforts and to strategically focus on the diversity and quality of their relationships.

If you want to effectively and consistently connect with others, be the kind of individual others want to connect with. Here are 10 best practices that will help you become an object of interest:

1. **Read, write, and explore—every day!** This is something I do daily, whether in my office or on the road. I intentionally

schedule time on my calendar to read a variety of topics, write articles or executive briefings/position papers or blog posts, and explore online. These three activities fuel each other by giving breadth and depth to the insights you gather. Set aside 15 minutes each day to do all three.

2. **Research and relate.** How often do we attend a meeting or networking function unprepared, without a clue as to who will be present or what is on the agenda? We walk in blind and empty-handed with little or no insight on the relevant topic. Be prepared. Block off 30 minutes in advance of a meeting or function to research key trends or the speaker/panel's bios. Come up with three to five compelling questions or discussion points that are thoughtful, hard-hitting, contrarian, or unique.

3. **Come out swinging.** Have you listened to a presenter or keynote speaker spend the first 15 minutes thanking the organization, exclaiming how delighted he or she is to be there, commenting what a wonderful city that city is, or sharing how God, parenthood, and apple pie made him or her the person he or she is today? Blah, blah, blah. By the time the introduction is over, the speaker has lost half, if not two-thirds, of the audience! Come out swinging with a bold statement, something catchy that bangs a stake in the ground and says you are worth listening to!

4. **Energize them.** While we are on the subject of bad openings, how about the snoozer? The ho-hum, monotone voice that makes you sleepier the longer you hear it? We could be talking about flying jets, and this person would still completely suck the energy out of the conversation! Don't be humdrum. Bring a slightly higher-than-relevant level of energy to every interaction. We're not all Tony Robbins, but if we are boring, people will disengage. Raise the tempo—genuinely.

5. **Be present.** Has anyone ever asked you a question and when you tried to answer, the person's eyes scanned the room looking for bigger fish to fry? Did you want to grab them and say, "PAY ATTENTION TO ME!" When engaging others, stay centered, present, and in the moment. Don't start thinking about your to-do list, your day's schedule, the proposal you have to create, or the 200 e-mails you have to respond to. Turn off the smart phone—it's for your convenience, not others'—and stay focused on the interaction at hand.

6. **Plant a seed.** If you tell me everything you know about a topic when we first meet, I'll take the earful I've gotten and move on (read "I'll be bored") and will have little interest in learning more from you. Conversely, if you tell me just enough to pique my curiosity, I'll either ask for more or seek you out to learn more. Plant the seed and leave someone wanting more by making a brief statement and then being quiet. If someone is interested, he or she will often come back with, "What do you mean?" or "Tell me more about that!"

7. **Paint a Picasso!** You've heard the adage that a picture is worth a thousand words; well, what I want you to focus on is the picture's texture and detailing and the feeling of the other person being transported into that picture! Don't tell someone there is a beach—describe it as aqua crystal-clear water that gently caresses the white sandy shore! Language is incredibly powerful; fight the dumbing down of corporate America by others who are simply too lazy to look words up and expand their vocabulary. If they don't understand a word, it's their problem; your authentic and genuine voice can do this without coming across as an elitist.

8. **Tell interesting stories.** This further expands on the idea that we can paint a Picasso. We can either show a picture or take someone there with a story. Most people may not

remember your points, but they will remember your stories. I often run into people who have heard my speeches or have read my book, and I am always amazed how, years later, they still recall and relate to my "2 A.M." stories or "meeting Joan at the YMCA at 6 A.M. on a Saturday" story.

9. **Appeal to their logical self-interest.** I often tell audiences that the worst thing you can do on social networks is to sell, because it unequivocally turns people off. Conversely, the best thing you can do online is to listen, engage, and influence others. Guess what? The same recommendation applies when you meet someone in person. You want to get to know people and give them a chance to get to know, and hopefully like, you. You'd ask better questions and appeal to their logical self-interest by always, always, always thinking about what's in it for them. What are they interested in, why are they asking this particular question, or why would they want to meet for coffee next week? Your interactions, responses, correspondence, and so forth, should always aim to improve their condition.

10. **Pace yourself.** Recently, I saw the same person at three different events—in the same day! She's a very competent chief financial officer (CFO), and, no doubt, networking is helping her cast a wide net of opportunity. The problem is that she discerns very little about the quality of her interactions at that pace. At every event, she's telling the same stories, jokes, headlines, and so on. Instead of helping, it's actually hurting her chances at being seen as an object of interest. Pace yourself and focus on quality rather than quantity. Attend gatherings of your peers or those of higher business stature. Or go where your potential clients will be, versus attending a gathering of your peers or competitors. Go where your strongest referral sources go or where others of particular insights or with unique attributes may gather. Remember, (1) NETworking is one letter away

from NOTworking, and (2) the diversity and quality of your relationships matter just as much as, if not more than, sheer quantity.

Someone I respect recently pushed me to think beyond what time it is to how much time I have left on this earth. And, more important, in the time that I have left, the person pushed me to think about how many people's lives I can affect. How many will be better off because they met me or heard one of my speeches, read one of my books or articles, or watched one of my videos? When I'm gone, will they say, "He was a great guy to know and befriend" or "He just networked a lot"?

If you want to connect more effectively and authentically with people, become an object of interest that others seek out!

How are you doing that today? How are your efforts working for you? How do you know? In the next chapter, we tackle strategic relationship planning as a solid approach to really understand where you should focus your relationship development skills, knowledge, and resources.

Relationship Economics Online Tools: Your ROI Reinvented

http://www.RelationshipEconomics.net/RE-Tools.html

How do you know if you're getting a high ROI on influence, integration, involvement, impact, image? Check out our ROI Reinvented tool, where you can answer a handful of simple questions and get an estimated value for each.

Enjoy!

3

Strategic Relationship Planning

Although most people agree that relationships are important, few actually bother to measure, quantify, or leverage them to their fullest potential. And even though every organization creates an annual sales plan—in which it crafts and strategizes around an annual marketing and operating plan—we've yet to find one that says, "For us to be successful in reaching these key goals and objectives, we need to identify, build, nurture, and leverage these relationships and here is how we'll get there."

In my consulting work with several marquee clients, I see a consistent trend of individuals and teams who confuse planning with strategy. Specifically, when focused on revenue growth, within their named accounts, geographic territories, or even global account management efforts, their prioritization of the relationships they choose to invest in is often purely based on a "foreseeable transaction."

Here is the challenge: Sociologists tell us that an average individual can proactively manage between 100 and 150 relationships. How do you know which ones to nurture? If you believe my notion that true relationship development (versus transactional networking) is about intentional investments you choose to make, how do you then prioritize which relationships you'll invest in? You certainly can't invest in everyone equally, so how do you or will you balance relationship creation and bridge those efforts to relationship capitalization?

Planning is extrapolation of the present. Specifically, what am I doing today, and how can I do more of it? In the revenue growth example mentioned earlier, the organization evaluates its current portfolio of products and services, market conditions, and its sales force and plans a revenue growth target. It then divides that target among its sales force, so Steve, who has a geographic territory or a handful of named accounts, will have to generate $10M in top-line revenue as his quota for next year.

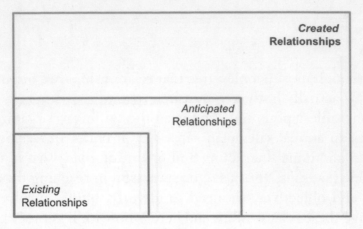

FIGURE 3.1   Existing, Anticipated, and Created Relationships

Steve then starts to panic because he generated only $7M in sales this year; he decides which accounts, transactions, and thus relationships he needs to reach his new target. What Steve and his organization are thinking about is often their "existing relationships," which for many is a very limited universe, compared with anticipated or, better yet, created relationships (Figure 3.1).

Strategy, on the other hand, is painting a picture of the future and developing a path to get there. Think of John F. Kennedy's proclamation of a moon landing in 10 years, when at that time, the country wasn't even close to accomplishing such a monumental task. Think of truly visionary leaders who join an organization and develop that vision of the future; they quickly nurture intracompany, as well as externally focused, relationships to recruit top-notch talent, fuel the vision and the mission with the necessary resources, and execute a set of priorities to bridge the current state with that future state.

Relationship strategy works the same way. What does that future vision look like? A much bigger universe that encompasses existing relationships, as well as the ones you'll need to anticipate and, in many cases, new ones you must create.

Unprecedented growth from a unique return on your strategic relationships is derived from developing a relationship strategy focused on the future.

As with any strategic initiative, the planning process is considerably more valuable than the actual plan itself. In this chapter, I discuss the eight-stage process that includes the templates, worksheets, and filtering mechanisms necessary to create a personal, team, and organization-wide strategic relationship plan. In the example section of a strategic relationship plan, I cover topics such as:

- *Relationship-centric goals*—business goals that you simply cannot achieve alone and must develop and nurture critical relationships to attain
- *Relationship bank*—existing relationships, with diversity and quality of those relationships as critical as the sheer quantity
- *Pivotal contacts*—those who have already seen the movie and have been through the pitfalls you're headed for; highly influential relationships you must seek to develop because they are instrumental to your future success
- *Relationship currency exchange*—the promised and delivered value in the favor economy
- *30-, 60-, and 90-day personal action plans*—critical to relationship development and a nurturing process based on a quantifiable and prioritized set of metrics

Fundamental Flaw in Strategic Planning

In 1972, Richard Rumelt, a professor of strategy at UCLA's Anderson School of Management, became the first person to uncover a statistical link between corporate strategy and profitability. He concluded that moderately diversified companies outperformed more diversified ones—a discovery that has held up after more than 30 years of research. His controversial 1991 paper, "How Much Does Industry Matter?" published in the *Strategic Management Journal*, highlights that neither industry nor corporate ownership can explain the lion's share of differences in profitability among business units. In short, he reinforced the notion that being good at what you do matters a lot more than what industry you are in.

This is in stark contrast to the 1980s, when the conventional wisdom dictated that an organization generates strategic plans at a business unit level and subsequently rolls up those plans in a portfolio fashion for the senior management of the company. In recent years, much of the strategy work has once again become centralized. According to Rumelt, most corporate strategic plans have little to do with strategy. Instead, they are simply three- to five-year rolling resource budgets and best guesstimates of market share projections, and they often create a false expectation that this exercise will produce a coherent strategy.

Strategic plans must outline a succinct pathway to substantially higher performance, making the need for strategic planning more event-based and mandated by the dynamic changes in one's industry. Planning should be based on available resources instead of becoming simply an annual exercise. Most companies link their strategy execution to that formulation by exploiting changes in the environment, such as technology, customer preference, regulations, cost of required resources, or competitive landscape.

If your strategy begins with identifying changes in your environment, then certainly reviewing changes in your current and available talent, the enhanced or diluted value of your brands, and the diversity and quality of your critical relationships—in essence, your soft assets—must also be included in developing strategies for exploiting those changes. Some may have long-term consequences, such as a brain drain with retiring, mature, and baby boomer generations. Companies must take a position now and invest in critical resources and processes to capture and capitalize on their soft assets before they are lost.

Strategic relationship thinking helps us take a consistent position in an uncertain world. Uncertainty and ambiguity will always be omnipresent. In many ways, they are the flip side of opportunity. If you are uncomfortable with uncertainty, you can always wait for others to take a first-mover position and ascertain their critical success factors. Although this does minimize risk, you will also lose the opportunity to take advantage of that knowledge at the edge.

Another fundamental challenge with strategic planning is that, in many circles, it is shortsighted. It is difficult to see a quantifiable ROI on your brand, for example, in one quarter. Typical budgeting processes start with a mission statement that outlines an often vague goal of the business, followed by a typical offsite strategic planning session to set the direction and high-level goals of the entire organization. These often form the framework for a six-month investment of critical resources such as human capital and time, not to mention 30-plus percent of a senior executive's and financial manager's bandwidth.

The Ford Motor Company discovered that this process can be a $1.2 billion drain. According to Jeremy Hope and Robin Fraser's book, *Beyond Budgeting*, a decade-old benchmarking study highlighted that the average company invests more than 25,000 *person days* per $1 billion of revenue in planning a performance management process. The often more intellectually engaging and analytically trackable issue of strategy can become an obsession for managerial attention because it is simply sexier to talk about strategy, even though a great deal of strategy literature highlights that focus and time are scarce resources.

It's critical to recognize the common temptation to attempt to fix what doesn't need fixing or to grossly ignore a critical component of the planning process. The common misconception that soft assets—similar to soft skills—cannot be quantified and as such cannot be planned for can deter even a well thought-out plan. Or, worse yet, people abdicate to the human resources (HR) or learning and development departments, but only in strict alignment with the current and anticipated requirements of the business.

Strategic Relationship Planning

Strategic relationship planning (SRP) is the process of transforming an organization's most valuable relationships into quantifiable performance, execution, and results. It is designed to help you identify fundamental key market opportunities and the resources you will need to meet these goals, including past strategic relationships and those necessary to achieve success moving forward. The plan enables an individual to achieve business goals and objectives and should be tightly aligned with those of the organization. Contrary to many plans disguised as management oversights, strategic relationship plans are driven by the efforts, analysis, and insights from individual relationship investments. What did you learn from those investments? Would you make them again if given the opportunity?

Here is another challenge to consider: revenue is a *lagging* indicator. It's the result of your past sales and marketing efforts. It's attempting to drive a car while looking in the rearview mirror. Yet, many organizations develop their future plans based on past performances.

Conversely, influence is a *leading* indicator. Who do I need to influence? Where are those centers of influence? How can I influence their thinking, perspective, and a logical call to action? These are all forward-looking questions. Now you're looking through the windshield trying to figure out a logical course of action and how to pick among several possible options.

SRP is intended to be that forward-looking perspective that drives your mind-set, tool set, and road map.

Eight Pillars of Strategic Relationship Planning

Eight fundamental areas where strategic relationships can and should have the biggest impact make up the pillars of an SRP. These pillars dictate where to compete, how to compete, and the quantifiable value of the strategic relationships you desire.

Pillar 1: Strategic Focus

What business are you in? What business *should* you be in? Although simple in their inquisitive nature, it is amazing just how complex these two questions can be.

What business you are in should answer, from a historical perspective, where you have been most successful, where you have produced the most professional products and services, and where your team's core competencies and expertise lie. Beyond those internal factors, the business you are in considers what the market has paid for and the value you have brought to the table.

What business you *should* be in is really what Dr. Roch Parayre at the Mack Center for Technological Innovation at Wharton School of Business calls "scanning the periphery." By changing the tools and focus from certainty to risk and from ambiguity to chaos, you elevate your perspective from lower risk and lower reward to higher risk and higher reward.

Relationship Economics @ Work:
Dr. Roch Parayre and Scenario Planning

The genesis of the scenario planning methodology, Dr. Parayre explains, originated with the oil industry. Big oil companies who relied on oil from the turbulent Middle East had to plan for different scenarios, such as war or embargo, that could affect their business.

(continued)

Relationship Economics @ Work:
Dr. Roch Parayre and Scenario Planning *(Continued)*

"We live in a world that is increasingly uncertain, yet most organizations plan as if the world were predictable," said Parayre. "We make forecasts. We plan for one view of the future. But when that view ends up not playing out as we'd planned, we are ill prepared for the alternative. Scenario planning not only reduces risk, it provides a much broader perspective on both opportunities and threats in your strategy."

Today, Parayre and his partners at Decision Strategies International, Inc., work with companies primarily in the financial services, pharmaceutical, and information technology (IT) industries—all industries that twist in the wind of some major regulatory uncertainties.

Scenario planning forces these companies to ask themselves if their current strategy is *future-proofed* across different scenarios. Relationships play an important role in this process because, for each initiative, the specific relationships needed for each possible outcome must be identified and nurtured.

For example, if you're a pharmaceutical company, the idea of an "Obamacare" health care system is clearly an issue.

"If you are a health care player anywhere in the health care value chain, you might have relationships with the kind of free marketers who serve you well in our current system," Parayre said. But because this value chain can change, you must also begin developing relationships with some of the government entities you might have shied away from in the past. If a single payer entity emerges, you will need to be able to leverage regional relationships in every possible way. If you have only built relationships that you need based on one set of assumptions about the future, you may be in bad shape if the future plays out in a different way.

"The relationship story is very consistent with the option story. The more options you have at the periphery of your core, the more you are prepared for multiple futures," Parayre said. "The same story applies to relationships. The more relationships you have as options, the more prepared you will be to leverage those relationships and deepen them if a particular future plays out."

As I cover in Pillar 7, competitive differentiation, later in this section, you must scan both internal and external influences in the short and long term and focus narrowly on your products and services and the broader market category in which you play. But beyond the competitive and market intelligence often encapsulated in a typical strategic focus, in SRP you must also include business intelligence, environmental scanning, and, to some level, social intelligence, the correlation between behaviors and relationships, as described in the book *Social Intelligence: The New Science of Success* by Karl Albrecht.

Said another way, the business you should be in is all about asking credible and trusted sources of strategic relationships the right questions. These sources could include current and prospective customers in an advisory board role, industry or functional insiders, and often ignored or underdeveloped cross-industry insights. You must learn from past interactions. What are your blind spots (what is happening now, best practices from other industries, and so forth), and who in your industry has a knack for identifying weak signals and early trends and acting on them ahead of the competition?

You must also examine present relationships. What important factors are you rationalizing away? What are perceived industry thought leaders and mavericks saying and doing? What are your customers and strategic suppliers really thinking? How can you get to them at a deeper, more candid level regarding what is happening right now?

Third, you have to anticipate surprises that can hurt you, and conversely, you need to uncover what can really help you. Can any emerging technologies help you change the game? Remember that there is a slight difference between incrementalism and innovation. Innovation is doing it *differently*. Incrementalism is doing it *better*. Some label incrementalism as continuous improvement, and in many instances that works fine. Is there a model way of doing something that you haven't explored because of present-day constraints? Competitive advantage is a highly fluid moving target, and a consistent review of your critical assumptions about your fundamental strategic focus is critical to long-term success. Strategic relationships can provide the much-needed independent perspective and perhaps unique insights on one's strategic focus.

Pillar 2: Revenue Growth

I continue to be baffled by the lessons we didn't learn from the Internet bubble of 2000. I don't care what business you are in; you cannot buy something for $2, sell it for $1, and make it up in volume!

How efficient are your sales, marketing, and business development efforts? How effective are they? Beyond 10 pounds of PowerPoint at the next leadership meeting, how do you know? Profitable revenue growth is about systematic, disciplined, strategic named or global account planning processes. Specifically, it is how to identify, nurture, and leverage your most valuable relationships for the specific intent of driving revenue at the most attractive cost of that revenue acquisition. How do you accelerate your organization's profitable revenue growth? I believe it takes a strategic relationship transformation focused on gaining mind share, wallet share, and—in the process—market share.

Relationship Economics @ Work:
Sales Transformation

One of the best practitioners of business relationships I know is Randy Seidl, senior vice president of Americas for HP's Enterprise Servers, Storage and Networking (ESSN) unit. We met several years ago. Although I was engaged to deliver the closing keynote by his counterpart, who led the channel program at a prior employer, Randy was an invaluable interview in my due diligence process of the sales culture he expects. In him, I saw a passion for revenue growth and sales execution. I saw a disciplined process to attract, develop, and retain the very best sales talent; and when expectations were not met, he was decisive in making the necessary changes.

We stayed in touch over the years, and when Randy joined HP, he quickly put in place a sales transformation game plan. Like any good leader, he brought his experience and value-based internal and external relationships to set the vision for a relationship-centric culture focused on sales execution. He promoted Kevin Purcell, a seasoned sales manger, to help drive the field efforts. Specific to revenue growth, Kevin and Randy's leadership team has built great relationships across this complex organization to deliver on Randy's expectations:

- Accelerate growth and exceed financial plan.
- Accelerate talent development; recruit the best.
- Accelerate showing up everywhere.
- Accelerate best partnering.
- Accelerate sales culture transformation.
- Accelerate efficiency and effectiveness.
- Accelerate leadership best practices.

(continued)

Relationship Economics @ Work:
Sales Transformation (Continued)

Randy and his leadership team have done well upgrading and improving the field sales force. They are constantly raising the bar on their strategic relationship development efforts. "We improved customer face time," commented Kevin. "Randy's leadership team improved the sales culture also with open confrontation, open communication, and open feedback with decisive execution. The team improved team account planning with the right people in the right roles prioritizing the right focus areas. The team reduced internal meetings during the week to focus externally on revenue-generating activities and sales calls."

"The best relationships—with the customer, the CIO, the partners, and internal to HP—are winning combinations," added Randy. "It's a work in progress, but I'm proud of the ESSN Americas team; our future continues to be bright as we focus on taking market share everywhere."

Pillar 3: Cost Performance

A very strong trend in the market today is that of supplier relationship management. Simply put, it delineates your broad-based list of suppliers in a pyramid-like format with the tactical, commodity-centric ones (you can get copper wiring from 50 different vendors tomorrow) all the way up to truly strategic, long-term suppliers instrumental to your success in the market.

Think of the different levels in this pyramid. Commodities are just that—commodity suppliers are all put through reverse auctions and will aim to drive a more attractive cost structure and leverage information technology to constantly scan the market for value chain disruption.

Conversely, you have foresight into strategic suppliers' advanced research and development efforts because they are an extension of your own research and development efforts. Collaboration often drives unique products and services to a very differentiated and sustainable market position. Cost performance in SRP also points to unparalleled asset management efficiency and effectiveness through critical relationships. If I am Sara Lee, for example, and have an on-site account team at the Walmart headquarters in Bentonville, Arkansas, not only am I tightly integrated with Walmart buyers but I can also optimize my asset utilization much more efficiently and effectively and exponentially increase my inventory turnover ratios.

Pillar 4: Process Optimization

There is a reason that a number of franchise concepts succeed: they follow a systematic, disciplined process for success. How do you build repeatable, predictable processes to scale your business? The answer is through strategic relationships.

World-class project and process management is independent of any one person, entity, or potential constraint. It is, however, highly driven by collaboration in constantly looking at what is working, why, and how it can be continually optimized to get the best outcome. That collaboration comes from internal pockets and external constituents with a vested interest in the outcome of that process. It is critical here to identify key touch points, milestones, and required resources along that process continuum. Then, look for quality gates of governance and compliance to best practices for the most efficient flow.

Pillar 5: Talent Development

Did you know that many of your current employees come with built-in relationships? You can exponentially enhance your talent acquisition efforts by focusing on the top-notch talent that you already have. There is a likely chance that your best employees know other highly qualified, capable talent for whom you are currently searching across the hall or across the globe.

Performance evaluation has to be one of the most dreaded events by both managers and employees alike. Givers don't want to do them—and neither do takers. They tend to all pile up in the last hour of the month, quarter, or year before HR calls and complains—and then they typically go something like this:

MANAGER: How are you?

EMPLOYEE: Things are fine.

MANAGER: How are the kids?

EMPLOYEE: Life is good.

MANAGER: You suck and that's it.

And unless you force the conversation back to the "you suck" part, these evaluations don't really become effective.

This is not the time to argue or declare, "Everyone hates me" and just move on. What we're talking about is *candor*, and it's the much-needed, less politically correct, much more productive way to retain and develop talent. After all, you can't do anything about a reputation you don't know you have.

"People gravitate toward those who create influence—people who are most self-aware. This includes asking tough questions such as 'What am I good at, not good at, passionate about doing? What am I really about? What do I believe strongly in?' People who are self-aware are at the highest levels of accomplishment," commented Dan Brown, a friend and former SunTrust executive.

Instead of performance reviews—a bunch of paperwork—I like strategic relationship 360-degree assessments. What do people around you think of your ability to engage and influence others? What do people above you think of the manner in which you identify and prioritize relationships to get things done, both within and external to the organization? What do you believe is your perceived value addition when you engage others on your team? Performance reviews make most of us think about how to fix, repair, or commit to remedial work. Strategic relationship 360-degree assessments can help you focus on what you're already very good at and how to capitalize on that strength. As my mentor Alan Weiss often reminds me, "We all grow by building on strengths, not by trying to metamorphose every weakness into idealized perfection. We're all imperfect. Success trumps perfection."

Bob Danzig, former head of the Hearst Newspaper Group and vice president of the Hearst Corporation, described the cream of the crop in every organization as *destiny shapers and future builders.* Only through strategic relationships and a systematic plan to identify and truly seek out the DNA of the future shapers of your team and organization will your organization succeed.

Pillar 6: Matrix Effectiveness

Organizations are complicated structures. With multiple reporting structures in different geographic locations and with different agendas, how do you get everyone on the same page to focus on execution? And more important, do you know *how* things really get done?

We believe that a highly decentralized and often informal network of relationships contributes more to actual productivity than the traditional organizational chart. Take a look at Figure 3.2. On the left is a very traditional organizational chart; many readers of this book are in one. It is hierarchical in nature and represents the classic command-and-control model originally conceived in military circles since before World War I. Conversely, the Relationship Dynamics Chart maps sources of information flow as indicated by the arrows highlighting centers of influence, sources of impact, and the true nature of

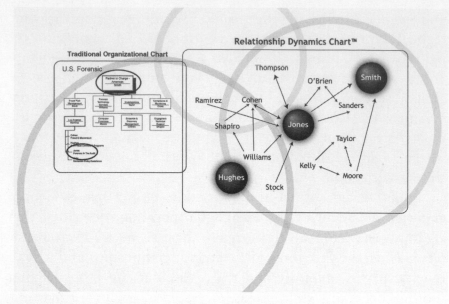

FIGURE 3.2 Relationship Dynamics Chart and Traditional
Organizational Chart

collaboration at work. Someone once called this process *mapping the watercooler*.

At the center of the Relationship Dynamics Chart is Jones. Jones has been with the organization for 10 years. She knows everyone, their spouses, their children, where they vacation, and their biggest assets and challenges both at and away from work. Conversely, Smith, as the leader of this team, has become so bogged down with administrative functions that he has actually become a bottleneck and an inhibitor to getting things done. In many ways, his finger is no longer on the pulse of the business.

Hughes is brilliant, but a raving introvert and a low talker. Because his ideas are seldom solicited or heard, his brilliance often slips under the radar and his insights are left undetected. As a result, he has become a highly underused resource when dealing with key performance indicators, balanced scorecards, and matrix forecasting.

Knowledge management is not a system—it's a process. Only by sharing the current highly influential role of Jones with others in diversified functional roles and geographic locations can you decentralize and capitalize on Jones's influence, as well as potential opportunities for shared knowledge and insights.

Pillar 7: Competitive Differentiation

The challenge with competitive differentiation is that it is a constantly moving target; it's never holistic and often not evidence-based. How do you really know what a competitor is up to? Sure, you can read white papers and analyst reports, but seldom are these insights based on hard facts provided by customers or users of the competitor's products.

The other challenge with most competitive insights is that you are often looking in the rearview mirror. It is very difficult to make real-time decisions, if not forward-looking ones, based not only on competitors' products and service offerings today but on some anticipations or predictions of the direction in which they are headed. Keep in mind that it is less expensive to innovate than to advertise.

Another insight someone gave me years ago—which I regret not following more proactively—is that your market is insightful and brilliant. Find, create, and invent ways to shorten the time from information to insight, insight to knowledge, and knowledge into results and performance between your market and your response to it. There is no faster path to success than through strategic relationships with market makers who have the ability to facilitate that accelerated access.

Pillar 8: Corporate Reputation

The fundamental drivers of corporate reputation begin with industry image. Regardless of how strong your company may be, some industries—pornography, alcohol, and even tobacco, to a lesser extent—will always have a negative connotation associated with them.

But outside of this, there are some very critical components of corporate image and identity that contribute to your reputation. They include character (culture, competitiveness); the respective abilities of the chief executive officer (CEO), employees, and resources leveraged by the company; the quality, value, and range of products and services; and the behavior of the leadership and the company's profit targets and various stakeholder values. The corporate reputation, as a result of all of these things, tends to become one of esteem, respect, trust, and confidence and is inherently either good or bad (Figure 3.3).

Whereas the components of the corporate image and identity are perceptual, a company's reputation is often emotional and the outcome a *superbelief*. Although no one company is always good or always bad, based solely on their reputation, we make decisions to buy their stock, buy their products and services, work for them, or refer our friends and families. And

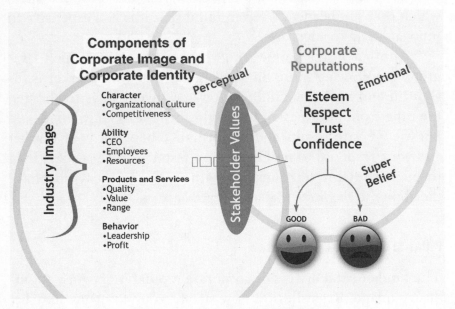

FIGURE 3.3 Critical Attributes of Corporate Reputation

although corporate reputation can take years to build, it can take just an instant to destroy.

Strategic Relationship Plan Blueprint

What follows is a blueprint for an annualized strategic relationship plan. In my consulting work, I modify this extensively based on the nature of the client's business, its key industry trends, and the quarterbacks who will lead the execution of these plans. But as a generic outline, the following provides a good starting point. Such a plan should be reviewed monthly for achievement of execution milestones and reviewed quarterly for strategic viability. You should also identify an accountable peer and proactively communicate with him or her about your progress. Develop a personal board of advisers to serve as a sort of air traffic control for some of the more challenging strategic relationship discussions.

Section 1: Looking Back—A Historical Perspective

Begin with a historical perspective of the previous year's marketing and business development efforts. Review what we refer to as your relationship-centric goals, which are business goals and objectives that mandate strategic relationships to achieve. Include not only the specific relationship development efforts you made to achieve each goal but your overall results for the previous year. Emphasize the *who* success stories here and ask the *who* questions I discussed earlier. This does not mean highlighting what you did to succeed, but instead which relationships most appropriately enabled you to achieve significant milestones and your overall success.

Next, quantify the outcomes of your collaboration efforts during the previous year. Keep the focus customer-centric by naming the client-specific colleagues and other partners you introduced and the results you accomplished through collaboration.

- What did you do last year to collaborate with a purpose, and what were the results of that collaboration? (Most people have a lot of meetings for the sake of having meetings without solving customer-centric problems.)
- Describe additional relationship-centric accomplishments made during the previous year.

Remember, specificity drives credibility. The more specific your answers, the more likely you are to capture the essence of the value of each relationship and identify specific behaviors that led to its perceived success.

Section 2: Looking Forward

As mentioned previously, the real goals of SRP are to become forward-looking and to future-proof. Invest the time and effort to consider the following objectives.

Your Current Relationship Bank

Set aside most individuals' desires to meet new people. Many do a terrible job getting their arms around the relationships they *already* have. Beyond the perception that it's all about quantity, they neglect to understand and truly leverage the diversity and *quality* of their relationships. They don't realize that the more diverse the sources of interesting and relevant contacts, the broader their sphere of influence. Likewise, the higher the business stature of one's diverse relationship bank members, the more likely it will be to gain access to and opportunities with influential relationships.

But you can't possibly improve anything you don't measure, so start with the fundamentals regarding the clarity, accuracy, and relevancy of your current portfolio of relationships by asking the following questions:

- How current is the information in your personal contact list? Are contacts appropriately categorized to reflect the diversity and quality of those relationships?
- Besides basic contact information, what initial insights have you captured regarding the nature of the relationship? What are your current plans to enhance the information you track on your most valuable relationships?
- How often did you review your entire portfolio of relationships in an effort to enhance that portfolio?
- How succinctly have you identified your ideal relationship profile, including key characteristics critical for lasting and consistent year-after-year personal and professional growth through those relationships as compared with short-term transactions?
- How aligned is your list of target relationships for the upcoming year with that ideal relationship profile?
- Did you neglect some key relationships in the past year? If so, what are your plans and time frames to reinvigorate them?

Relationship-Centric Best Practice: Relationship Resource Allocation

I don't know about your business, but my consulting and speaking work slows down twice a year: midyear around July and during the second half of December around the Christmas holiday. I use these slow times for introspection, focusing on what is going well in my business and how I can raise the bar on my client engagements, thought leadership, and personal development.

(continued)

**Relationship-Centric Best Practice:
Relationship Resource Allocation (Continued)**

I also take the time to physically print out the list of my most relevant relationships—my own relationship bank—in search of highly influential net-new relationships I've developed, identifying which ones I intentionally invested in and which ones I unfortunately neglected. This process helps me think about and prioritize my relationship investments for the next six months. I make an A-B-C list of no more than 10 relationships in each category and commit to getting caught up live and, in the process, finding a way to add value to their efforts.

Those relationships that I've invested in but unfortunately have not seen gratitude, reciprocity, or an innate sense of paying it forward simply get deprioritized. I simply am not willing to continue to give valuable time, knowledge, talent, or access to my portfolio of relationships to those who either don't get it or are unwilling to equally invest in creating value in our relationship.

Your Most Valuable Relationships

You don't have the bandwidth to invest in everyone equally, so how do you prioritize which relationships you'll invest in? On any given day, you can contact 50 people—but which 50? How are you balancing internal versus external relationships? In my experience, if it's dysfunctional within the organization, external contacts will surely see what is clearly broken.

- Who are currently your top three relationships? Think of customers, partners, colleagues, suppliers, or industry contacts at large. And don't forget to include both inside and outside the organization.

- How intimately do you understand their business, market, and foreseeable challenges and opportunities?
- Which industry publications do you read? Which thought leaders or analysts do you know with whom you can collaborate and anticipate some of the key challenges and opportunities?
- What are your plans to increase your knowledge base of this client's business? How well do you know the internal and external sources of knowledge, insights, and influence in their business or particular requirements?
- How did you invest in nurturing the relationships at multiple business stature levels this past year? Fundamentally, it's a risk to put all of your eggs in one basket when it comes to relationships at a single point of failure. If you have only one contact in that client department or organization, what happens if that person leaves? Will you be forced to go back and start all over again?

This is a good place to talk about the strategic relationship bowtie effect. As a team, when we first begin to identify and nurture a relationship, we're typically the focal point to the other side—think of the customer's company, where you've called on a single point of contact (Figure 3.4).

As you develop and nurture multiple relationships within that customer account, it's critical to align those multitudes of relationships with counterparts in your organization. In essence, reversing the bowtie to create a relationship shoestring model (Figure 3.5).

- How would you rate the diversity of the business relationships between the two firms?
- What are your account protection and relationship development plans for the coming year? Others are surely competing for the perceived value that you provide; do you

FIGURE 3.4   Early Stage of a Team's Relationship: Bowtie Effect

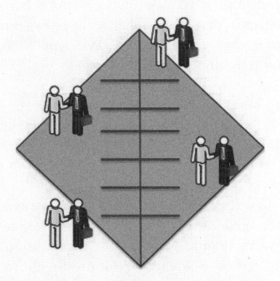

FIGURE 3.5   Developed Stage of a Team's Relationship: Shoestring Model

know who they are and your unique position? How can you continue to build a barrier to entry by others? In what specific manner can you continue to bring innovative ideas and products to minimize their needs or wants to explore other options or relationships?

- Has this client referred you to other relationships? Do you know why or why not?

- Are the results from your relationships with this client producing a positive trend in your business, as evidenced by increased profitability from work with this client? If it's an internal relationship, is the quality of your interactions increasing? Are you being perceived or described as the go-to person? Why and how or why not?

- Asked independently, how would this client describe your relationship as well as overall reputation?

- How battle tested is your relationship with this client? Remember, relationships and trust in particular can take years to develop and only single incidents to dilute or destroy. How solid is your levy against rising waters of missed commitments, and could it survive a Katrina-sized incident of poor contingency planning, lack of communication, the blame game, and a disaster of unparalleled financial or reputational outcomes?

Relationship Currency Exchange

With every interaction, we all promise value. As that value is delivered, you begin to exchange *relationship currency*. It's very similar to cash in its liquidity, but it also has a shelf life. People may or may not remember what you did for them 6, 12, or 18 months ago, but they are likely to remember the asset you were a week ago. So the timely nature of your relationship currency exchanges is critical. Therefore, ask:

- Who are your top referral sources? How do you proactively add value to each interaction? Why would they introduce you to their most trusted relationships?

- How do you thank these sources for their referrals?

- What quantifiable business have you been able to send to each of them? What efforts will you make next year to increase referrals you make to others?

Your System for Following Through

I'm simply mesmerized by how many individuals, teams, and organizations simply do not follow through on their initial interactions. Consistent, professional, and value-based follow through is often the difference between initial interactions becoming a relationship of mutual benefit versus a one-time, often transactional meeting. It's also important to reinforce that follow up is a transaction; follow-through is a process to ensure that value *promised* is, in fact, value *delivered*.

- What is your system for proactively following through with key relationships and the ones you develop?
- Describe your plan in the coming year for how you will prioritize your relationship pursuits and the criteria for which you will make key investments. How often will you work on this process, and how will you enhance it?
- Describe your plan for establishing a reputation for content. How will you become a thought leader in your chosen field?

Section 3: Return on Involvement

Strategic relationships, by definition are proactively sought, identified, nurtured, and in a win-win manner, leveraged to create performance, execution and results. As such, you must get involved—proactively, intently, and consistently—in your organization, industry, market, civic and the community in which you live. The challenge becomes one of bandwidth and a constant evaluation of the impact your involvement creates.

- With what organizations are you proactively involved and why? Describe your level of involvement in the past year and plans for expansion or deletion (there is no middle road) of your contribution to that particular organization. (Figure 3.6.)
- What quantifiable impact did you create from that involvement? Did the relationships you developed through that

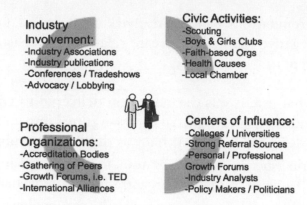

Industry Involvement:
-Industry Associations
-Industry publications
-Conferences / Tradeshows
-Advocacy / Lobbying

Civic Activities:
-Scouting
-Boys & Girls Clubs
-Faith-based Orgs
-Health Causes
-Local Chamber

Professional Organizations:
-Accreditation Bodies
-Gathering of Peers
-Growth Forums, i.e. TED
-International Alliances

Centers of Influence:
-Colleges / Universities
-Strong Referral Sources
-Personal / Professional Growth Forums
-Industry Analysts
-Policy Makers / Politicians

FIGURE 3.6   Sample Relationship Involvement Matrix

involvement result in any business or potential referral sources? What efforts did you make to refer business to individuals in those organizations? Elaborate why or why not.

- To what extent did you expand your intrafirm involvements with that organization?

- To what extent did you coach and mentor associates in relationship development activities? How did you help associates learn how to more effectively relate to client challenges and opportunities and enhance their return on that involvement through your influence?

- Describe your plans for the coming year to assist associates with their relationship development efforts and to help them obtain valuable experiences in key interactions throughout the year. List specific associates you plan to include in client and referral source meetings and events.

Reputation Capital

As mentioned earlier, performance trumps all. Strategic relationships create that extra edge necessary to win—personally or professionally. If you've ever watched an Olympic 100-meter track and field race, it's often won by fractions of seconds. Relationships are that extra edge. Reputation creates that extra edge on an on-going and much longer-term basis. Positive and well regarded reputations can create market gravity or pull; conversely, negative reputations create relationship resistance and market friction.

- To what extent was the value you delivered to clients and referral sources recognized for its eventual impact as having been delivered by you? What was the return on objective?
- Describe specific actions you took to enhance your personal, as well as your team's and organization's, intellectual capital.
- Describe speaking, writing, or industry involvements that directly contributed to your thought leadership position. How were you a servant leader in a charity or a community?

Pivotal Contacts

As previously mentioned, and something I discuss more of in upcoming chapters, pivotal contacts are the relationships you aspire to have. They are often individuals who are two business statures above your current perceived reach. Their time and access to influential relationships are well protected. In my experience, they are passionate about execution and pride themselves in their subject or domain expertise.

- Describe the three most effective approaches you have identified in expanding your portfolio of relationships.
- Identify the most valuable and most diverse relationship asset you gained in the past year. What are your plans to enhance these in the coming year?
- How would you describe your relationship liabilities in the past year? What will you do to mitigate similar risks in the coming year?
- How will your efforts affect the desired outcome for a key relationship you value most?
- How did you share firmwide intellectual capital with clients and referral sources?

- Describe the marketing campaigns you designed, developed, and deployed to create air cover for your relationship-centric efforts.
- What specific assets (time, capital, and human) did you invest in your overall relationship-development efforts in the past year, and what investments do you anticipate for the coming year?

Relationship Signature Index

Twenty unique attributes define the personal imprint that we as individuals, teams, or organizations bring to every relationship. They are often behavioral in our approach to prioritization and investment in our most valuable relationships, collaboration with others in search of desired solutions or outcomes, relationship-centric risk identification and mitigation, our perceived versus actual reputation among our intracompany peers, and key influencers external to the organization.

- What are your relationship strengths? In which areas would you like to improve?
- Compared with your peers of equal or greater business stature within the firm, how would you rate your reputation capital?
- How important are strategic relationships to you, and why?
- What initial resources can the firm provide to help you achieve your relationship-centric goals?
- What are your quantifiable 30-, 60-, and 90-day milestones?

I'm often reminded of Winston Churchill's and Dwight Eisenhower's remarks that the planning process itself is more critical than the final plan produced. If you went through this high-level overview, what did you discover about the investments you're making (or are not making) in identifying, building, nurturing, and leveraging critical relationships to your success? To produce the ultimate results that you're seeking, you must clearly understand the following:

- What business outcomes you are trying to achieve
- What performance you need to enhance to achieve those outcomes
- What skills, experiences, and behaviors you need to enhance that performance

In the next chapter, we look at the science of relationships, which may help explain why we tend to gravitate and collaborate with some colleagues more than others.

Relationship Economics Online Tools: Relationship Assessments

http://www.RelationshipEconomics.net/RE-Tools.html

I'm really excited to have worked with David Ryback, Ph.D., corporate psychologist, and my coauthor on *ConnectAbility*, to create several relationship assessment tools. Check out free versions:

- **Relationship Signature Index**^{TM} **(RSI)**—an individual assessment of your unique relationship development style
- **Relationship DNA**^{TM}—a team-based assessment of how well the group works together
- **Reputation Perception Assessment**^{TM} **(RPA)**— how your relationship development efforts are perceived by others

Enjoy!

4

Understanding the Science of Social Network Analysis (SNA)

Relationship economics is about understanding both the art *and* the science of business relationships. It has been my experience that although many get the art—30-second introductions, remembering names, building rapport—few truly understand the science. The concept of Social Network Analysis (SNA) has been in existence since the 1930s and is the intersection of psychology, anthropology, sociology, organizational design, and mathematics—specifically, graph theory. It has nothing to do with Facebook, Twitter, or LinkedIn (more on those in Chapter 10). Its roots are ingrained in academic circles and are too complex for many to comprehend, much less apply to teams within corporations.

Many experts have attempted to bridge the gap in an effort to explain these concepts in everyday terms. For example, in his popular book *The Tipping Point*, Malcolm Gladwell highlights the critical importance of social networks to the general public. Through illustrative stories, Gladwell uses examples of how social networks create an enormous amount of influence and acceptance of ideas and trends. (Gladwell describes Paul Revere, for example, as one of history's great "connectors" because of his relationship with various revolutionary leaders along his route and his acute understanding of the British situation.)

In this chapter, I translate SNA into practical, proven best practices in five functional areas where relationship economics is most applicable.

Brief Overview of Social Network Analysis (SNA)

SNA, in its simplest term, is the process of mapping and measuring relationships and flow among people, groups, organizations, and other information/knowledge-processing entities. SNA provides both a visual and a mathematical analysis of human relationships. The term has been used as a metaphor for more than a century to convey complex sets of relationships between members of a social system. In 1954, Jay Barnes, a social scientist, began using this term to denote patterns inside and outside founded groups such as tribes or families and social categories such as gender or ethnicity. In recent years, SNA has evolved from suggestive metaphors to a true analytical model in various methods and research circles (Figure 4.1). Analysts are able to deduce key insights from a deep dive of "whole to parts" from structures to individual interactions and from behaviors to attitudes. By studying the whole network, which contains specific ties or relationships between individuals, key assumptions can be made as to the frequency, quality, and expansive nature of an interaction between two individuals.

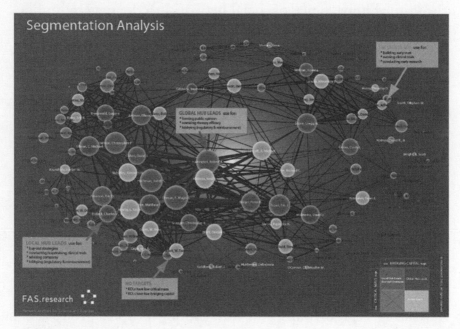

FIGURE 4.1 Sample SNA Diagram

Think about it: Why do you socialize with some coworkers more than others? Why do some colleagues' names appear more often in your Sent e-mail folder than others? Give me a copy of a person's checkbook and calendar and I can tell you the breadth and depth of their relationships. The same could be said for several key attributes of individuals with whom you tend to engage considerably more often than others. A number of those attributes could be easily explained by your role or realm of responsibilities.

Other attributes of our most valued links simply include people who *get* us. These are the people who are a lot like we are and with whom we have chemistry. If you have been through any of the behavioral or psychological assessment tools such as Myers-Briggs, HBDI, or DiSC, you realize that similar profiles naturally gravitate toward each other. In short, ENTPs (extravision, intuition, thinking, perception) like associating with other ENTPs.

The shape of a social network—whether small or more expansive, both internal and external—can also highlight the true collaborative nature of an individual or a team. In other words, a group of individuals who communicate and collaborate with only one another already share the same knowledge and, to a greater extent, the same set of contacts. Conversely, a group of individuals with connections to a broader, more diverse array of social worlds is more likely to have access to a broader knowledge base and, by deductive reasoning, access to greater opportunities to overcome obstacles.

This is why it is critical to prioritize diversity as a strong asset in your portfolio of relationships; the broader your social network, the bigger your relationship bank and sphere of influence.

Phil Ostwalt, a national partner of the forensic practice of KPMG LLP, is one of those rare individuals who genuinely believes in and consistently practices both intrafirm and externally focused, value-based relationships. And in some ways, his extensive social network is a strong asset to his professional success. Both within the firm and outside it, Phil is well known, respected, trusted, and consistently seen as not only a viable source of knowledge but someone with access to others who can provide very real and quantifiable value based on their breadth and depth of knowledge. By collaborating beyond geographic and functional limitations—a key success attribute of social networks—Phil and his colleagues developed a poignant white paper titled "Cross-Border Investigations." It integrated global best practices introduced as a key component to good corporate governance by Adam Bates, global chairman of KPMG Forensic. The result of their global collaboration is a highly relevant, timely, and strong illustration of the vast and decentralized expertise within the organization. This is an example of an ideal outcome of the productivity gains delivered by effective social networks.

The next valuable asset is the *quality* of your social network. This represents not only a strong connection between individuals, but also, through sheer time and a broad base of experiences, a wider pipeline for information, knowledge, talent, key insights, and access to influential individuals (see Chapter 8). As two people connect over time, the pipeline between their networks broadens and creates bigger opportunities for them to interact more often and introduce each other to additional contacts. The more relationship currency that is contributed to the pipeline, the bigger the network becomes.

Think about individuals you have known and worked closely with over the years, perhaps in various jobs, markets, and business statures. Would you agree that the quality of your relationship with those individuals has strengthened because of frequent interactions and exchanges of value-based information? You tend to develop a stronger bond with those who have referred to you consistently profitable business over the years. You feel genuinely closer to those on whom you have counted for an independent perspective or unique insight. In essence, the depth of those relationships and their relevancy toward your specific goals and objectives nurture certain predictability in what you say and do on a consistent basis over time. We define this as *mutual trust*.

Connections within social networks are also critical for those individuals who exercise influence or act as knowledge or relationship brokers within their own social networks—as well as between diverse networks—to fill structural holes. Have you ever heard someone say, "John is a go-to person. He may not have the answer, but he certainly knows someone who does." Or, "Sandy is an amazing connector. Not only does she know everyone, but she takes pride in connecting the people she knows."

Relationship Economics @ Work:
Rob Cross and Rod Beckstrom

One of the leading authorities in the area of SNA applications is Rob Cross, associate professor at the University of Virginia's McIntire School of Commerce and author of *Driving Results through Social Networks: How Top Organizations Leverage Networks for Performance and Growth*. Rob's ideas are reinforced in Ori Brafman and Rod Beckstrom's book, *The Starfish and the Spider: The Unstoppable Power of Leaderless Organizations*. Both books compare and contrast the traditional organizational chart and what we refer to as a *Relationship Dynamics Chart*, as shown in Figure 4.2.

As readers of this book can appreciate, an organizational chart helps control chaos. Yet very few people believe that this is how things really get done. The hierarchical nature of an organizational chart, by sheer design, builds geographic, divisional, and functional silos that simply are not conducive to collaboration, communication, or identification and implementation of best practices across the organization.

(continued)

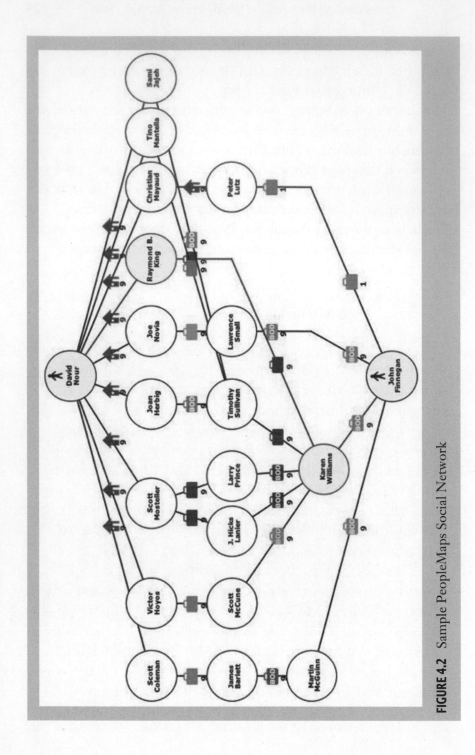

FIGURE 4.2 Sample PeopleMaps Social Network

Brafman and Beckstrom masterfully compare the starfish—a highly decentralized organism—to a highly centralized command-and-control model of a spider. Cut off the spider's leg and you'll have a crippled spider. Cut off its head and you have a dead spider. Conversely, cut off one of the five legs of a starfish and it is likely to regenerate. Cut off all five and, in some species, you will produce five different starfish.

Have you ever wondered why it is so challenging for a true superpower such as the U.S. military to find one man and his group of hoodlums hiding in caves on the other side of the world? It is a classic case of a highly centralized command-and-control model trying to adapt to a much more nimble, highly decentralized cell. War, Brafman and Beckstrom explain, has to become more than just a military campaign. It must become an economic and political campaign as well.

Brafman and Beckstrom highlight three ways to defeat a decentralized organization:

1. Draw them into discussion. (Blame, antagonism, and taking a hard stance seldom work.)
2. Centralize the opponent.
3. Decentralize yourself.

Characteristics of a highly decentralized model are its source of energy, driven by catalysts; ideology-centric circles or pockets of influence; and a very specific set of protocols and rules for membership that include breadth, frequency of circles, the extent of the network, funding of the network, and self-governance. The social networking diagram highlights not only sources of influence but the flow of information, the frequency of exchanges, and disconnected executives on the periphery—often due to the administrative nature of their roles and grossly underused resources disconnected from much of the interaction.

Organizational Application of SNA and Resulting Impact

So how does the concept of SNA apply to organizational efficiency and effectiveness? As illustrated in the Relationship Dynamics Chart shown in Figure 4.2, an individual's social network is often defined by their personal and professional strategy, relationship investment resources (time, effort, capital, etc.), and key relationships they choose to invest in at any particular time.

Intracompany social networks, interestingly, are often in direct conflict with managerial behaviors and organizational design. It has been my experience that performance evaluations and compensation or other incentives, as well as predetermined management practices, usually diverge from or preclude collaboration among departments, divisions, or parts of the business. As discussed in the matrix effectiveness section in Chapter 3 and illustrated in Figure 3.2, Jones, at the center of the diagram, is often and rather excessively sought out, making her a potential bottleneck.

Do you remember playing the gossip game in elementary school? The first person whispers a phrase in the ear of his or her neighbor, and so on, around the circle until the last person is asked to repeat the message, which is inevitably a gross distortion of the original phrase. The same thing happens in social networks. People add their own experiences, interpretations, and context to information they receive. Take recruiting practices, for example, in which many managers are involved. This, too, could lead to a cluster of expertise because it deals with a very tightly connected group of people with the same knowledge base. Or, if several people who share a past come together, it can be very difficult for an outsider to break into the inner circle. This is an especially common practice in most venture capital–and private equity–backed early-stage companies.

One of the most impressive aspects of Cross and Parker's research on the hidden power of social networks is their analysis of 60 strategically important networks in a wide range of household name organizations over a five-year period. In areas such as consulting, pharmaceuticals, computer hardware and software, consumer products, financial services, petrochemicals, heavy equipment and machinery, and yes, even governments, they clearly illustrate the broad-based application of social networks in developing customer, people, and operational world-class environments.

Five Functional Areas Where SNA Can Be Most Applicable

There are five fundamental areas that I believe can greatly benefit from the quantifiable value of business relationships. Each area is driven by relationship-centric goals, heavily influenced by those with a reputation for expertise and responsiveness, and each is instrumental to the short- and long-term success of your business.

1. Revenue Growth

Now more than ever, smart, strategic, profitable revenue growth is critical to organizations of any size. Make no mistake about it—performance trumps all. You as an individual, your team, and your organization all have to *consistently* deliver quality products, exceptional professional services, and an unparalleled customer experience. Otherwise, the rest is a moot point. A strong social network can help extend the market capitalization of your performance. Its applications are invaluable (1) within the organization where you need the support of your colleagues to deliver on the promises you make in the market; (2) with distribution channel partners who can help uncover previously untapped market opportunities or extend your reach with exponential value-added services; and (3), of course, with great customers. Social networks can help you focus on your core competencies while you explore innovative business and revenue models. These opportunities can come from unlikely sources, and the most efficient way to tap into them is to through as diverse a social network as possible.

As Michael Rene, former chief strategy officer at Choice-Point, explains, "It is difficult for large, complex bureaucratic companies to innovate. It is much easier for small, nimble, highly focused niche players to not only improve an existing product, process, or go-to-market strategy, but to also truly come up with a marketable, customer-driven innovation." Your access to these pockets of brilliance is exponentially enhanced with a broad-based social network. In the next chapter, I highlight sources of value creation.

Keep in mind that strategic relationship development takes time, effort, and investments. The value of these relationships may not show up in this or next quarter's pipeline, but if cultivated correctly, they will create a significant long-term return. To make long-term relationships successful, you need an organization with unique skill sets, capabilities, and relationship-building styles. Building a strategic relationship plan can drive unparalleled efficiencies in how you share information, transfer critical knowledge, and make long-term, mutually beneficial decisions. Tempering the corporate enthusiasm of short-term revenue results with long-term prosperity will be a challenge and one that you, as the relationship quarterback and the internal advocate of the customer, must master.

Another application of SNA for revenue growth is when a new product is being launched or the company is attempting to enter a new market. Uncertainties of customer preferences in the first example and creative and accelerated market access can be overcome if you can identify key centers of influence. With the product launch example, consider who the highly connected individuals are who will try new products; then blog about them, and create notoriety at an accelerated pace, driving market pull in the process. There is an intentional reason Apple invites key people to each new product launch announcement. Within hours, whatever Steve Jobs and his team announce spreads throughout the Web and thus the market like wildfire. Similarly, when entering a new market, if you can identify the most valuable connectors in a social network, it will accelerate your ability to create awareness and intrigue—think of this as your best opportunity for more "at bats."

2. Leadership Development

With few exceptions, not enough informal or formal mentoring occurs in corporations today. As the generation before ours retires, these leaders leave a very real void in the next generation of leadership. Today, more executives retire earlier in their careers and take many of their valuable insights and much knowledge with them when they go. Key intracompany relationships developed in mentoring programs not only can enable much of that crucial knowledge transfer but can continue to develop it into world-class processes and competitive differentiators.

A fundamental core competency of a true leader is the ability to gather multiple sources of information, extract insights from that information, make sound decisions, and then effectively communicate those decisions to the diverse makeup of the broader organization. In many companies, managers and leaders are taught to *functionally* become the best they can be—the strategic value of financial stewardship or the value of real-time information from a technology platform—but are taught nothing about how to effectively build and leverage relationships across diverse operating groups.

Relationship-Centric Best Practice: Shared Leadership?

Have you noticed that the current business climate has produced several interim chief executive officer (CEO) and even interim head coach positions? I've often wondered if

(*continued*)

Relationship-Centric Best Practice:
Shared Leadership? *(Continued)*

that sends confusing signals about the organization's direction or focus, particularly when their tenure drags on. And do their underlings view the interim role as a big "vacancy" sign? Does an interim leadership role point to the CEO or the board's inability to create a coherent succession plan or a strong bench of talented, well-rounded leaders?

If you've ever had trouble finding the right person for that leadership role, perhaps because there wasn't one particular person with all the necessary capabilities, experiences, and interests, you can relate.

Unfortunately, many leaders are one-dimensional—great skills in some departments but not in others. Many incredibly successful and well-trained GE executives, for example, have less-than-stellar roles as CEOs of other firms. They may bring a renewed sense of management professionalism or fantastic cost-cutting expertise, which is crucial at the beginning of their tenure but often not for the duration they serve.

With the complexity of organizations today and the required sensitivity to governance, performance, and transparency, perhaps it's time to rethink the logic of the super-hero leader and larger-than-life CEO. Perhaps it's time to build a range of skills in the C- and V-suite, each impactful in different points in the initiative or the organization's growth continuum.

How? Here are three options to consider:

1. **Consider spreading the responsibilities across several people.** Allow the most qualified person—rather than the most senior person—to step up to the leadership task. This gives all competent people the chance to demonstrate their leadership prowess.

2. **Consider rotational leadership assignments within the firm.** The chief financial officer (CFO) positions often have been such roles; why not use rotational leadership for that strategic initiative role or new products launch, customer executive sponsor, or a new market entry opportunity?

3. **Bring in a competent outsider to lead the assignment and recommend the next quarterback.** Outsiders often bring a fresh perspective and are uninhibited by the traditional political posturing. Good ones build and nurture great relationships to uncover the true passion and strength of each leader involved.

To lay the groundwork for this type of organizational flattening, create a relationship-centric climate in which people develop the courage to take on new assignments and fail without fear of retribution. Leaders and managers alike must be thought of as resources rather than authorities. It's a fundamental difference between a *trust-and-track* culture versus a *command-and-control* one.

Traditional leadership development that is corporate driven also typically leaves it to the corporation to match the mentor with a mentee. Within social networks, mentees are taught how to broaden their portfolio of relationships and expand that mentoring beyond the formal to the informal. This turns your entire leadership development from a top-down organizational structure to a side-and-out structured model. Effective social networks start from the bottom and move out in every direction.

The key is to build an environment where you move from performance evaluations that are viewed as a *have to do* and instead build personal SWOT (strengths, weaknesses, opportunities, threats) profiles and a formal mentoring program to help key individuals become not just better managers but better human beings.

Another often misunderstood or underapplied concept in not just leadership development but also personal and professional growth holistically is the incredible value of a personal brand. To this day, I recall the cover story of *FastCompany* magazine on September 1997 with the lead article from Tom Peters: "The Brand Called You" and its tagline: "You Can't Move Up If You Don't Stand Out." Both that article and much of the research I've done on the topic point to several fundamental attributes of a personal brand. It must be:

- Distinctive—uniquely *YOU*.
- Memorable—only if you want it repeated to others.
- Respected—people will deal with others they know, like, and trust; it's time to add one more to this list: respected.
- Following—are you a best-kept secret?
- Resilient—strong brands overcome adversity; think about Tylenol, Toyota, or Michael Milken.
- Timeless—fads come and go and there is a reason it's called "15 minutes of fame."
- Reliable—can others count on you *consistently?*
- Deliver—as mentioned previously, performance trumps all.

As you develop your brand—which I believe is a lifelong process—you must also do four things to build your brand equity:

1. *Deliver consistently.* Nothing else matters; if you become known for something, you must deliver on that brand promise consistently. Otherwise, it becomes diluted and undervalued.

2. *Upgrade constantly.* This is one that I've learned from multiple mentors. If you stop learning, growing, expanding, and extending your horizons, your brand becomes stale, outdated, and worthless. Think of professional athletes

who don't give back or achieve anything after their playing career is over.

3. *Invest wisely.* Take a candid inventory of your assets and liabilities, and develop a path to continue to build on your strengths. I consistently invest in conferences, workshops, and thought leadership gatherings to raise the bar on my own efforts.

4. *Protect passionately.* Corporations spend millions of dollars protecting their brands. You must be as vigilant in knowing how your brand is discussed, shared, perceived, and sometimes infringed upon.

Relationship Economics @ Work: Dale Silvia at Cisco Systems

According to Dale Silvia, director of human resources for the Americas U.S. CDO REM at Cisco Systems, many mentoring programs are typically an organizationally sponsored, mechanical approach that is limited by formal relationships and partnerships.

"Instead of waiting for the organization to structure a formal program, we teach our people to seek out their mentors and engage those individuals who will help them better understand the areas in which they currently need help," said Silvia. "There is nothing wrong with formal mentoring programs per se, but they can oftentimes be self-limiting. If you give people the know-how, you give them the permission and tools to go get what they need. You are flipping the pyramid upside down and suddenly you have a broad base of people that you can at least informally call your mentoring group. That is two-way sharing."

At Dale's business unit, newly hired undergraduate and graduate engineers participate in an extensive leadership

(continued)

Relationship Economics @ Work:
Dale Silvia at Cisco Systems *(Continued)*

development program that relies heavily on the principles taught in relationship economics. Specifically, new hires are taught how to make deposits in relationships so they can draw on them when they need help.

"I take these new graduates, give them direction and the permission to seek out the key people in the organization, and I challenge them to build relationships that will help them and others become more successful over time," said Silvia. "They all come back and tell me what value it produced for them. Over months or years of doing this, you can really see the personal and professional growth."

Silvia's message to the next generation of leaders is clear: "I tell them to go out and become famous for something. Build those relationships in a positive way. Show people what they can do. Go out of your way to help those people and you will have a solid foundation throughout your career because you will have people who want you to succeed."

It comes down to human capital, Silvia claims. It comes down to that personal connection and the perseverance to exercise that over time. Not in a greedy fashion, but in a way that you, those around you, and the entire organization will benefit.

3. Strategy Execution

As I have said before, there is no shortage of strategy formulation. The problem is strategy execution! Every executive with whom I have worked has challenging stories about how the brilliant 400-page strategic analysis of their business—prepared by high-priced consultants—could never be implemented because the company lacks the resources and talent to convert academic exercises into actionable steps.

Public service organizations rely heavily on their basis of knowledge, which is often gathered through tenure, especially given the current challenges as baby boomers, who make up the largest percentage of the workforce, retire. Over the next decade, as many of these baby boomers retire, companies may find that there simply isn't a replenishable pool of equally talented and knowledgeable workers. In a situation where knowledge is not valued until it begins to cascade through the organization and then leak out through retirement, it is critical to find a way to map those subject matter experts by their peers. SNA can become a useful decision support tool for the planning and execution of these key strategic initiatives.

The questions then become how do you identify critical expertise, how do you map the source of that expertise, and how do you establish a practical knowledge transfer process? The answer is a peer evaluation through parallel queries with each recipient responding by selecting from a list of names. The result is a critical list of key players who can (1) help with the development of up-and-coming key players and (2) uncover a number of surprises in key organizational resources.

It is interesting that subjectivity is ultimately reduced with peer evaluations, and the popularity contest inevitably diminishes. As you attempt to identify communities or practices of expertise, you tend to highlight strategic vulnerabilities in critical skill assets that you need and don't have or those that are few and far between. Through this process, you can identify isolated and highly underused individuals and develop a precisely targeted training and knowledge continuity plan for carrying key strategic initiatives across geographic, functional, and business unit boundaries.

One of our clients is using Yammer—the "Twitter-like" micro-blogging platform—to ask its employees a very simple question each and every day: What problem are you trying to solve? Think of the massive knowledge base of the hundreds if not thousands of solutions to the problems employees of an organization tackle each day. Now think about how many hours those employees would save if they were to leverage the collective knowledge of the organization.

4. Adaptive Innovation

In Chapter 8, I cover adaptive innovation in much more detail. For now, think of it as a real-time sensor constantly giving you data points, which allows you to do things differently (real innovation) and not just better (incrementalism). SNA can help with two aspects here: one is within the organization and the other is external to it.

As a new divisional leader, how do you quickly uncover and leverage knowledge, experience, and specific expertise across the disparate parts of your organization in an effort to not only retain your best customers but also expand your mind share and wallet share within each of your most profitable client companies? First, map your relationship dynamics chart by learning who individuals go to for information. Who has deeply rooted departmental, divisional, or company-wide information specifically focused on getting things done? Don't just map the subject of the content of e-mail exchanges—map the *connections*. Look at who is copied and the frequency of exchanges compared with others in the organization. Beyond a charming personality, who is *functionally* missed when not there? With objective information, you can identify not only those who are most connected but those who collaborate instinctively and in the daily course of performing their functions.

Most of my clients are surprised by this phenomenon, yet it somehow reaffirms their intuition that social networks are often much more valuable than systems or databases for learning and sharing information. Silos, despite efforts by leadership to the contrary, are very much alive and well established within many organizations, and there are hidden revenue or cost-saving opportunities that could be derived through strategic relationships. Of particular interest to several clients has also been the fact that some of the most connected people are those who rank lower in the company's traditional hierarchy. But as leaders, they are well served to prioritize those relationships because of their influence within the group.

Other defining characteristics of social networks are individual roles, including realm of responsibilities, length of time at the firm, current position, and nature of their department or functional role. Innovation should be promoted across the entire organization. It is the quantifiable value of collaborative relationships that fuels innovation. Remember that it is not necessarily the best ideas that rise through the company's bureaucratic ranks and become market-leading products and services, but rather the ideas backed by the most influential relationships in the organization.

External to the organization, SNA can help you map key market influencers and the connections among them. Think of them as tentacles in the market and how you can leverage them as "signal scouts" to bring faint market signals to you. If you can develop the individual skills, tools, and processes to quickly analyze and act upon these signals, adaptive innovation can help you reinvent your revenue or even business models (more about this topic in Chapter 8).

5. Large-Scale Change and Mergers and Acquisitions

At some point, your 3 percent organic growth, although perhaps respectable in your industry, will become less than attractive for the organization. Therefore, the senior leaders or the board may recommend a more aggressive, inorganic growth strategy that encompasses a strong spring of deal flow, preacquisition, due diligence, and postacquisition integration, typically driven by the project management office.

Make no mistake—there is seldom a merger. Instead, there is typically an *acquisition* and often the integration of disparate employee teams into an expansive geography. Separate functional groups working in different locations drive incredibly inefficient and often dysfunctional redundancies in their implementation of various programs and initiatives.

Information technology (IT), although a broad-reaching shared service, is often a good but unfortunately painful example of this scenario. Infrastructure, large projects, pockets of unique expertise, mandates by business units, and the critical nature of the organization's operational efficiency based on a consistent and productive IT strategy make matters worse. After any acquisition, IT leaders often recognize that a reorganization and reprioritization are not only necessary but critical to seamless continuity. The goal is often to break down us-versus-them silos and get people in Europe, Asia, and the Americas talking to one another, not only to improve IT services, but to create efficiencies in the desired output. So, how do you break down silos and get people talking? First, map out social networks of intracompany relationships to reveal who is most overworked, most isolated, and most connected without alienating any particular employees or teams. Then, convey the painfully clear value of collaboration or lack thereof.

You would be amazed at how many people are disconnected across functional lines by physical distances or even with those working on key projects. Some are to be expected, but others can cause enormous pain and redundancy in an organization. Often, reorganization is needed based on functional groups as opposed to teams of experts. For example, if the enterprise resource planning deployment team does not fully understand the critical steps in the process, nor do they develop the relationships with the frontline users of that technology to extract candor regarding what is really broken and how to fix the process before implementing the technology, the implementation is sure to fail.

Many cross-functional social networks often become enablers to more effective communication and unity in their respective parts of the bigger picture. Geography creates a very real disconnect, which team-building sessions can help overcome. Last, strategic knowledge communities in areas such as project management, process reengineering, and client services previously unknown to the senior staff can emerge.

Relationship-Centric Best Practice: Campaigning for Change versus Governing Change

Regardless of your ideology, many would agree that political campaigns often tout both the need and a plan for change. Our most recent presidential campaign heavily emphasized hope and change, but I would submit it was 80 to 90 percent about hope—hoping for a better economy, hoping for a more inclusive nation, hoping to overcome racial barriers and create a historical milestone we can all be proud of.

The challenge is often the change part of the campaign. As much as we talk about change and may aspire to change a nation, an organization, a team, or even an individual, change is messy. Change is committees and approval processes. Change is long hours and what often seems to be an endless debate. In politics, it's partisanship; in our organization, it's compromise. Any way you look at it, it's difficult and requires steadfast leadership, unfazed by those who may find it unpopular.

I often meet senior executives who have a vision for fundamentally changing the relationship development behaviors of their organizations. After all, that's where the real impact or change they seek will come from—a change in behavior by an individual, a team, or the entire organization. When we first meet and begin to work together, I see a commitment and a passion for change. They "campaign" within the organization, among the senior leadership team,

(continued)

Relationship-Centric Best Practice: Campaigning for Change versus Governing Change *(Continued)*

internal stakeholders, and external board members. They map out a path to get there and commit to "doing whatever it takes." Does that sound familiar?

Then the reality settles in of governing for change. They get pushback from the status quo opposition. They get budgetary concerns from the financial stewards or operational concerns from the bowels of the organization, which has "never done this or that before." They get compliance guidelines, human resources evaluation reports, and calls from the inevitable board member who simply "doesn't get" what the senior leader is trying to accomplish. Dissent begins to creep in, and the leader loses strategic relationship management efficiency and effectiveness in keeping that vision of change on track.

The leader now begins to backtrack and redefine the truly visionary change he once had, to one of incremental improvements over a longer period. The vision of doing things differently—implementing real change—becomes one of doing things better—incrementalism. The accelerated time to market becomes "let's take it slower" and "let's not ruffle any feathers."

There have been countless books written on change, making change work, or making it last. Many are valid, but many also miss a critical factor in both envisioning a truly changed environment and governing to get you there: strategic relationships, influencer marketing, and reputation tentacles on the front line of where change must take place.

Change isn't easy or often fun. Changing behaviors, and relationship development behaviors in particular, requires both a campaign for change and also steadfast governance for and about change—in mind-set, tool set, and road map.

5

Relationship-Centric Goals for Revenue Growth

In Chapter 1, I mentioned that most traditional networking is often deemed ineffective because of a lack of relationship-centric goals. These are business goals that a team, individual, or organization simply cannot achieve without a systematic and disciplined focus on their most valuable relationships. In this chapter, I examine the most prevalent area for the quantifiable outcome of relationships: revenue growth. Strategic, intentional, and profitable revenue growth needs both an infantry for the day-to-day interactions (building relationships is not a spectator sport), the Navy SEALS for the more surgical efforts, and the air force for the coverage from above. Relationship-centric goals should further quantifiably reduce your customer acquisition costs, help expand your current market reach across multiple markets, or help segment your access deeper and wider in your current markets. Here, I address how to establish equity relationship-centric goals for the purpose of business development, particularly for nonbusiness developers.

Fundamental Difference between Brand Awareness and Business Development

Product-centric companies are forced to effectively delineate their unique differentiators. Unfortunately, professional services organizations, such as the Big Four accounting firms—as well as a multitude of law firms, engineering, and construction companies—also struggle with the same challenge. For example, how are the legal services of one international law firm really different from those of another? Although many such organizations attempt to highlight the breadth and depth of their talents, unique set of processes, and successful past engagements that contribute to the broad-based experiences, they all have the same basic ingredients. It is the savvy professional services organizations that realize the orchestration of relationship assets at a multitude of business stature levels and geographic locations is what really sets them apart.

Your overall revenue generation engine has many interdisciplinary activities at work that all drive toward a common cause. They must operate as a cohesive function of your organization and create forward motion. The revenue generation engine focuses on customer and market acquisition and retention and includes two main components: the pretransaction phase before they become customers and the posttransaction sale after they've chosen to invest in you, your brand, your firm, or your value promised. It is amazing how often individuals, teams, and organizations take the posttransaction element for granted. Let's take a look at both of these stages.

Before They Become Customers

Within customer acquisition, relationships are the fundamental enablers or drivers in several key areas. It is important to remember that relationships are not a substitute for performance; rather, they are complementary to it. In fact, performance trumps all. To be successful, you have to begin with a product or service that performs superbly in the market. Once you have a strong core product or service, it is easy to build around it.

I have never known a business that can survive without performance. If you are an environmental consulting company and you can't provide accurate audits, you won't stay in business for long. Dell was initially known for its simplified product mix and mostly positive end-user support experiences. However, when the product mix became entirely too complex (do we really need 30 different laptop models?) and its quality of support diminished, both its reputation and market share weakened dramatically. Even the dry cleaner around the corner from my house will lose my vote of confidence and subsequent business if it can't meet my expectations, as well as my *preferences* (medium starch on hangers) consistently. At its core, your product or service has to perform. Once you have that in place, relationships can greatly aid that revenue generator.

It has been said that "Nothing ever happens until someone, somewhere, sells something." Beyond its complexity and evolution over the years, any success in sales remains a very relationship-centric function. Although people buy from people they like, trust, and respect, the sales function often has a very transactional nature about it. A purchase order or invoice is made up of a document and transaction that solves an immediate problem. This is not to be confused with the campaign, which must be developed to create the sale. But at the end of the day, we define *sales* as very transactional.

In contrast, business development transforms an organization and has a longer-lasting impact. What is transactional in sales can become transformational in business development. Take the Big Four accounting firms: Deloitte, Ernst & Young, KPMG, and PricewaterhouseCoopers, for example. Most are multifaceted, with tax, audit, and advisory services. Tax and audit services can be transactional. But advisory services, dealing with financial, long-term consulting, and often strategic issues, are perceived to be highly transformational.

Many companies could greatly benefit from strategic business development. Think of it in terms of parallel swimming lanes. The fundamental difference between branding (air cover), sales (transactional), and strategic business development (transformational) is that business development is long-term and designed to enhance your current market position, extend your market reach, or create new opportunities altogether.

Relationship Economics @ Work: David Goldsmith of MetaMatrix on the Seven Unique Types of Alliances

David Goldsmith, president and cofounder of New York–based MetaMatrix Consulting Group, has defined seven kinds of alliance relationships, all contributors to your personal and professional success. In all my work with decision makers, I find it important that everyone know early on in the game what type of relationship is being developed. This common language, drawn from a variety of sources, makes progress happen fast.

1. *Affiliate relationship*—a partnership that allows two parties to work together with minimal risk to either party. For example, one company may promote another one on its web site, where both parties have a limited investment and risk in the relationship.

2. *Ad-hoc relationship*—a type of relationship that is normally formed for the purposes of solving or looking into a particular challenge. In politics, for instance, you'll hear that an ad hoc committee has been established to review the need for a new sewage plant.

3. *Consortium*—occurs when a group of people combine their resources, enabling them to achieve significantly more than any individual could individually. Associations and chambers of commerce are a very well known type of consortium. Each member contributes just a few dollars per year, and in return receives the benefits of all the funds provided by the members.

4. *Project joint venture*—a relationship in which two parties agree to work together in such a manner that resources from both parties are used, but on a limited scale. The hiring of a printer to print a brochure or when two parties put on an event are examples of such a relationship.

5. *Joint venture*—a type of relationship that requires that both parties commit to working together to the degree that if one fails, the other fails, and if successful, they both partake of the reward.

6. *Merger*—when two parties agree that joining together as one would be better for everyone involved and the combined efforts would produce more than each one could individually.

7. *Acquisition*—differs substantially from a merger in that in an acquisition, one party believes that the relationship would be best for both when joined even if the other disagrees.

When an organization or an individual looks to develop a relationship, it's extremely important that all parties understand what they're actually trying to achieve. Mistakes are avoided and the desired outcomes are achieved at an accelerated pace by defining what each organization desires early on in the dialogue. Think about it this way: If you see a marriage as a joint venture but your partner sees it as a project joint venture . . . well, you're in for trouble.

In the revenue generation engine, successful business development requires the most astute capitalization of strategic relationships. Channel or distribution partners in domestic, or particularly in international, markets must become an extension of your reach, yet consistently convey your unique value proposition. That arm's-length reach in the market alters your direct contribution to one of success through influence, often without authority. Only by arming your partner with the appropriate resources and a succinct and accelerated path to incremental and profitable revenue growth will you be able to develop a channel-friendly organization.

One of the best in the technology business development arenas is my good friend and long-term colleague Charles Daniels, formerly of SGI (Silicon Graphics). Charles and I joined SGI a week apart back in the early 1990s. I was responsible for several named accounts, while Charles masterfully and proactively managed the SGI channel program. His calm yet results-driven demeanor, high-touch and high-care personal characteristics, and professional attributes made him—as a direct sales rep, as well as with his channel partners—an absolute joy to work with.

In every opportunity, Charles was a consummate diplomat, not only in creating win-win-win opportunities between the SGI sales force, channel partners, and ultimately the end customers, but by excelling in a multitude of roles, including that of a catalyst, a mediator, an enforcer, and certainly an influencer. The results of Charles's strategic relationship management efforts can be described only as exemplary, as evidenced by his nine trips to the coveted Presidents Club, composed of the most elite 10 to 15 percent of the entire SGI sales force.

Relationship-Centric Best Practice: Feet on the Street

Nothing will ever replace feet on the street.

Develop the necessary processes, acquire channel-centric talents, and proactively invest in your most valuable channel relationships because they can drive an estimated 20 to 40 percent of your overall revenues at a fraction of your selling, general, and administrative (SG&A) expenses.

Several of my consulting clients deliver exclusively through a channel network (direct sales reps are creating demand for the company's products and services) or lead with a channel partner when possible. In many industries, distribution partners are at the very edge of the market; they speak with or see clients daily and in the process gather invaluable insights about market preferences and trends. Individuals and organizations who develop intimate, trust-centric, value-based relationships with their channel partners can tap into these insights; those who actually embrace the market insights through trusted relationships and deliver innovative products and services in response to those customer demands are the ones often head and shoulders above their competitive peers.

Feet on the street do more than create distribution channels; they can also act as tentacles in the market, bringing critical signals back.

After They Become Customers

An often undervalued, undermined, and certainly underdeveloped part of an organization is often the postsale part of the revenue generation engine. Many struggle to automatically throw a customer, which they have worked so hard to acquire, over the wall to a customer service department.

The truth is that the real selling begins *after* the sale. It is my belief that quality, customer service, client service, and account management should seldom be a department, but rather a fundamental mind-set of the entire organization. A recent survey highlighted that, on average, you have a 1 in 2 chance of earning incremental business from existing or past clients and a 1 in 18 to 1 in 30 chance, depending on the industry, average sales cycle, and average sales price, in winning that business from a prospect unfamiliar with your past performance.

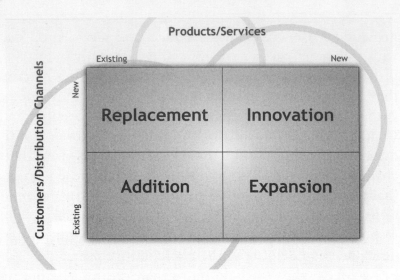

FIGURE 5.1   Up-Sell–Cross-Sell Matrix.

Your relationships and ability to systematically nurture and keep your finger on the pulse of that customer voice become a quantifiable return on integration. By seamlessly incorporating the presales and postsales functions of the revenue generation engine, you further establish greater barriers of entry by key competitors and sustain a diligent client protection strategy in the process.

Figure 5.1 illustrates an outbreak strategy where the *x*-axis represents your existing products and services and the *y*-axis represents your existing customers and distribution channels. Each end of this 2×2 matrix represents existing and new, respectively.

The easiest thing to sell is more of the same products and services to the exact same customer base. We call that *addition*. Next are your *expansion* strategies, which include selling new products and services to your existing customer base. And by far the most challenging business development cycle tends to be selling new products or services to new customers or channels, what we call *innovation*.

For the bottom two components in Figure 5.1—addition and expansion—functional relationships (as defined in Chapter 1) will suffice. Ideally, many unknown risks have been mitigated through their previous interactions, which have established trust with you, your firm, and the performance of your products and services. Examples of these functional relationships are operations managers or purchasing agents.

The top two components in Figure 5.1—replacement and innovation—will demand strategic relationships to influence at the executive or perhaps even the board level. At this stage, the conversation is greatly elevated from the *what* and *how* to the *why*. Strategic relationships also demand a reduced sense of self-interest and heightened level of strategic problem solving and strategy execution.

Why Many Accountants, Lawyers, Consultants, and Engineers Struggle in This Area

As evidenced by my work with a broad base of professional services clients, many technical professionals are often terrible at selling themselves. Many accountants, attorneys, consultants, and engineers don't think of themselves as salespeople—and they don't want to! Their DNA, through their academic and educational foundation and their professional development, seldom includes the notion of strategic relationships and business development best practices.

I genuinely believe that a very small number of people are born with these best practices and insights into what works. Very few companies and learning and development organizations bring a disciplined approach to the knowledge, skills, and evolutionary development of revenue-generating skills for non-business development professionals.

Relationship-Centric Best Practice: Follow the Money

If you want to know someone's motivation, follow the money. In 9 out of 10 professional services organizations, performance evaluations and compensation plans are not congruent with the needs and desires of the leadership team to drive sales and revenue. Even the word *sales* is seen as or thought of as derogatory and somehow demeaning and beneath their professional accreditation. Yet if you consistently look at individuals who become partners in law firms or senior leaders in these professional services firms, they not only unequivocally deliver exceptional service but are also able to attract and retain a consistent book of business.

Many people in the accounting and engineering professions, for example, are not typically extroverts; it's just not in their DNA. They are not the relationship-initiating types. Many would rather dive into 400 pages of Sarbanes-Oxley compliance papers or endless technical specifications than attend a networking event where they have to shake hands and exchange business cards.

In addition, such interaction simply was not part of their education. Networking and relationship building are not taught in our schools. They aren't part of the accounting or finance curriculum, and aren't covered by companies upon employment. Law firms seldom teach strategic relationships, and when they do, they often focus on the *art*. They encourage associates and partners alike to immerse themselves in various civic, professional, and community organizations, yet very few are able to convert relationship creation into relationship capitalization or monetization.

If you can change the perception of transactional, quick-hit sales to a more strategic, longer-term perspective of business development, this competent group of professional services providers will not only listen but will embrace practical, pragmatic advice in building and profitably nurturing their respective businesses. By the way, it has been my experience that this group is very good at building relationships based on competency and trust. The challenge often remains creating the initial access and nurturing relationships to extend and expand current engagements.

Here is another dangerous trait I saw working with a professional services firm this past year. In a part of the organization, some 30+ partners have the title and a preponderance of the responsibility for delivering the work. Yet less than a handful of the partners are actually bringing in the work! The rest are simply latching onto the engagements the few rainmakers bring in.

As part of my due diligence process, it became very clear rather quickly that both at the individual level and, in large part, at the firm level, the overarching mentality is that if you simply do good work, new business will come in. These people actually think sales is demeaning and beneath their professional pedigree. They refer to business development as "marketing" and have built a rather large—and ineffective, I may add—marketing department so that they don't have to do any heavy lifting.

There is a big problem with this mind-set, which is their biggest hurdle: their particular kind of work doesn't lend itself to up-sell or cross-sell opportunities. That means when this engagement is done, this particular client doesn't have an immediate need for them to continue. So they're counting on (1) this client remembering their good work and referring them to others and (2) key members of this organization going to other firms and remembering them and their good work. Guess what? Neither is happening. My client certainly has built a strong reputation over the past three decades, but as the market gets soft or as many of their clients retire and new economic buyers take the reins, my client's good reputation is heavily undervalued.

It's painful to watch. Make no mistake about it—these are very competent, capable, seasoned professionals who are very good at what they do. They're simply very bad at putting themselves out there, nurturing relationships, and bridging those relationship creation efforts to relationship capitalization. So, I've made it a personal mission to take a handful of the 30+ and mentor and coach them one-on-one to create the right behaviors, insert the appropriate skill sets, and help them measure and analyze their progress to prove that without net-new relationships, very few net-new customers will come in the door. One of the partners actually introduced me to the managing partner of a law firm they work closely with as "Hitch for Companies"—referring to the hit movie with Will Smith where he plays a matchmaker.

Flaws in Professional Certification Processes

If you look at many of the professional certification processes such as those required for a certified public accountant (CPA), attorney, project manager, and even the medical profession, their curriculum for accreditation seldom includes content focused on the systematic, disciplined process for the development of strategic business relationships. None of these processes motivate, encourage, or praise individuals for the art and science of building, nurturing, and leveraging relationships. Instead, and rightfully so, they credit ethics, operational efficiency, and human resources (HR) policies. They applaud continuing education in compliance but frown upon the very essence of their survival and success, which is business development and building strategic and quantifiable relationships.

And when it comes to compensation, whatever is spent comes directly out of the partners' pockets, so asking them to dedicate resources to building their business development skills is often frowned upon as unnecessary. Or they hire rainmakers—people who have networking in their DNA—to drive revenue for them. But these people are few and far between and can provide a false sense of security. For example, if a power networker brings a huge international deal to a firm that keeps 20 people busy for two years, the firm may be led to believe that it is succeeding—but how will it develop 10 more of these types of deals?

Competency and Trust as Critical Components of Reputation Capital

As mentioned earlier, as you promote value and deliver it, you begin to exchange relationship currency. And as the delivery of that value is recognized, you start to accumulate *reputation capital*. The two fundamental pillars of reputation capital are competency and trust.

Competency

Strategic business development involves a multitude of constituents and partners, and your success heavily depends on competency. Any alliance partner you engage with will ask, "Where else have you done this? Where have you been successful with this project, team, individual, and organization?" So that you are prepared to answer these questions, perform your own competency assessment to quickly gauge what your fundamental product and service strengths are. Clearly define your current state (where you are today) and a future state (where you aspire to reach). The difference becomes your developmental gap.

This level of competency assessment creates a road map for personal and professional development.

> ### Relationship-Centric Best Practice: Client-Centric Teams
>
> An extremely positive trend in many professional services firms is the breaking down of the traditional functional, geographic, and expertise-centric silos to one of a matrix organization with client-centric teams. Having gone through this process, prominent Atlanta law firm Alston + Bird was able to create a client team encompassing a multitude of legal disciplines for one of its major clients. By using its global talent, they were able to overlay client teams over their usual functions (legal, real estate, accounting, and so forth) to solve the client's issues and exponentially increase their billable fees. This client-centric focus makes relationships both inside and outside the law firm that much more productive. Today, the firm has more than 30 similar client teams in place.
>
> Similarly, for years, PricewaterhouseCoopers has had a client relationship partner on site at large accounts such as Home Depot, with a partner serving as the quarterback and orchestrating the firm's global resources to deliver its exceptional expertise to Home Depot's unique challenges and opportunities.
>
> Remember: Value creation is derived from value-chain disruption. If you don't disrupt your market, customers, and suppliers, your competitors will!

Trust

Think of the concept of a *trust barometer*. If I am one of your channel or distribution partners, for example, you are asking me to put my reputation on the line to walk you into my end customers. That is huge on the trust barometer. Components of that trust start in an organization, but often come down to trust between individuals. We all start out with a certain level of credibility and, over time, can choose to enhance, reinforce, and cement that credibility by consistently executing and delivering on promises made, or we can choose to dilute it by incongruence and inconsistency between our thoughts, words, and actions.

Trust, as an outcome of your competency simply defined, is predictability in what you say and do over an extended period. The challenge with trust is that it takes years to develop and moments to destroy. Individuals, teams, and organizations have to make it their lifelong focus and mission to establish and protect their position on their trust barometer. And that trust barometer is applicable to a whole host of constituents. Take employees, for example. The first time you lie to me as a boss, I won't trust you again. The first time you mess with my expenses or break our contract, you have diluted that credibility and broken that trust. Conversely, if you are consistently candid and forthcoming and you foreshadow what others should expect from you, you can build and solidify this fundamental pillar called trust.

Relationship-Centric Goals

Whether your specific goal for building and nurturing relationships is acquiring and retaining clients, launching a new product or service, or entering a new market or buying a company, relationship-centric goals are goals that you need others to help you achieve. Specifically, these are business relationships with colleagues, clients, suppliers, media, analysts, and the business community at large. There are three types of relationship-centric goals: direct, influence, and equity goals.

Direct Goals

Direct goals are black-and-white goals that are clear, simple to understand, and to the point. They are quantifiable, directly related to how you are measured, and generally on the 12- to 18-month horizon.

Examples
- Buy a $20 million discrete manufacturing company in Atlanta this fiscal year.
- Transfer internally to the New Hotel Opening Team by mid-July.
- Transform 50 percent of revenues over the next two years to come from direct distribution.

Influence Goals

These are goals that you have less personal control in achieving. They often require other things to fall in place on your behalf, such as the influence of others. To achieve these goals, you will have to influence key situations or align your efforts with key influencers in the organization. When setting these types of goals, go beyond your comfort zone. What do you want to achieve 18 to 36 months from now? How will you know when you've arrived?

Examples
- Expand my portfolio of thought leader relationships to really help us accelerate our innovation efforts by four new members this calendar year.
- Achieve an 8 out of 10 customer satisfaction rating on the next survey.
- Earn 20 to 40 percent of new business from key European markets by the middle of next year.

Equity Goals

Equity goals are often intangible and difficult to quantify. These include areas such as branding and building a go-to person reputation or increased market awareness. What positive things do you want people to say about you? What is your personal brand? What are you doing to research, package, build, and market your brand for more responsibility and positive visibility within the firm and the community in which you live and work? If you look back three to five years from now, what will you have accomplished?

Examples
- Establish a go-to person reputation for connecting entrepreneurs with capital.
- Develop a reputation in my department as the one who really gets it, has great follow-through, and is extremely driven.
- Create a reputation of having outstanding personal integrity in the mergers and acquisitions business.

The Challenges

Goals are fundamentally more achievable if they are written down and reviewed. For goals to be effective, they must also be quantifiable and have a time frame. Remember that if you can't measure it, you're unlikely to track your progress and you won't be able to make course corrections along the way.

It is also critical to filter your goals for realism. Next time you write down a goal, ask yourself these three questions:

1. *Are your goals realistic?* Even clearly defined, fact-based goals can be frustrating to pursue if they are not realistic. Don't confuse the need to push oneself with what is truly attainable.
2. *Are they achievable within your sphere of influence and control?* What other factors contribute to the attainability of your

goals? Are your goals dependent on things outside of your control or influence?

3. *Are they documented, measured, and analyzed along a defined time line?* Goals must be consistently documented, measured, analyzed, and appropriately responded to along the way. If the goal is not documented and if quantifiable metrics and time lines are not identified, how will you measure your progress against them? If you don't measure your progress, how will you analyze what's working and what's not with each relationship? If you don't analyze effectiveness, how can you make any course corrections in your relationship investment strategy and tactical execution?

Relationship-Centric Best Practice: Daily View of Your Goals

Sit down, find some quiet time, and really think about the specific, quantifiable goals you want to achieve. I've taped mine to my bathroom mirror so that every morning when I'm getting ready for work, I know where I'm going, what I'll do when I get there, and what I am aiming to achieve.

6

Pivotal Contacts for Leadership Development

M ost leadership development programs are very myopic in their approach. They train high-performing individuals on how to become the best in their functional roles, yet they underemphasize the most central issue of fundamental and lasting leadership: the ability to engage an increasingly diverse workforce with generations of deep-rooted beliefs, expectations, and pet peeves. Beyond cultural diversity, pivotal contacts are key individuals who can accelerate one's ability to achieve key goals, strategies, objectives, and tactics (GSOT). In this chapter, I quantify accelerated execution, give succinct examples of sources of pivotal contacts, highlight hubs and spokes, illustrate sample profiles, and review a scorecard of how to identify your most valuable pivotal contacts.

Myopia in Leadership Development

Typically, our view of leadership development encompasses the escalation of current high performers into an environment where they can develop a broader set of competencies and capabilities. In many organizations, the senior leaders aim to manage the perception of the issues, form coalitions, and use relationships to influence change in the organization. Without "relationships and influence," they are without arrows in their managerial quivers. In my experience, however, we have found that many leadership development programs fail to include the quantifiable and strategic value of business relationships, not only as another bucket or segment of the curriculum, but also as part of the encompassing framework in the development of the next generation of corporate leaders. In other words, you could be the most astute financial leader, operations leader, manufacturing executive, or complex project owner, but if you lack the ability to proactively and systematically identify, build, and nurture personal, functional, and strategic relationships to influence others, I am not convinced of your fully realized long-term success in any organization.

According to former SunTrust executive Dan Brown, "[Little] *l* leadership typically focuses downward: I have four managers reporting to me, and they have 20 people each reporting to them. Though this type of leadership plays an important role, it typically focuses on accomplishing something you are doing as a team. Big *L* leadership deals with influence. How am I working with my peers and people above me? How do I formulate a coalition with this person, or this person? It usually doesn't take as much time to formulate a relationship or influence . . . people at lower levels. But once you create that influence above, you really become a leader.

"When I was at SunTrust, I had a project that wasn't going well. A subordinate in rank who worked for another manager asked me about it. After I explained the situation, he said, 'I can help you get that done. It's stuck and one of my peers is holding it up. I'll fix that. I have a relationship with that person. I will fix that and it will help you and it will help us all around.'

"I started taking him to lunch once a quarter. This was obviously a person in the business who could break down barriers and get things done. He could generate solutions for people outside of his group," Dan added.

The increasing diversity of today's workforce makes it that much more critical that our future leaders can effectively engage those who don't look, sound, or think like us and lead them toward a common set of strategic goals and objectives. In addition to providing cultural diversity, key individuals with unique perspectives and insights can accelerate any leader's ability to achieve results. We call these people *pivotal contacts*.

In researching dozens of *Fortune* 500 leadership development programs, we found many to be myopic in their perspective and focused purely on safe topics such as strategy, financial engineering, and global expansion. Many try to elevate your thinking, executing from the purely tactical (*what* we are doing) to the more strategic (*why* we are doing this). Then there is the holistic approach that questions not just the ability but the social responsibility aspects as well. Although extremely beneficial to current high performers and those perceived to be high potentials, these questions don't include a systematic, disciplined approach to functional and strategic relationships.

Strategic relationships are seldom part of any personal evaluations we have reviewed to date. Nor are they part of any compensation model we have seen, at least no compensation plan that actually moves one's needle (a 5 percent variable is not really an incentive). They are not part of a human resource organization's competency maps or formal mentoring programs aimed at raising the bar on key functional leaders today. Unless the appropriate metrics and rewards are in place to accurately align the organization's goals and objectives with those of the individual in a highly relationship-centric environment, how will we overcome this fundamental and often myopic perspective of world-class leadership development programs?

Relationship-Centric Best Practice: Politically Savvy

Take a look at the following excerpts from a world-class leadership development program. The foreword asks:

- How do you know when your team is winning? How do you know when they are losing?
- What do you look for in a leader?
- What questions do you ask to separate the high performers and high potentials?
- Why has your team been successful?

(continued)

Relationship-Centric Best Practice: Politically Savvy
(Continued)

Throughout close to 400 pages of concepts, case studies, exercises, and reviews, the notion of business relationships as a strategic asset is mentioned in less than a single paragraph. We exert a great deal of energy developing a strategic mind-set, constructing plans, and investing in field execution, yet many simply do not believe that corporate politics is worthy of their attention.

I am often reminded of Plato, who said, "Those who are too smart to engage in politics are usually punished by being governed by those considerably dumber than themselves." Become astute in describing the motivation and key forces in human nature and organizational structures, which make the political system both necessary and unavoidable. Not only are there political structures in every organization, but they tend to be highly influenced by a select group of insider relationships. Their key lieutenants, both formal and informal, within the organization, as well as key external advisers, can provide unparalleled access to opportunities with those who have invested in deep and broad-based relationships. Only by establishing personal credibility and direct or indirect business value to those in highly influential roles will you be able to formulate a professional, polished, and ethical win-win solution for long-term viability and success within your organization.

Inclusion as a Strategic Asset

Although many forward-thinking companies have a diversity initiative—a change initiative that specifically addresses the core dimensions of differences or an initiative to improve workplace conditions—few really talk about relationship diversity and what goes on every day under the radar. Diversity has to be understood as more than affirmative action. Diversity is about trust, respect, and productivity. Relationships can often power and elevate these three elements through inclusion of unique perspectives and independent insights. Innovation is accelerated to shorten time to market; personnel acquisition costs and the cost of a bad hire are reduced; and a very distinct and quantifiable differentiation is created between strategic execution and yet another corporate agenda.

I am reminded of a mentor of mine who once said, "Each of us, having walked a very distinct path, could get us where we are today." When brought together around a common cause, we also bring very different understandings, experiences, and unique capabilities to view the same set of challenges and opportunities. In essence, we are the products of the advice we have taken over the years, and our past influences often solidify or frame our recommendations in the future. The more diverse those experiences, the more inclusive of a broad-based set of constituents and the more likely a successful outcome of any challenge or struggle.

Diversify Your Portfolio of Relationships

There are three critical attributes in what we call your relationship bank, that is, the portfolio of relationships you already have. I'll elaborate more on this in the next chapter, but for now, I need you to really think about those who already know, like, and trust you. The number one attribute you have to keep in mind constantly is the diversity in which you build relationships.

In delivering between 50 and 80 global keynote speeches and working with a dozen consulting clients each year, I see more and more clients not diversifying the relationships they build. They become completely dependent upon one large customer, one geographic region, a single supplier, or one dominant distribution channel.

Think about it for a second. What happens if that one primary relationship deteriorates? Would your world come to a screeching halt?

We often hear about diversification in the context of our financial portfolio but seldom in our relationship portfolio. Like many, if your 401(k) became a 201(k) in the past few years, you know that diversifying your financial portfolio—selling a few stocks here, buying some bonds or CDs there—is a lot easier than diversifying your portfolio of relationships.

Let me start with some of the inherent risks of not diversifying your portfolio of relationships:

- Some risks are obvious. If that supplier or client changes strategy, goes in a different direction, goes out of business, or curtails spending, there will be a gaping hole in your profitable growth curve.
- The bigger risk is what I call the adaptation risk. You get so close to a client, supplier, or partner that you begin to customize your processes, products, or services to satisfy only that relationship. You change your recruiting or training practices, your marketing strategy, your product specs, or your service delivery methods. Then you wake up one day to realize that you've alienated the rest of the market. No other relationships adhere to or value your new direction, and the destination becomes bleak.

Some habits are hard to break, right? After all, that huge contract is difficult to ignore. That huge customer and all of its executives want all of the products and services that you offer— they want all of you! You become friends and end up spending all kinds of time, effort, and resources with just that one relationship.

So what's the answer? How do you balance investing in your most valuable relationships, yet diversifying that portfolio? Here are three best practices:

1. Set intentionally net-new relationship goals and objectives for yourself. Attend new events, work with different groups and organizations, and read about and explore previously uncharted territories. In short, get out of your comfort zone and try new experiences where you'll have a chance to meet like-minded quality people.

2. Become more selfish—with your time, talent, and investment efforts. I'm blessed that through my speaking and consulting work, I get a chance to meet a lot of great people. But the exact reason why they appreciate the quality of my work is the same reason I can't afford to have coffee or lunch with all of them. Diversity in your portfolio of relationships requires constant trade-offs between relationship investment choices. Make those investment choices wisely.

3. Build new personal brand attributes attractive to different relationships. I'm launching a thought leadership series with some of the brightest minds in global academia. Their research, unwavering commitment to education, and lifelong learning are of great value to my clients. Joint position papers, webinars, and speaking engagements with this group will push me to think differently about strategic relationships.

Listen, diversification is tough. It's as much letting go of some things as it is learning and engaging new opportunities. The goals are to meet, grow, learn, and prosper. Remember how I began this section—the more diverse your portfolio of relationships, the broader your influence footprint.

Pivotal Contacts

Certain individuals can help accelerate your ability to achieve your goals—not just meet your goals, because many people can get there by themselves, but truly *accelerate* your achievement of them. For example, on your own, it might take you six months to reach the chief executive officer (CEO) of Company X to offer your suggestions on how to accelerate revenue growth in Asia-Pacific. Alternatively, the chief financial officer (CFO) of that same company could personally walk you into the CEO's office in less than two weeks. That is accelerated access, and it can be obtained by knowing the right people, or those whom we call *pivotal contacts*.

Pivotal contacts are thought leaders among their peers. They have developed deep subject matter expertise, have proved themselves in situations requiring a balanced approach between strategic vision and tactical execution, or simply have access to influential relationships. They are commonly referred to as movers and shakers in a given role, company, vertical industry, or city. They are rising stars and key influencers, and they often lead the most critical projects within any company. They are highly thought of in board meetings, get mentioned in industry trade publications, and make numerous appearances in industry forums. They are always invited to speak at the company's off-site strategy session or cross-industry conferences for their unique best practices. They are published writers, authors, or subject matter authorities and are considered pillars of their organization or industry.

Relationship-Centric Best Practice: "Most Influential"

Google "most influential 40 under 40," and you're likely to find pivotal contacts that someone, somewhere, has already sought out. The *Inc.* 500, the *Training* magazine

Top 150, and yes, even the "10 most influential players in the concrete industry" are all examples of those who, in many ways, have seen the movie and suffered through the pitfalls you're headed for.

Yet many look at such lists and simply think to themselves, "That's nice." They often ignore these gold mines of industry, geography, or subject matter insiders. Proactively seek out the people on these lists. Find value-based reasons to get introduced to them and, more important, become an asset to them. These individuals will exponentially increase your visibility, level of access, and perceived influence in your desired market.

Regardless of any particular function you currently serve or aspire to reach, a pivotal contact's formal decision role tells you a great deal about his or her business stature. Of particular interest are two critical areas: formal decision role and level of access (Figure 6.1). The person's formal decision role is one of the following.

Decision Maker

Ask most people and they'll tell you they know what or who a decision maker in the business context is—"it's the person who signs the check," I'm often told. But dig a little deeper and few really understand the key challenges consistently good decision makers face and critical attributes they develop over the years. In the context of strategic relationships and pivotal contacts, decisions are critical elements in these leaders' daily lives—from corporate strategy, talent progression, investment options, and distribution channel to research and development (R&D). So, mastering decision making is easy for them—or is it?

FIGURE 6.1 Pivotal Contact Attributes

Do you want to nurture meaningful relationships with pivotal contacts who are true decision makers? Become astute enough to understand the biggest obstacles to high-quality decision making they face on a daily basis. What are some of the biggest challenges to decision making you face as a consumer, as a leader, or for your organization? Key concepts such as presumed associations, anchoring, and pattern matching dramatically affect the business relationships decision makers are interested in.

Approver

In my experience, these are highly valued lieutenants. They often work very closely with the decision maker and are strongly plugged in to the key fiscal year priorities, project imperatives, and highly influential people involved in the desired outcome. They are privy to the broad-based outcome the decision maker is seeking, as well as the realistic limitations or barriers to get there—think of internal bureaucracy; budget issues (often a priority issue and seldom a financial roadblock); or other lack of resources (human resources, capital, or time).

Their title and reporting structure within an organization are irrelevant. What matters is if their evaluations of possible options and recommendations are trusted and respected. The best ones I've ever worked with are creative and will work with you in a highly iterative process to position your value-added proposition as the best possible solution.

If they like you, invest the time and effort to get to know you, and trust you—often due to your past performance—they will recommend to the decision maker that they buy from you, not just monetarily for your products or services, but also for your ideas, perspectives, or perhaps tackling that initiative a little differently.

Convince them of your value-based relationship approach and you'll fast-track your access to the decision maker.

User/Evaluator

It is critical to walk a fine line here. Ignore this group, and they have the potential to become cancerous in your efforts to achieve critical mass of valuable relationships. Aim to develop a highly cordial and engaging relationship with those who will ultimately put your value proposition to the test.

Early in my career, I witnessed the exponential rise of a certain engineering software company. Its sales model was one of recruiting highly assertive salespeople who were extremely aggressive, outright pushy, and abrasive, and who operated with a "buy from us or we'll go over your head" mentality. If the evaluation of their software was in any way jeopardized by the engineering manager's bowling night conflicts, they wouldn't think twice about going over his head and the vice president of engineering to reach the company president and get a deal signed.

Needless to say, this company—largely due to a sheer ignorance or dismissal of emotional and social intelligence—alienated a great number of users and evaluators. Even though it was often successful in its customer acquisition campaigns, in countless accounts, the retaliation of the user community led to its ultimate demise.

Don't Know

It is actually okay not to know a pivotal contact's formal decision role, but it is dangerous to assume without verifying. One of the worst things you can do is invest in the wrong relationships. This is not to say that you should be manipulative or spend time only with those from whom you can benefit. It is simply to say that you don't have the ability to invest in everyone equally. It is critical that you succinctly identify the key attributes of contacts that you will find most helpful. Assume a 5 percent differential in your pivotal contact's formal decision role and we've proven a 22 percent detriment in lost time, effort, and valuable resources in various projects, business development campaigns, go-to-market initiatives, and customer retention and expansion strategies.

Sources of Pivotal Contacts: Hubs and Spokes

Pivotal contacts are also often hubs in their chosen fields. Here are some other common traits:

- *Time*. To pivotal contacts, *time* is a valuable asset and they don't like to waste it. You're not likely to see these people hanging out by the watercooler, chatting it up.
- *Execution*. Pivotal contacts are passionate about *execution*. Seldom will they get excited about a 100-page analysis of a challenge. They are much less interested in everything you

know and much more intrigued by what they need to know to get things done.

- *Gatekeepers.* Pivotal contacts are protected by very capable gatekeepers. The old days of the cliché secretary are long gone. Today's executive administrators and administrative assistants are polished, well-educated, professional, well-paid, and very good at what they do. They take pride in being professional administrators and are focused on optimizing their executives' valuable resources.

- *Mutual trust, respect, and value.* Pivotal contacts build relationships based on mutual trust, respect, and value. Often, the only source of access is through a referral by a trusted source. These include lieutenants inside the organization or highly valued external advisers, but certainly those who have filtered out the time or resource wasters.

- *Private.* It has been my experience that pivotal contacts are well-known, yet *private* individuals. You may hear of their accomplishments, but seldom about their personal lives—including their family matters, political views, or downtime interests.

Pivotal contacts are often one to two business stature levels above your current perceived reach. If you are a manager, for example, a pivotal contact could be a vice president. If you are a director, they could be division presidents. If you are a senior executive, pivotal contacts could include the CEO, board of directors, or senior vice president of the parent company. Pivotal contacts can also be peers in other departments or of higher stature in other organizations, such as private equity firms.

The other critical attribute of pivotal contacts is their level of access. How well are they known, respected, and trusted? Are they perceived to be of quantifiable value? If not regarded highly, their access will be extremely limited. A pivotal contact's level of access can be categorized in four distinct areas.

Unrestricted Access

Meet almost any chief strategy officer, astute executive in investor relations, strategic general counsel, or those few in human resources who can align business strategy with investing in an organization's human capital and you'll quickly recognize their unfettered and unrestricted access. Although many complain about not having a seat at the table, the roles characterized here earned that seat through exemplary performance in their respective functions and their canny ability to quickly assess opportunities and risk and communicate critical matters to the appropriate executives.

Restricted Access

Restricted access could be due to a functional role such as that of product engineer, which doesn't necessarily lend itself to private conversations with a CEO. This could also include geographic limitations; for example, a remote office in Albuquerque, New Mexico, has trouble accessing executives at the corporate office in downtown Manhattan.

New members of an organization may have restricted access because they haven't earned their stripes or don't yet have the proper professional maturity. Or, perhaps they have stumbled in the past and have lost their access because they abused it and broke someone's trust. In some cases, individuals' access is limited because their superiors are potentially threatened or annoyed by them.

It is critical to understand *why* a pivotal contact's access is restricted because there are certain reasons, such as experience, that can be made up for and others that are truly insurmountable.

No Access

This is another group not to be ignored, because they can often be a great source of firsthand knowledge and insights from the street-level rank and file. This group is often passionate about their contributions, and their lack of access could be easily overlooked when they have a high degree of domain expertise. Think of that frontline project manager or engineer or that first-year associate out of law school.

Don't Know

See the earlier section on formal decision roles. The same issues absolutely apply. Remember that it's okay to not know—but if you assume the person has access and you pursue that pivotal contact, you will waste a lot of cycles and resources.

**Relationship-Centric Best Practice:
Diversity as a Strategic Asset**

Sit down with your list of relationship-centric goals. Pick one goal and identify as many diverse buckets of people as you can who could be instrumental to your success. Then, for each bucket, write down specific names of individuals and why you think they could be relevant.

For an example of the "buckets" exercise in the preceding best practice box, let's consider this goal: I want to buy a $20 million discrete manufacturing company in Mexico City by December 31. Diverse categories of pivotal contacts instrumental to your success would include sources of deal flow and creative financing, people who can fulfill gaps in your management team, and the creation of a board of directors or advisers. Sources for these functions could include:

- *Attorneys.* In this case, you don't want just any law firm, but one that specializes in midmarket mergers and acquisitions.

And you don't want just any attorney at that firm, but ideally the firm's managing partner. Managing partners are one to two business stature levels higher than someone you can reach on your own, and they often have a broader perspective into the ongoing activities, efforts, and key relationships of the firm.

- *Accountants.* Build a relationship with a managing partner of a firm that does the audit and tax work for this vertical market (same reason as preceding source).

- *Consultants, marketers, and other strategic service providers.* You might be surprised to learn the breadth and depth of the types of deals these folks see daily.

- *Retained search executives.* These people are in the human capital business and have very broad portfolios of relationships. The good ones have unbelievable access to influential executives and extensively invest in relationship development activities, such as social events, vacation homes, and highly experiential outings.

- *Private equity, wealthy individuals, or merger and acquisition advisers.* This includes those in the business of finance. If they don't have the capital themselves, they know people who have access to it. They would also make strong choices for your board of directors or advisers.

Relationship-Centric Best Practice: Relevant Contacts and Reciprocity

Once you have identified the "buckets," focus on individual contacts and how they relate to your goals. Identify 10 such individuals. Print them as a simple list on one page with your goal and contact information, and give it to the most valuable relationships you develop. This approach will allow you to leverage one of the most fundamental characteristics of value-based relationships—that of reciprocity.

It is not critical that you know exactly who a pivotal contact is, as long as you are able to describe that person's role. Do your homework on these people and search for commonalities, opportunities to engage, and, most important, avenues in which you can become an asset to them.

Relationship-Centric Best Practice: Pivotal Contacts and Philanthropic Causes

Pivotal contacts who have achieved material success in life are often attracted to two fundamental opportunities that often provide your best path to reach them.

First, many are deeply passionate about a philanthropic cause. Often, these causes are related to a personal experience, such as a child with autism, an elderly parent with Alzheimer's disease, or the great results they have experienced firsthand, thanks to the American Cancer Society or American Red Cross. Put yourself in a position to quantifiably contribute to their passion.

Stuart Johnson, a friend and respected corporate attorney in Atlanta, is not only a fellow Eagle Scout but also extremely passionate about the scouting mission. Beyond his professional success and respected circle of friends and admirers, Stuart deeply believes in making a very real difference as an active board member in the scouting organization.

(continued)

Relationship-Centric Best Practice: Pivotal Contacts and Philanthropic Causes (Continued)

Harry Volande, former executive vice president and CFO of Siemens Energy and Automation, annually led the Light the Night Walk for the Leukemia and Lymphoma Society. This past year, they raised $1.4 million. When little Chloe Baker, a leukemia survivor, is around Harry, you feel his compassion, as evidenced by his ear-to-ear grin in the presence of this beautiful little girl and her sheer resiliency.

Second, consider inviting pivotal contacts to highly experiential events. It is one thing to own a Porsche, but it is an entirely different experience to drive one at 160 mph around Road Atlanta. Create exclusive and memorable experiences for key pivotal contacts you aspire to meet.

For example, our good friends John and Pam Moye in Denver own a beautiful villa in Tuscany. What a great opportunity to invite close friends to experience the tranquil beauty of the Italian countryside in this day and age of hustle and bustle in our daily lives. Jim and Elizabeth Munson regularly attend 20-plus black tie events per year, often inviting those they deem most interesting to a number of unique and sought-after gatherings.

Pivotal Contact Prioritized Matrix of Relationship Investments

If you genuinely believe that pivotal contacts can, in fact, accelerate your ability to achieve key goals and objectives, it is not difficult to see that prioritizing those relationship investments will become a fundamental challenge. On any given day, you can pursue a plethora of pivotal contacts, all of whom could be great assets. But how do you know which ones? A traditional analysis model looks in the rearview mirror to make forward projections. But with changing goals and objectives and constant shifts in the position and business stature of those pivotal contacts, this prioritization is a classic scenario for a perfect storm and certainly a moving target.

An intelligent approach to this prioritization is a simple, yet practical, matrix based on breadth and depth, relevancy, spectrum of access, required investment effort, and anticipated return on impact. Let's look at each.

Breadth and Depth

Consider the individual's breadth and depth in your target industry, geography, and functional expertise. How much of a mover and shaker is this person? In the matrix in Figure 6.2, the left-hand side characterizes *specialists*. The more you shift to the right, the more *generalist* the characterization becomes.

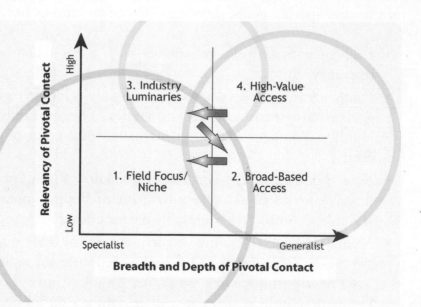

FIGURE 6.2 Pivotal Contact Prioritization Matrix

Specialists are niche players who are narrow in their focus (for example, a neurologist). *Generalists* are the jack-of-all-trades, generic connectors who know a lot of people and shake a lot of hands (for example, politicians). Both groups know a lot of people, but the neurologist is typically very focused on his or her chosen field and will primarily have contacts within that field. Conversely, a politician can talk about anything with anybody. Breadth and depth contributes to how pivotal a contact truly is.

Relevancy

How relevant is the individual to your immediate and quantifiable set of goals and objectives? Although a given person may be able to introduce you to a U.S. senator, this connection doesn't solve your immediate revenue challenges.

On the *y*-axis of the graph of Figure 6.2, there is a scale from low to high relevancy for your immediate goals and objectives. This matrix allows you to identify and, more important, prioritize the four types of pivotal contacts that are directly relevant to your specific goals, strategies, objectives, and tactics.

- *High-value access (4)*—generalists with a high degree of relevancy.
- *Luminaries (3)*—specialists who are highly relevant to your goals, strategies, objectives, and tactics. They not only are highly visible but should be a particular focal point of your efforts.
- *Broad-based access (2)*—generalists who know a lot of people or have broad-based access to a lot of people, many of whom are completely irrelevant to your efforts.
- *Niche (1)*—specialists, and as such, experts in their respective fields. However, they have a low relevancy to your desired relationship-centric outcome. Although it is good to know these individuals, you will seldom see an immediate impact from their relationship investments.

We recommend prioritizing your pivotal contacts according to the matrix in Figure 6.2, that is, by high-value, luminaries, broad-based, and niche (4–3–2–1).

Spectrum of Access

This is often a question of business stature and broad-based reach. Some people can get you in to see a mayor, whereas others have access to a country's president. An individual's spectrum of access expands from local to regional to national to global (Figure 6.3).

This does not refer to a solitary incident or a point in time. We're not talking about you scalping a ticket for me in the nosebleed section of a global economic forum, but instead identifying who has that consistent, genuine level of access.

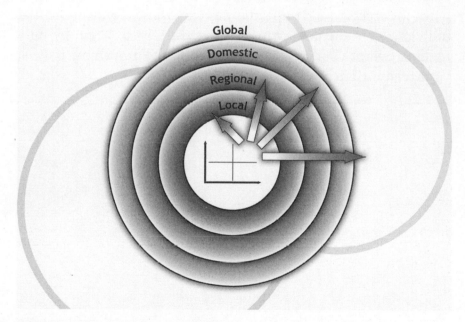

FIGURE 6.3 Spectrum of Access Radar

Required Investment Effort

What kind of investment of time and effort would it take to get to someone who has access to the president? During a recent political fundraiser at the home of a wealthy executive, it became very clear very quickly that only those with access to long-time party supporters had been extended an invitation. Generous contributors sat at the candidate's dinner table while the rest of the attendees were fanned out according to their spectrum of access radar.

It requires one level of investment to create the kind of access that gets you into a political fundraiser, but it requires a whole different level of investment to get invited to the Oval Office. Think about it: What would it take for you to get to the CEO of GM, for example? What kind of relationships would you need to gain that level of access to those kinds of circles?

Pivotal contacts are instrumental to your personal and professional success. By prioritizing your focus, efforts, and relationship investments, you can create and capitalize on accelerated paths for access to and opportunities with these highly influential individuals. In the next chapter, I discuss how to begin by fully making use of your existing portfolio of relationships, that is, your relationship bank.

7

Relationship Bank for Strategy Execution

The desired outcomes of any strategic initiative—profitable growth, delighted customers, a motivated and prepared workforce, efficient and effective processes, and, of course, satisfied shareholders—are directly related to how well an organization can link personal actions to its strategic direction. Contrary to popular belief, this takes more than just people. It takes the *relationships* of those change agents to really make things happen.

As I mentioned in earlier chapters, the idea of relationships is not a stand-alone concept; it's an enabler or an enhancer. Think of your relationship bank as the rocket boosters attached to the shuttle to get you into outer space. If strategy is the selection of several choices for the best possible outcome, your relationship bank becomes an enhancer in the evaluation of those choices and the enabler in the execution of key tasks for the best outcome. In this chapter, I discuss 10 schools of strategy formulation, barriers to strategy execution, and the three critical components of an individual's, team's, or organization's relationship bank: diversity, quality, and the required investment efforts.

No Shortage of Strategy Formulation

Strategy formulation is not in short supply. Marty Gupta of CAP Consulting Group often refers to the 10 schools of strategy from *Strategy Safari* by Henry Mintzberg (Figure 7.1):

1. *Design* (1957-plus)—where strategy formulation is a deliberate process of conception owned by the chief executive officer (CEO), kept simple and easy to communicate, and where structure follows strategy, with SWOT analysis (strengths, weaknesses, opportunities, threats analysis) as

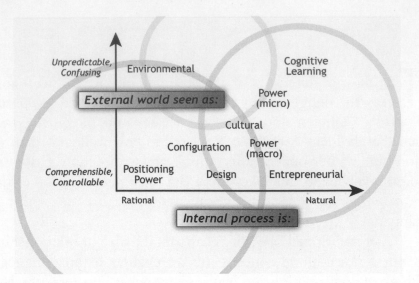

FIGURE 7.1 Ten Schools of Strategy

its centerpiece tool. This is often used for organizations coming out of a period of change into operating stability, where empirical information is available, and with organizations that can implement a central strategy.

2. *Planning* (1965-plus)—through a formal process, formal training, and formal analysis involving lots of numbers by the CEO and the staff. Strategies are often full-blown with objectives, budgets, programs, and operating plans. It is usually very controlling and includes scenario planning and strategic control tools. It is often used for stable, predictable, and controllable situations.

3. *Positioning* (1980-plus)—focused on an analytical process, it is one of the most common approaches, as it is highly analytical with market growth and share matrix, an experience curve, Michael Porter's five-force analysis, and value-chain analysis as its common tools. Porter's strategies often dive into cost leadership, differentiation, and focus of the business. Often used for predictive, established, and stable situations.

4. *Entrepreneurial*—one of a visionary process and leadership where strategy is rooted in the experience and intuition of the leader. The strategy is based on searching for new growth-oriented market opportunities and dramatic leaps forward in the face of uncertainty in a malleable organization. Often used in controllable, comprehensible, situations.

5. *Cognitive*—heavily involved in the mental process with analogies, metaphors, and models. Mapping becomes valuable where strategies emerge as perspectives. Tools include the Myers-Briggs personality test. It is often used in unpredictable and uncertain situations.

6. *Learning*—derived through an emergent process where strategy is evolutionary and emergent and as such can't be controlled. Focus is on learning and knowledge creation, using tools such as systems thinking, core competencies, strategic intent, and knowledge management. It is often used for unpredictable and uncertain situations.

7. *Power*—relies on negotiation where strategy is shaped by power and politics. Micro-power sees strategy formation as the result of persuasion, bargaining, and perhaps confrontation among parochial interests and shifting coalitions, with none dominating over any significant period of time. Macro-power uses alliances and social networks inside and outside the organization to control or cooperate. Micro-power works in uncertain situations, whereas macro-power requires more stability.

8. *Cultural*—formation as a collective process of social interactions. The focus is on corporate culture, values, beliefs, and behaviors and uses tools such as socialization, indoctrination, and ideology to perpetuate existing strategy.

9. *Environmental*—often a reactive process, using an ecological strategy model where the environment is the central factor. The organization must respond to these forces or

be selected out, where the environment is read and adapted to. It is often used in highly uncertain situations.

10. *Configuration*—one of a transformation process focused on strategic change or change management: life cycle analogy with the recognition of the need for transformation without destroying the organization. Tools include incremental change programs, reengineering, and top-down transformation.

Frustrations of Strategy Execution

The breakdown of a great many approaches to delivering strategic outcomes, which are fundamentally designed to satisfy shareholders, delight customers, create efficient and effective processes, and build a motivated and prepared workforce, is a lack of strategy execution.

Much of this strategy execution pyramid begins with an organization's mission (why we exist), its core values and beliefs (what is important to us), its vision (what we want to be), and its strategy (our game plan to get us there). See Figure 7.2.

I call this nothing more than *wall art*. Have you ever seen these often vague and nebulous statements not only spouted out but actually worshipped and accepted as the be-all and end-all to the company's overall success? Many companies go as far as framing these and glorifying them in their corporate hallways, yet ask three individuals in different geographies or functional silos of the company and they will give you three very different answers on where the organization is headed.

Can you imagine driving a car without a dashboard? Most would agree that this would be ludicrous, yet many organizations don't operate in real time using input from a *strategic dashboard*. Not only should the status of current strategic implementations help you gauge your progress, determine whether you are on the right track, and close the gap between your

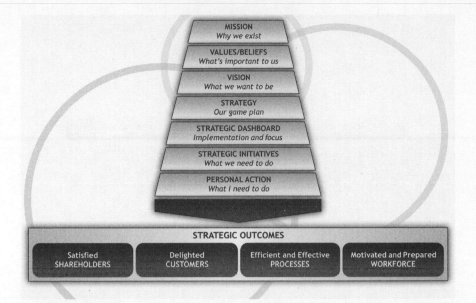

FIGURE 7.2 Strategy Execution Pyramid

current and future state, but it should also help your organization better focus its valuable resources, such as limited capital and critical relationships.

What are some of the strategic initiatives outlining what we need to do and who is responsible for asking whether we *should* do certain things? Specific actions we need to take are seldom ever tied to corporate-mandated strategic initiatives, nor is the dashboard we discussed earlier used to track their progress.

For some reason—perhaps fear of the global war on talent—we continue to lower the bar and accept less. We reward tenure over performance and, as such, reject the notion of holding the entire organization, specific teams, and certain individuals accountable for their lack of willingness, ability, and sheer will and determination to make things happen.

Figure 7.3 highlights four common fundamental barriers to strategy execution: vision, management, people, and resources. Let's examine each one closely.

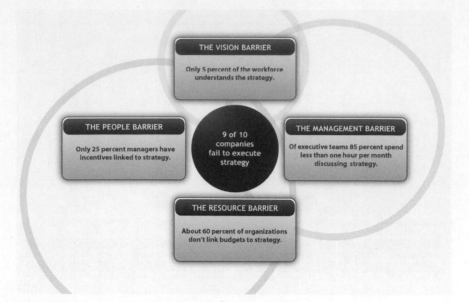

FIGURE 7.3 Barriers to Strategy Execution

- *Vision barrier.* In our research, we have found that only 5 percent of the workforce really understands the company's strategy. Down in the mailroom, where the simple execution of the strategy is critical, there is often the biggest disconnect between everyday actions and broader strategic initiatives. This ultimately reduces efficiency and effectiveness and halts the communication of a common vision.

- *Management barrier.* Some 85 percent of executive teams spend less than one hour a month discussing their strategic options.

- *People barrier.* Only 25 percent of managers have incentives linked to strategy. If you want to know someone's motivation, follow the money. Which performance-based approach will move their needle and get their attention to execute—*consistently*? This applies to a broad-based audience previously made comfortable by the welfare state of a presumed paycheck.

- *Resource barrier.* Some 60 percent of organizations don't link their budgets to strategy. Is there any real surprise that 9 out of 10 companies fail to execute on their strategy?

Relationship Bank as a Key Enabler

So, if these barriers are the problems, what is the solution? I believe change agents or catalysts at their fundamental core are relationship-centric. Don't confuse vibration with forward motion, though. Nothing will ever trump performance, and as such, if you choose to deliver less than what the market expects, you will ultimately lose. Conversely, with execution, performance, and results, an organization's change agents can leverage their relationship banks to institutionalize the desired changes.

Most people do a terrible job of leveraging their existing relationships. You have already spent years, if not decades, working with key individuals you already know and who already know and trust you, yet you haven't touched base with them in years. Did those relationships really fade, or did they simply grow cobwebs?

Your portfolio of relationships is your most valuable asset. Within that portfolio, three characteristics are of extreme importance: diversity, quality, and quantity. Look at the people you already know, and let's categorize them in several areas.

- *Relevance*—see the relationship value pyramid later in this section
- *Geographic*—Atlanta, Northeast, West Coast, Europe
- *Function*—recruiter, legal, finance, venture capitalist (VC)
- *Stature*—higher than you, lower than you, the same as you
- *Organization*—American Management Association, Rotary, parent-teacher association (PTA)

- *Other (non-work-related)*—friends, neighbors, nonprofits, church
- *Time known*—less than 1 year, 1 to 3 years, 3 to 4 years, 5 to 10 years, 10-plus years
- *Maintenance effort*—time spent maintaining this relationship: One hour a month, two to three hours a month, one hour a week, two to three hours a week
- *Interaction frequency*—never, sometimes, often, frequently, very frequently

Unless you can categorize your portfolio of relationships into distinct groups, it will be difficult to gauge any meaningful or comparable quality scale. Furthermore, to create impactful connections, you must effectively align your current relationships with the ones you want and need.

Similar to pivotal contacts, in which the decision role and level of access are critical attributes, three critical components within your relationship bank can help you effectively prioritize the breadth and depth of your relationships today. In short, they should help you answer the question: Do you have *contacts*, or do you have *relationships*?

They are:

- Your relationship value pyramid
- The level of influence of each member
- Invested time and effort you are proactively making in each

Now we'll take a closer look at each relationship.

Relationship Value Pyramid

Let's begin with the depth and relevancy of your current relationships. For years, I have searched for a process to systematically distinguish the broad-based business stature of my existing

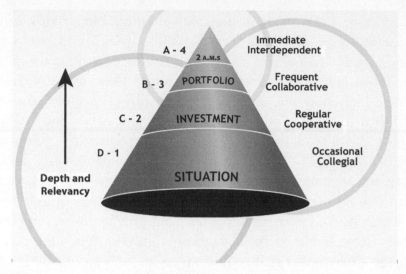

FIGURE 7.4 Relationship Value Pyramid

relationships. Unable to find one, we created the relationship value pyramid (Figure 7.4).

Before we look at each of the levels, it is important to point out that this graphic does not imply that some people are more valuable than others; everyone has value. Instead, the purpose here is to focus on the relevancy of each person in this chapter of your professional life, the nature of your current relationship, and the frequency with which you are likely to interact.

Situation

Your interaction with these people is occasional; your relationship, very friendly and collegial. You interact with them because you need to for a particular project, or you interact with them in a specific department- or event-based situation. If that situation were to change, more than likely so would the nature of your interaction and relationship. Think of past neighbors, colleagues, project teams with outside consultants, or an industry association you no longer actively participate in.

When possible, automate your outreach to this you-never-know group. Well over 100,000 opt-in subscribers who may have heard me speak at a conference or attended one of our training sessions receives our sought-after monthly newsletter. They may not think of relationship economics to solve a critical business challenge today, but you never know when a CEO will read the article in a recent edition—"Tomorrow's Social CEO"—and call me to inquire about my enterprise social market leadership road map. Similarly, you can't afford to ignore what we believe is 50 percent of an individual's portfolio of relationships, because you really never know when these dynamic roles, market opportunities, and event-driven situations will become an asset to your efforts. Yet this is also too broad an audience for any concerted effort. Instead, seek out the up-and-comers who are quickly becoming pivotal contacts in their chosen fields and aim to become an asset to them.

Investment

Your interaction is regular, and your relationship is cooperative. Members of this group are a lot like you. As mentioned earlier, investments are those individuals with whom you have a high degree of behavioral and psychological profile similarities. Take the time to get to know them better, collaborate more frequently, and develop a closer relationship. The tactics and the ethics of your relationship with this category are of critical importance, for they are most susceptible to *perceived* inappropriate relationships. Those who are most like you will draw out cries of favoritism, nepotism, and foul play.

You may have a strong relationship with this group and cooperate with them on key initiatives, but they may or may not be of the highest value to your relevant goals and objectives. Remember that the aim is to heavily invest in those who can influence the achievement of your goals or create access to those who can directly help. This group should ideally make up 25 percent of your portfolio of relationships.

Portfolio

These are the go-to people in your portfolio of relationships. They are subject matter, geographic, or functional experts. Your interactions are frequent, and your relationship is very collaborative. The relationship is one of equal stature and perceived value added. If value is diminished in one scenario, it is easily replenished in another.

These are high-value targets. To build deeper relationships, focus on close family ties and interactions or on non-work-related interactions over an extended period. This group should ideally compose 15 percent of your portfolio of relationships.

2 A.M.S

Not only will this group not get upset if you call them at 2 A.M., they will come and bail you out of jail! Your access to them is immediate, and you have a very interdependent relationship.

These are former bosses, mentors, coaches, and other select people with a very real vested interest in your well-being and success. These people are the real gems in your portfolio of relationships. Protect them at all costs, take care of them, never let them down, and constantly aim to remain an asset to them. These are mentors who can provide pearls of wisdom and valuable access to pivotal contacts most relevant to your goals. They know you very well, so leverage their insights as sounding boards and gauge your personal and professional strengths and weaknesses from their candor. Never embarrass them or even hint to the outside world any weaknesses or shortcomings they may possess.

Your lifelong mission should be developing relationships with the people in this group, and they should make up the remaining 10 percent of your relationship portfolio. It has been our experience that senior executives who heavily guard their most intimate relationships have single-digit 2 A.M.s—a very select few whom they have known for years. They have vacationed together, have been childhood friends or college roommates, or have met through a special circumstance. To be clear, these 2 A.M.s are *professional* relationships beyond your close personal friends and family members.

Level of Influence

The second critical attribute in your relationship bank is the level of influence of your key members. Their level of influence is critical because of the notion of credibility by association. If they are respected, trusted, and held in high regard, when you become an asset to them, will that level of influence be an asset to you in return?

Six levels are identified in Figure 7.5, ranging from a very high level of influence to none and "don't know." (Which prompts the question, How can you tell if someone has a high level of influence?)

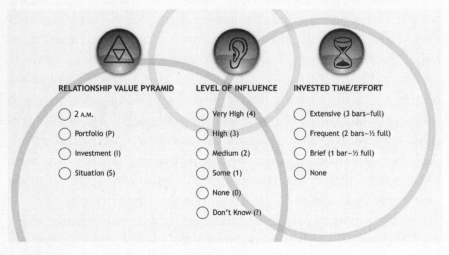

FIGURE 7.5 Relationship Bank Attributes

Look around. Listen intently. Observe. Are their ideas being implemented? How are they thought about or spoken of in this contact's absence? Would an unscientific survey of 5 to 10 colleagues provide any insights? Are they able to accomplish critical functions or tasks often without authority over others? Are they clearly and consistently in the inner circle of what's happening versus asking what just happened?

Time and Effort Invested

The last attribute in this area is the time and effort you have invested with this individual in your relationship bank. Keeping in mind a holistic perspective, would you consider your investments *extensive, frequent, brief,* or *none?* To truly realize the full potential of any relationship, you must invest the time and effort to really get to know the other person and to truly understand what he or she holds dear. You have to become savvy in the realm of that person's currency.

Diversity, Quality, and Required Investment Efforts

To effectively leverage the quality scale, you should begin by categorizing your existing relationships according to this pyramid. Twice a year, print out your entire contact database (from your Outlook, Act, Palm, BlackBerry, and so forth). Preventive maintenance of your most valuable relationships will reduce the likelihood of failure of future relationship currency exchanges when needed the most. Go through each individual contact, and ask yourself the following questions:

- When did I last speak to or see this person?
- Is this contact still at the same company, location, and function?

- Is this a person in whom I have previously invested with no return on that relationship investment, or is it someone whom I have neglected and need to prioritize in the next six months?
- Is this person still relevant to my goals and objectives or someone whom, similar to my closet, I have neglected to clean out?

Please note that I am not advocating discarding people simply because they are no longer of value to you! Instead, I am suggesting that we are all busy and pressed for time. You simply cannot invest your finite resources (time, effort, and capital) on everyone equally. If, in any given day, you could interact with 50 people, for example, how would you prioritize which 50 out of the hundreds, if not thousands, you know? Some would simply say, "The 50 people I have to deal with at any given time." Unfortunately, this is very narrow-minded, because many of those are situational relationships that will change as your circumstances change. All the while, you are neglecting critical members of your relationship bank. Although we have addressed the relationships you need, it is also critical to point out the fundamental value in proactively seeking to understand relationships others need with you. Are they transitory or enduring, and how can you nurture those relationships accordingly?

Here's a question for you: What was that really important project you were working on in the fall of 2000? Conversely, who was that manager who really invested in you, who cared about your personal and professional development and took you under his or her wing to make sure you turned out okay? Most people don't recall those critical project deadlines or deals, but they will never forget the key people who have molded their careers, characters, and lasting relationships.

Relationship-Centric Best Practice: Relationship Value Pyramid

Sit down, find a quiet time, and dust the cobwebs off your past relationships. Document all of the different *buckets* where you currently have or previously have had great relationships. Of particular interest are investment, portfolio, and 2 A.M. contacts. We often find that, when dealing with 2 A.M. contacts, it really doesn't matter how long you have been apart. With many relationships, you can simply pick up where you left off, and five minutes into that initial phone call, it will seem like you just saw each other the day before.

Take an inventory of your relationships. Jog your memory and create a list of people you know in each section. Identify the source of the contact, individual members, and their relationship relevancy. Start with your most immediate interactions—let's call them "The Today Chapter" of your life.

The Today Chapter
- Current colleagues (people you pass in the hallway every day)
- Industry and civic associations
- Personal friends, neighbors, poker night friends
- Sports leagues/golf club members, kids' involvement
- Faith-based acquaintances
- Other

The Yesterday Chapter
- Most recent job (colleagues, clients, suppliers)
- Former industry associations

(continued)

Relationship-Centric Best Practice: Relationship Value Pyramid *(Continued)*

- Last neighborhood, civic organization, nonprofit board
- Other

Education
- Undergraduate/graduate school, law school, medical school alumni
- Executive education program members
- Study abroad contacts
- Other

Special Circumstances
- Travel/vacation friends, Peace Corps members
- People met through tragedy/disaster (9/11, Katrina relief)
- Awards/achievements recipients and members (Presidents Club members, Olympic torch relay participants)

Your Past
- Childhood friends, neighbors
- Parents' friends, colleagues
- Other

We have become such a transient society that many of us lose touch with more than 90 percent of the people we work with when we change jobs or move to another city. We get bogged down with the day-to-day grind of our new roles and simply forget the people with whom we spent hours, if not days, weeks, and months on projects, those whom we really appreciated getting to know.

The good news is that old friends don't go away; they simply fade. Google them. Call someone else you know who may have stayed in touch with that person. Find them and reconnect, reengage, and create a reason to see each other again whether the other person is on the next street, in the next town, or clear across the country.

To summarize this section on the importance of your relationship bank, keep in mind the following topics and focus on achieving the following:

Categorize your current relationships. Who are the influential people you already know? How long have you known them? How much time and effort do you invest to nurture those relationships? Are you leveraging the most quantifiable value from each? You can't improve what you can't measure. Begin by categorizing the relationships you already have. Don't forget— relevancy and diversity are the two most valuable assets in your relationship bank.

Build and nurture your key relationships. Once you have categorized your existing relationships, you can set out a course to nurture and leverage the crucial ones in which you've deemed it appropriate to invest. What did you bring to the table for your most valuable relationships? Expand your bank by getting involved in diverse projects, teams, and organizations. Openly share your goals and objectives, and solicit best practices from those you trust and respect. Share best practices as often as possible.

Make bank account enhancements. Like the clothes in your closet, do an inventory of your relationship bank every year. Prioritize those who have invested in your success and deprioritize those in whom you have invested but haven't seen a return on your relationship investment. Proactively seek out those of higher stature, subject matter expertise, or different focus.

So far, we have covered relationship-centric goals, which are business goals that will require a relationship with others to achieve, and pivotal contacts as individuals instrumental to your personal and professional success. We have also discussed key metrics to be used for your existing relationship bank. A logical question at this point is, "How do I connect the people I know to the ones I need to get to know better in a nonthreatening value-based approach?"

Glad you asked. Read on.

**Relationship Economics Online Tools:
Your Relationship Value Pyramid Template**

http://www.RelationshipEconomics.net/RE-Tools.html

Here is a quote from a reader, which inspired this tool:

Relationship Value Pyramid was an aha moment for me and loved the concept. What I was looking to create for myself after this section was an Excel template with just the most critical contact information by person, drop-downs for Situation, Investment, Portfolio, or 2 A.M.s, and a section for their Level of Influence. This would quickly help me prioritize where my time goes.

Enjoy!

8

Relationship Currency for Adaptive Innovation

It has been said that it is less expensive to innovate than it is to advertise. Yet most organizations are satisfied with incrementalism—a me-too way of doing things *better*. In contrast, true innovation is about doing things *differently*. It focuses on the investment of an organization's most valuable asset—its portfolio of relationships—to capture and leverage best practices across the organization and across the globe. In this chapter, I define *relationship currency*: what it is, how it really works, and how to leverage it most effectively toward adaptive innovation.

Exchanging Relationship Currency

Exchanging relationship currency is how you bridge the gap between the trusted relationships you currently have and the influential relationships you need. Its most simple definition is a gift of time, talent, knowledge, or an influential relationship that is exchanged between individuals with the intent of adding quantifiable value. As you rekindle old relationships or seed new ones, your key goal should always be to uncover what is important to each person in the relationship so that you can make an appropriate *deposit* of relationship currency. Here are some simple methods.

Become More Interesting

Did you know that only an estimated 27 percent of all Americans have a valid passport? Travel, whether domestically or abroad, is a perfect opportunity to expand your horizons, provide unique perspectives on very different social styles, and in the process, hopefully provide you with a new outlook on not only how we as U.S. citizens view the world but also how the rest of the world views us. Developing an interest in the performing arts or a passion for a philanthropic cause can also expose you to opportunities that provide unique value to a variety of personal and professional interactions.

As a member of the Society of International Business Fellows (SIBF), I had the opportunity to participate in the new member program trip to Hong Kong, Beijing, Shanghai, and Xi'an. Not only did we enjoy breathtaking views, but we also attended panel discussions with:

- Cynthia Watson, chairwoman of the Department of Security Studies at the National War College
- Sameena Ahmad, Asia business and finance correspondent, the *Economist*
- Eden Woon, chief executive officer (CEO), Hong Kong General Chamber of Commerce
- Jonathan Anderson, managing director, Asia-Pacific Economics, UBS Investment Bank
- Shai Oster, correspondent, *Wall Street Journal*, Asia
- Jamie Florcruz, Beijing Bureau Chief, CNN
- Kenneth Jarrett, U.S. consul general, Shanghai

I had the chance to experience a very unique and firsthand perspective on the challenges and opportunities in China alongside a very talented group of senior executives, many of whom have become great friends. That experience has helped me engage some of my most valuable client relationships with relevant and insightful perspectives regarding that region.

While I was there, the cultural influences I experienced— such as a private concert by the Peking Opera at the exclusive China Club, Beijing, and tour of the Forbidden City (and not to mention rappelling off the Great Wall, where Genghis Kahn broke through many centuries ago)—enlightened and humbled me regarding the vast amount of opportunities available to expand one's sheer capacity to grow personally and professionally.

As a direct result of the relationships I developed during and since this trip, several SIBF members have become consulting or speaking clients, as well as invaluable referral sources. I've presented keynote speeches at SIBF Annual Conventions and have developed professional relationships with other speakers and thought leaders from their Washington Briefing to the more recent Middle East new member programs.

Build a Personal Brand

What is that brand of clothing with the famous swoosh mark? How about the shop around the corner with the $10 cup of coffee? How about the red can of soda that we all order by name? As previously mentioned, companies spend billions of dollars annually to enhance their brand equity.

Regardless of your profession, when others engage you, buy from you, work with you, or trust and invest in you, they are in essence buying three things: your product or service, the perception of the company behind that product or service, and the brand called *you*. This is not unlike corporate brand equity. Your personal brand equity also differentiates you from competing mind share and wallet share among a sea of sameness.

Only by elevating yourself above this noise and (hopefully) creating personal brand attributes such as competence, intellect, solid judgment, integrity, and dependability will you be selected for critical projects and true leadership roles and viewed as one who will create access to strategic relationships.

Become Known for Content

You may have heard that it is better to be known for content than it is to simply be known. When I say *Good to Great, Execution, In Search of Excellence, Blue Ocean Strategy, The 7 Habits of Highly*

Effective People, *Blink*, or *Freakonomics*, what comes to mind? To many, it is the thought leaders behind these well-known works.

When you develop compelling and unique content, you become known. Combine that with relevant, practical, pragmatic context in which the consumers of that information can use your content to improve their conditions, and now you're sought after. You are asked to speak, moderate panels, and share your experiences, unique insights, and independent perspectives. Think of a trade show. You can *exhibit* there; you can set up a booth and pass out marketing materials. You can *attend* the show and sit through content sessions. Or you can *speak* or *moderate* a panel at the event. Which do you believe would have the greatest impact on your personal and professional brand?

Each has its respective value, but the last alternative often leaves a much more meaningful and lasting impression. So, how do you get invited to speak? What value do you contribute to the event? What forward-looking or contrarian perspective can you bring? That is your highly valuable and unique content and relevant and pragmatic context.

Content takes research, packaging, and marketing in the form of position papers, published articles, columns, and commercially published books. Content plus context is constantly in demand. Yet people amaze me; many true subject matter experts in their respective fields have never written or submitted their unique perspectives on topics that they are passionate about. What they don't realize is that by being perceived as thought leaders in their fields, they would create an unparalleled market pull for their respective organizations—and personal brands.

As a mentor often reminds me, "If you don't toot your own horn, there is no music!" How are you combining content—your unique ideas, insights, and perspectives—with context and applying it to specific situations of others to improve their condition?

Here are some examples of how relationship currency works and the relevant deposits you can make:

- You are talking to a colleague who was recently transferred to your division. He notices something from your college on the wall and mentions that his son is interested in applying to that same school. As an alumnus, is there something you can do to assist your colleague? Can you make a call to someone in admissions or provide a campus tour? By the way, no one has perfected the campus tour experience quite like Nido Qubein, president of High Point University in High Point, North Carolina. His highly student-centric approach provides every student an opportunity for an extraordinary education in a fun environment with caring people.
- You are having coffee with a client when she mentions how busy she has been working on a charity silent auction and how she desperately needs unique donations. Offer to call a neighbor who is a strong sponsor of Cirque du Soleil and entice her to become similarly passionate in the campaign.
- You read in the paper that an old friend has been promoted to a new vice president position. Call to congratulate him, and offer to introduce him to a senior executive at your company to explore possible synergies.

It is critical to remember that what people do for a living is not who they are. If you don't give people a chance to get to know you, how do you expect them to trust you? Someone protested recently, "But trust comes with time and experience in dealing with that person. Aren't you really looking for faith?" Well said! People want to believe that you are credible *today* and believe in you *tomorrow* as you begin to deliver some of the value you promised *yesterday*!

Remember a simple process that has been proved since the beginning of time: *Like Me—Know Me—Trust Me—Pay Me!*

- If you like me, you'll invest time and effort to get to know me.
- When you get a chance to know me, hopefully opportunities will arise for you to experience that you can trust me.
- Only when you feel that you can trust me will you pay me—monetarily for my products or services, as well as my independent perspectives.

Get to Know People—Ask Better Questions

If you are determined to go beyond the superficial and really begin to get to know others, you must start by asking better questions, beyond the obvious, "How have you been? How was your weekend?" Instead, try:

- If you were going to create a new role here, what would it be and why?
- What are you passionate about when you're not at the office?
- What are the top three goals you want to achieve this year?
- How are you measured?

Only by changing your behavior to stop winging it and becoming more disciplined and intentional with your questions will you really get to the core of who your colleagues really *are* versus simply what they *do*.

Get People Out of Their Offices

Most offices have stiff chairs. Most coffee shops have comfortable couches. Get people out of their office and engage them—

really engage them—over a cup of coffee. If you don't like coffee, drink tea. If you don't like tea, drink water. If you have a corporate cafeteria, take them there. It's never about the meal. It's about the opportunity to engage, interact, and get to know each other better outside the day-to-day grind.

You Can't Clone Yourself, but You Can Clone Time

Most people look perplexed when I say this, but think about it: If you are meeting someone for a 10 A.M. cup of coffee (and if it's appropriate), why not invite someone at 9:30, visit with them, and overlap the two visits by 15 to 30 minutes so you can introduce the two people you are visiting with to each other? This gives them a chance to meet and extend their own portfolio of relationships. Just remember that no one likes surprises, so run the idea by both parties beforehand. Also make sure to discuss sensitive, personal, and no-other-party-relevant topics on your individual times.

Start by Making a Deposit!

Your relationship currency exists in an account that is very similar to your checking account, and you can't write a check from an account in which you have no money. You can't make a withdrawal without making a deposit first. You also can't deposit $100 and attempt to withdraw $1,000. These principles are equally consistent in your business relationships. We have all experienced far greater ease in asking for a withdrawal if we have previously made the necessary deposits.

It is absolutely mind-boggling to me how many people will ask for a favor when they haven't earned the right to do so. I am not advocating that you keep score. When I meet someone, I'm not gauging whether we can do business together; I'm looking to understand whether this person gets, appreciates, and leverages the real value of relationships. Reciprocity is a natural and unmistakable law in relationships. Maybe not today, tomorrow, next week, next month, or next year, but those who truly understand the dynamics of the *favor economy* will find a way to eventually reciprocate.

Relationship-Centric Best Practice: Relationship Currency Deposits

To summarize relationship currency deposits and discover how to transform relationship creation into relationship capitalization, keep in mind the following simple, yet critical, precepts.

- *Reciprocate first.* If you begin by really getting to know and truly investing in everyday contacts with meaningful relationship currency deposits, the world becomes your ATM.

- *Establish value-based relationships.* Aim to deliver value in every interaction. By focusing on what is of particular value to others, you can sharpen your unique value-added proposition. When you introduce two people to each other and they benefit from that introduction, you have made deposits in *two* accounts.

- *Build a personal brand.* In a sea of sameness, being interesting, being known for content, and building a personal brand will differentiate you from the others. By becoming more interesting, you add value to each interaction. Content is far more valuable than self-promotion. Personal branding can exponentially extend your reach. Research it, package it, market it, and perfect it. People are buying *you*!

- ***Return on involvement.*** Carefully pick the organizations in which you choose to invest—whether professional, civic, or community. Get engaged or get involved by taking on the most visible roles in areas such as membership, marketing, or programs.

30-, 60-, and 90-Day Personal Relationship Plan

Only a fundamental change in your behavior will create a lasting impact on your relationship development success. To adopt even some of these four ideas to the extent that you are comfortable will help you make many of these best practices yours.

1. *Make a real commitment to start pervasively integrating relationships in your everyday interactions.* Relationship development is not a spectator sport. Attend a function from the sideline and you'll largely miss the opportunity to meet those critical individuals who can dramatically improve your situation. Start by inviting a colleague to an industry function where you already feel comfortable with your surroundings.

2. *Set quantifiable goals.* Remember, most New Year's resolutions fail because they don't include a quantifiable way to measure one's progress. Build a 30-, 60-, and 90-day plan with quantifiable goals, objectives, and action items. Prioritize them into three categories: *serious* (if you don't do it now, it will hurt you); *urgent* (if you don't get to it, it will become serious and hurt you); and *growth* (fire prevention and opportunities for scale).

3. *There is no magic bullet when it comes to building and nurturing lasting relationships.* And when you make mistakes or

unintentionally ruin a relationship, there is no pause or re-start button. Relationship building is not speed dating; it takes time, effort, and investments. Many are either un-willing or unable to take this journey. If you're unwilling, neither I nor anyone else can help you. If you're unable, we can address that with coaching, training, mentoring, and supporting technology. You simply have to decide if this aspect of your personal and professional development is important enough to make the necessary investments to do it right and do it well.

4. *There are absolute and very real trade-offs in the process.* I have two young children, and it is always a heartbreaking choice whether to (1) spend time that I won't get back attending another networking function or (2) go home to my beauti-ful wife and kids whom I miss throughout the day. There is no easy answer, and as hard as many try, real balance is dif-ficult to obtain. The opportunity cost forces me to do my homework before attending any event. Ideally, I'll have a good idea of the speaker's bio, the nature of his or her con-tent, and the interests of the audience. If one of these three is not aligned with my personal or professional goals, I don't go. I have elevated my efforts from simply activity-based networking to value-based relationship development in the organizations I belong to, events I attend, and travel commitments I make.

Understanding and beginning to exchange relationship currency is the critical first step in your relationship economics transformation process. The more you use these techniques, the more confident your mind-set, the sharper the tools in your tool set, and the clearer and crisper your individual road map will become. Make the commitment to invest the time, effort, and resources in the next 30, 60, and 90 days to make a real change in how you build, nurture, and leverage key relationships toward your personal and professional success.

Relationship-Centric Best Practice:
30-, 60-, and 90-Day Personal Plan

Over the Next 30 Days

- Clean, centralize, and update your current relationship bank and create a relationship value pyramid. Take the time to go through and assign categories, think about how much time you have or need to invest in each, and if they're not relevant, export these contacts into a separate spreadsheet, apart from your active, day-to-day list.

- Identify your top three goals for the next 12 months; inventory your relationship currency assets.

- Given your goals, identify and begin profiling three pivotal contacts and higher business stature relationships you currently have.

- Get to really know those pivotal contacts over coffee or a meal.

- Find an opportunity to become an asset to those pivotal contacts early and often.

Over the Next 60 Days

- Translate your value-added proposition into something that has a recognizable impact.

- Arm your current relationships with ammunition to introduce you to a pivotal contact.

- Meet with a minimum of one pivotal contact, working toward achieving a key goal.

Over the Next 90 Days

- Build a pipeline of contacts met, sources of those contacts, outcomes of each meeting, and any next steps.

(continued)

Relationship-Centric Best Practice:
30-, 60-, and 90-Day Personal Plan *(Continued)*

- Leverage one contact to extend your reach to as diverse an audience or network as possible.
- Connect a minimum of three individuals you've met with each other.

Remember These Three Best Practices:

1. Build a "mastermind group of partners" who believe in the real value of relationships. Schedule regular meetings and keep each other accountable. Everyone gets busy, so the involvement has a tendency to drop off. Stay vigilant and get committed to supporting each other; continue to learn, grow, and prosper— personally and professionally. If you excite or disturb people to raise the bar on their performance, they'll keep coming back for more!
2. Bring your personalized plan to a weekly meeting and build on this foundation.
3. Start small, with easy or comfortable topics. Success builds on success, so start by attending one event per week or strive to meet one or two new people per week.

Less Expensive to Innovate Than to Advertise

An organization's most valuable asset is its portfolio of relationships. How an organization's staff members invest in those relationships to capture and leverage best practices across the organization determines how successfully they will be able to reach true innovation.

What qualities are shared by the candy and beverage company Cadbury Schweppes, Indian automaker Tata Motors, Caterpillar, Apple, Adidas, Toyota, and Christian Dior? According to the Booz Allen Hamilton Global Innovation 1000, they are but a few of the world's relationship-centric innovators. By nurturing highly decentralized and knowledge-driven cultures—regardless of whether you are the earth-moving equipment giant, the nimble conceptualizer of the iPod Nano, or the German purveyor of quality, yet fashion-conscious, sportswear—these smart spenders get a higher return on their research and development (R&D) investments than many of their highly innovative peers.

Although there is seldom a simple relationship between an organization's overall R&D expenditure and its corporate performance, adaptive innovation consistently leverages strategic relationships to uncover new innovative practices as well as reinforcing metrics such as the number and quality of patents controlled.

Take Apple, for example. Do you really believe that Steve Jobs was the first to think of recording audio on a memory stick? On the contrary, for close to a decade, Sony enjoyed enormous success with the Walkman. It was by far one of history's most successful product launches, executions, and extensions of a consumer products company. But it took Steve Jobs, the Apple DNA, and its relentless focus on the customer experience to not only put the Walkman out of business but introduce a new market maker in the iPod. By understanding the limitations of the Walkman—compared with the expansive ability to deliver hundreds, if not thousands, of CDs, individual songs, and even more recently, television shows and entire movies on the iPod—Apple disrupted the value chain between content creation (the artists), content delivery (traditional music industry channels), and the enormous end user of audio and video content.

When you innovate, it is critical not only to engage in a broad-based scanning of the competitors, market, and business drivers but also to extend that scan into the larger environment and collective social intelligence.

Adaptive Innovation

To adapt to one's dynamic market demands, the organization's relationship-centric DNA must focus its innovation investments on a succinct understanding of the customer's needs coupled with strong marketing and investment planning. In adaptive innovation, seven critical metrics can be greatly enhanced through the systematic and disciplined capitalization of intracompany and external strategic relationships.

1. Sales growth
2. Gross margin percentage
3. Gross profit growth
4. Operating margin percentage
5. Operating income growth
6. Total shareholder returns
7. Market capitalization growth

The broad-based identification and leveraging of company-wide expertise in a multitude of functions, developed over time, can create a very sustainable competitive advantage. Adaptive innovation must be fueled by those at the edge of business, often closest to the voice of the customer. Those investments made for longer horizons focus on creating profitable growth.

Adaptive innovation also forces the organization to focus on and invest in its most valuable asset—its portfolio of both intracompany and externally focused relationships. In all of the organizations I have worked with over the years, I have yet to meet a chief best practices officer. So, whose role is it to capture and leverage the pockets of best practices that abound in any organization?

Through innovation, a company aims to leapfrog the competition and truly shape an entire industry. Adaptive innovation is about doing things *differently*. This approach requires a relationship-centric culture with the courage to fail and learn from those failures. It is not about simply imitating the strategies of others through traditional value-added propositions, but rather the shaping of one's own destiny.

It is important to note that innovation is a process with multiple enablers, contributors, and positive components. A single ad never works. Advertising often just contributes to the noise. But when you innovate, the market seeks you out.

Relationship-Centric Innovation Value Disruption

Value creation is derived from value chain disruption. If you don't build strategic relationships to disrupt your value chain, someone else will. As such, adaptive innovation can be characterized as a series of logical processes and critical relationships often interdependent on one another (Figure 8.1). These sequential processes are:

Stage 1: *Seeding*—market research and conceptualization of often far-fetched ideas

Stage 2: *Prioritization*—selective decision process

Stage 3: *Product development and product road map*

Stage 4: *Commercialization*—adapting, bridging, and aligning with those dynamic customer demands

These are links in a value chain. And for adaptive innovation to work, these links must be seamlessly integrated and deliver a very high level of consistent performance over time. Relationship-centric DNA focuses heavily on not just the

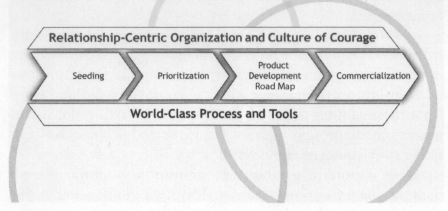

FIGURE 8.1 Adaptive Innovation Value Chain

passing of the baton between those critical stages but being able to do so without knowledge drain. An organization's relationship-centric DNA mitigates market risks and also hones an organization's capabilities in project prioritization and subsequently commercialization. This is ideally coupled with a sharp understanding of not only what its customers want but what they need.

Adaptive innovation can also greatly benefit from *co-opetition*, where promising ideas are jointly developed and advanced through a consortium. Agility, systematic seeding, and broad-based involvement, including that of the senior leaders (such as Steve Jobs at Apple), in the conceptualization and further refinement of new ideas are other critical characteristics we've seen in this area.

Portfolio of Relationships as a Differentiating Asset

Another fundamental enabler to relationship-centric innovation is the critical, yet often missed, notion of location. Face-to-face meetings are still critical for the effective exchange of ideas, and nowhere is this exchange more valuable for technology companies than in Silicon Valley. Paul Romer, professor at the Graduate School of Business at Stanford University, argues that geography absolutely matters and that technology ideas with their genesis in Silicon Valley have an exponential advantage over those brought to market elsewhere.

Have you ever wondered why some of the most successful VC firms that back some of the most compelling ideas are often obsessed with the 50-mile radius between San Jose and San Francisco? On a quarterly basis, PricewaterhouseCoopers releases its MoneyTree Report, which consistently points to more than 25 percent of all venture investments in the United States going to Silicon Valley ideas and ventures.

Strong portfolios of relationships create a highly differentiating asset in this scenario based on two fundamental factors: (1) first-mover advantage and (2) a noticeably higher return on any of those investments. Some of your best future employees are friends of your current employees. As such, their personal relationships outside of work become a huge determining factor in where they choose to work. And besides, who wouldn't want to work for a rock star of a company like Intel, Apple, or Google (all of which are within a 50-mile radius of San Francisco and San Jose)?

Stephen Adams, an assistant professor of management at the Franklin P. Perdue School of Business at Salisbury University, has studied the rise of Silicon Valley. In his research, he points to the fact that venture capital attracts a lot of ideas, which in turn attract a stronger portfolio of relationships. This genesis of an ecosystem fascinates newcomers who are plugged into existing relationships of seasoned professionals, which allows the right teams to assemble great technology ideas much more quickly than anywhere else in the country. They understand, embrace, and apply adaptive innovation at a much faster rate. They test ideas, fail, learn, reinvent, repurpose, and reintroduce groundbreaking approaches much faster than anywhere else in the world.

That's not to say that Silicon Valley is immune to challenges in establishing and developing sound relationship economics practices. The logic of first-mover advantage and greater-than-average returns is also very real along Route 128 in the suburbs around Boston, as well as in many other parts of the world with residents who also know how to commercialize great ideas. There are also fundamental challenges with innovation in places like Silicon Valley. In times of trouble, such as during the Internet bubble of 2000 or the housing crisis of 2007 and 2008, the Valley tends to catch a worse cold than the rest of the world. Right after the bust, for example, there was a period of time in which Silicon Valley was seen as overcooked and overdone. The amazing thing is how resilient it has proved to be. Every time there is a failure, it recovers and becomes even more durable.

Fifty years ago, the silicon chip was the growth engine of Silicon Valley. Until the late 1970s, the Japanese memory chip manufacturers stole the show. With the advent of personal computers, data storage software, and more recently the ever-expansive World Wide Web, new media, and online commerce, we continue to paint the portfolio of relationships within Silicon Valley as a *wow*. Even with the evolution of technology, personal connections continue to build on the momentum and the ability to consistently adapt models to changing market demands. Deal flow, which is the lifeline of VC firms, is most often driven by the breadth and depth of your portfolio of relationships. More important, value promised and value delivered encompass the exchange of relationship currency.

In all great industries, geographies, organizations, teams, and especially inner circles—beyond the aboveground economy—the fundamental driver linking business innovation to economic prosperity is often the undocumented, unspoken, and underground favor economy. Like cash, relationship currency has immediate and extreme liquidity in its value.

9

Transforming *Us* and *Them* into *We*

In his book *Winning*, Jack Welch writes about a lack of candor in corporate America. The same is often true with business relationships. We tell people what they want to hear—not what is going to help them become better leaders or even better human beings. We talk about accountability, yet we tolerate mediocrity (at a number of iconic U.S. corporations) and then wonder what the key factors were driving the same company to its eventual demise.

Exemplary professional conduct shouldn't be the exception. Why do we talk about *business ethics* when it should be just *ethics* in general? You either have them or you don't. You seldom meet someone who is incredibly ethical in his or her personal life, yet laundering money, bribing customers, and engaging in corporate espionage against competitors at work. Likewise, quality shouldn't be a *department*—it's a *mind-set*. It is an attitude and an organization's deeply rooted belief system that "We will produce the best product or deliver the best service we can, every time, while we continue to raise the bar for ourselves."

One of the most visible areas in need of candor today is in large-scale change management, sometimes brought on by mergers and acquisitions. A Bain study highlighted that less than 30 percent of mergers and acquisitions are deemed successful. A Mercer/*BusinessWeek* study found that, out of 150 deals valued at $500 million or more, more than half actually *destroyed* shareholder wealth as judged by stock performance. And only one-third contributed marginally to shareholder worth.

In this chapter, I cover the fundamental role of change agents and the strategic value of their business relationships with the very organizational departments in need of that change. I discuss the 100-day action plan that every company needs in a large-scale change initiative or mergers and acquisitions event and the critical role of strategic business relationships on the influential and the influenced, both inside and outside the organization. In short, I discuss how to transform *us* and *them* into *we*.

Strategic Relationships of Key Agents in Navigating Change

Let me start by making a distinction between problem solving and real change management. Problem solving is fixing things. As you can see in Figure 9.1, if you start with the status quo, something happens to create a less-than-desired state. When you fix that issue and return the situation back to its previous status quo state, you've resolved the problem. Fix it a little better and you have resolution plus.

Conversely, as you can see in Figure 9.2, in *real* change management, if you start with the same status quo, a pulse point of change elevates the situation/the expected norm to a new height of performance, expectations, execution, or results. If you develop a culture that constantly creates these pulse points, now you have constantly enhanced positions—you're constantly raising the bar on your own as well as the team's or organization's growth.

A component that is critical to driving everything from process optimization to altering the mind-set of the people

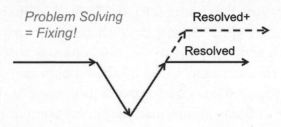

FIGURE 9.1 Problem Solving

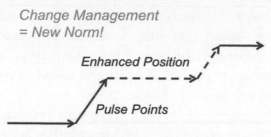

Change Management
= New Norm!

Enhanced Position

Pulse Points

FIGURE 9.2 Real Change Management

whom the change will surely affect is the team of employees chartered to help the organization navigate through this often challenging journey. These change agents are leaders in their organizations, free of hierarchical bondage, and are often able to move across a multitude of departments, business units, and divisions in search of simpler processes. They are highly motivated and well-trained employees and absolutely key to implementing better procedures for the maximum output from any organizational investment in limited resources.

Pick this team for their technical skills alone, and in many instances, they will fail. Pick them for their tenure and knowledge of the organization, and they are likely to come up short. Pick a team wholly cut from the same cloth (with similar psychological or behavioral profiles), and they are likely to dismiss those who bring different perspectives in regard to a prioritization of strategic initiatives. They will miss critical components necessary for a successful transformation of the organization. Pick them carelessly, and the cost will not be too dissimilar to that of a bad executive hire—at least 10 to 12 times their combined annual salary. And that doesn't take into consideration the corporate reputation and perceived inability of the leadership team to assign a competent, credible, and emotionally intelligent team to lead the very change communicated to be strategic to the organization's future.

Consider, for example, a manufacturing client that assembled a team of change agents to drive its lean operations initiative.

The group reported directly to senior executives and was staffed with a team of young, energetic, fresh-thinking new hires—real innovators. Unfortunately, senior leadership failed to recognize the covert and overt pushback by the business units' NIH (not invented here) culture and silo mentality.

As a result, operations managers with very real organizational power felt invaded by "a group of kids who simply didn't 'get' how we do things around here." The management team was left with few choices other than to abandon the change initiative after just a few months. The change agents did not focus on fostering strategic relationships—those that could influence the broader mind-set and help position their great ideas as "a fresh set of eyes on a stagnant industry and its complacent workforce." They did not establish themselves as trustworthy in combining their credibility (knowledge of highly efficient and effective processes combined with empathy) with the value of experience from a highly tenured team. Trust leads to candor, candor leads to prudent risk taking, and risk taking leads to innovation.

My experience with a variety of organizations that have succeeded in crafting and executing real change suggests that it is critical to have strategic and intentional relationship development competencies of a carefully constructed change agent team. There are three essential components:

1. *Quantifiable impetus for change and the opportunity cost of status quo.* To understand the essence of *why* we must change, people must believe in the real, financial impact on their lives if they *don't* embark on this journey. Without that understanding, the idea of change itself will seldom strike the necessary chord to move. Another fundamental challenge is that of the status quo, which does not represent alternatives to change but rather the most destructive option of all—that of simply doing nothing. Unless the opportunity cost of the status quo is likewise presented in

real dollars and cents, very few will want to move away from their current comfort zone.

2. *Careful recruitment and development of the change agent team.* Clearly articulating the benefits and opportunities team members will receive because of nontraditional career paths, particularly when selecting high performers already well respected within the company, sends a clear signal that management takes the program seriously. This group must possess both the raw analytical power to solve complex business problems as well as highly astute interpersonal skills, including empathy, strong communication skills, perseverance, and creativity in the face of challenge or ambiguity. This is particularly critical when dealing with conflict. They must be constructive and seek to strike a balance between young MBA types and seasoned managers with proven track records within the organization.

3. *Close relationship development and nurturing between the change agent team and the influential members of the organizational areas targeted for transformation.* Alan Weiss has often coached me that, "With eighty percent completion of anything—move. The remaining twenty percent seldom matters." By developing a close working relationship with the shop floor, your buy-in rate as a critical success metric for real change increases exponentially.

Encourage open, candid communication that keeps key influential team members actively engaged in the change process and involves them in complex problem-solving sessions. This helps build personal connections to and ownership of the solution. Testing proposed ideas and making iterative modifications creates small wins, which can be transformed into standard tools and processes and can serve as a flywheel of momentum for the rest of the organization. Communication and collaboration serve as an enabler, not just to inciting change, but to leveraging relationships to overcome barriers to lasting impactful change.

Network of Influencers as a Strategic Asset in Change Management

Several years ago, one of my professional services clients decided that it needed an organizational overhaul. Coordination of best practices and efficient and effective collaboration across service lines was dismal at best. Critical team members who needed to be at the edge of the business engaging current and prospective customers were anything but engaged. The client responded with a new organizational structure and drastically changed the work environment to support a community feel where service line subject matter experts were in close proximity to business development, marketing, and delivery resources. Team members could mingle and collaborate and engage customers easily, casually, and candidly in key discussion forums.

If you're trying to promote collaboration, as was the managing partner of this firm, proximity certainly helps, as does a visually appealing space. Unfortunately, in this case, it failed to spark any meaningful innovation or deeper relationships with key customers. Recently, management decided to revamp the organization and the workspace once again.

This example should ring with some familiarity for any organization that responds to sheer dysfunction without truly understanding its root causes. Decentralization, as mentioned earlier, could help organizational or leadership bottlenecks in decision making. But if you're struggling with poor or nonexistent communication, inflexibility, or lack of real collaboration from disparate sides of the organization, it's time to break down functional, geographic, and project-based silos.

Keep in mind that there is seldom a magic pill. The ideas offered by organizational effectiveness specialists look great on paper (believe me, as I sat in a meeting with 12 of them recently at a *Fortune* 500 client), but they often produce disappointing results. Yet, like the blossoms of the Japanese cherry trees on the Potomac River in Washington, D.C., each spring, reorganizations come and go with amazing regularity, often without significantly boosting the organization's effectiveness.

One of the inside jokes at Silicon Graphics (SGI) years ago was that, "It's not a reorg; it's a wardrobe," as evidenced by countless shirts from a multitude of three-letter divisional name changes that were so frequent, many in the field organization could seldom keep up. (We were all convinced that someone on the leadership team owned the promotional company that provided the plethora of trinkets.) Constant organizational changes seldom produce any real or lasting benefits for end customers.

Business process reengineering (BPR) and total quality management (TQM) are two other common initiatives of the past that ignored the highly influential, yet nonorganizationally structured social networks of change agents. Knowledge sharing through collaboration is by definition impossible in isolation. In transforming an organization's willingness and ability to change, the relationships of those change agents are critical to anything actually getting accomplished.

Companies that invest resources such as time, talent, and capital to understand and leverage internally influenced as well as externally influenced social networks greatly improve their chances of creating lasting and highly impactful organizational and behavioral change through the leadership of their change agents. As a team, if the change agents can map critical, informal, yet highly influential networks and identify and leverage key connections—particularly across traditional organizational charts—they can independently isolate root causes, filter best-in-class options, mitigate risk through targeted pilot campaigns, and deliver small wins that can serve as momentum makers or future change shapers.

Beyond Influencers to the Influenced

As we discussed earlier, one of the best approaches to spreading a viral change campaign is to court key influencers. But recent research also confirms that the *influenced* may be as critical as the *influencers*. James Coyle, assistant professor of marketing at Miami University's Farmer School of Business, recently conducted a study that found that trying to track down key influencers—people who have extremely large social networks—can, in some ways, limit a campaign and its viral potential. Change agents instead need to realize that the majority of their audience, not just the well-connected few, is eager and willing to pass along well-designed and relevant messages.

Science News Online reports on related topical research by two social network theorists: Duncan Watts, now a researcher for Yahoo!, and Peter Sheridan Dodds of the University of Vermont in Burlington. These researchers tested the conventional wisdom that experts on a subject matter who love to talk can persuade dozens of others to adopt their opinions. If this were true, an excellent communication strategy would be to find those few critical people, convince them of the value of your change campaign, and leave it to them to persuade others.

Although this theory sounds good, it shouldn't be your only approach. The researchers compared how far an idea would spread depending on whether it started with a random individual or with an influential individual who was connected to a lot of other individuals. They found that highly influential individuals usually spread ideas more widely, but not *that* much more widely. More important than the influencers, the researchers found, were the *influenced*. Once an idea spread to a critical mass of easily influenced individuals, it quickly took hold and continued to spread to other easily influenced individuals.

Dodds compares the spread of ideas to the spread of a forest fire. When a fire turns into a conflagration, no one claims that it was because the spark that began it was so potent. Instead, a fire takes off because of the properties of the larger forest environment: dryness, density, wind, and temperature. So what's the takeaway? According to the study, the best way to increase the odds of a person-to-person transmission of an idea is to make it a good idea. Some things are just fun to talk about. One of my favorite quotes by Seth Godin is to simply "Be remarkable—that which is worthy of remark!"

Are your efforts to change an individual, a team, or the organization at large worthy of remark? How can you ensure that beyond the network of influencers, the influenced are armed with just the right message to create the broad-based viral effect you need to broaden your reach and your return on impact?

Change through Mergers and Acquisitions

During a mergers and acquisitions event, both financial and strategic buyers rightly focus on the strategic, financial, and governance aspects of a transaction so as to further their goal of maximizing shareholder value. I recently met with a partner of a private equity firm who succinctly described the competency and capabilities of the group of professional services providers they use in both their pretransaction due diligence and their postacquisition integration—what he referred to as his A-team. From a global law firm to Big Four accounting, top-notch real estate agents, and a very recognizable retained search for the human capital component, they spare no expense in ensuring that world-class teams are on their side of the table when pursuing strategic acquisitions.

What's missing from this success formula? Someone to examine what ultimately becomes the greatest source of wealth creation—the strategic and quantifiable value of the relationships both inside and outside the target acquisition companies. Is it any surprise then to learn that in 2009 alone, three of this firm's portfolio companies have declared bankruptcy? Although there are certainly unique circumstances in each organization, when they announced the acquisition of each entity, it was the rage of the local business community. The lawyers and accountants had certainly done their part in the valuation of the hard assets. But the critical soft assets, such as discretely strained intracompany relationships between members of the leadership team, the dissatisfaction of their distribution channels with the direct sales model, and the lack of repeat or referral business from their vast customer base, should have all been yellow flags to further investigate and certainly prioritize in their 100-day action plans.

In our experience, conducting considerable due diligence regarding these relationships is as crucial as paying close attention to the balance sheet, cash flow, and expected synergies from the deal. By asking management a series of questions about their strategic relationships, investors can contribute to the smooth transition to a more unified company. This results in a better merging of the cultures, prevents the loss of A-team players, and creates a stronger human capital bench for the joined entity—all of which will ultimately create far greater shareholder value from the transaction. Why, then, are these strategic relationships so often neglected?

During many roll-up opportunities, strategic and financial investors largely rely on bankers (often the chief advisers to the company) in the pending transaction. Understandably, investment bankers tend to focus on the financial aspects of the deal and believe that addressing the strategic relationship issue comes much later in the postacquisition integration process, if at all. As a result, the quantifiable and strategic value of these relationships is often grossly underestimated and their value can easily be disrupted, if not destroyed, in most common practices after the merger and acquisition event.

Lack of Candor and Stand in Corporate America

A multitude of surveys done in the late 1960s showed that 70 percent of U.S. residents believed that corporations could generally be trusted to act responsibly. Even after the economic boom of the past two decades, this figure has fallen to around 45 percent. Particularly because of times of crisis for the business community and the demise of candor and trust, improvement in accepted practices and relationships among auditors, analysts, executives, and a multitude of stakeholders becomes difficult to visualize.

Many of us experience a very real lack of honesty in corporate America daily. I submit that there is also very little *stand*. We're so conscious not to offend, not to polarize, not to leave anyone out, not to discriminate, and not to differentiate, that many of us go through a day, week, month, year, or lifetime without saying *anything* at all. If you don't stand for something, what *do* you believe in? What is it at your core that you are so fundamentally passionate about that you are willing to sacrifice a secure paycheck, benefits, and your precious vacation?

Relationship-Centric Best Practice: Protecting Unique Cultures

Kraft Foods Canada purchased a small West Coast coffee company with its own unique culture. The acquisition's ultimate success was largely due to executives at Kraft having graduated from the school of hard knocks in this area.

Kraft's sheer size and traditional approach to institutionalizing acquisitions could have proved detrimental, yet

(continued)

> ### Relationship-Centric Best Practice:
> ### Protecting Unique Cultures *(Continued)*
>
> the upfront candor of the Kraft management team helped coffee company executives understand that Kraft was buying their brand, while at the same time adding its systems infrastructure and cultural best practices. By not painting a false picture of what was to remain true in the small company, Kraft avoided the possible misperceptions and consequently mass exodus of the critical human element of the coffee company.

In examining more than 1,000 Match.com ads, Dan and Chip Heath, brothers and authors of *Made to Stick*, made an amazing discovery. Their research yielded clever headlines on personal ads such as "*Hey*—If that's your opening line, you better be hot" and "Looking for Love—Duh! You're on Match. com." But even more striking was that well over 600 of the headlines simply said *nothing at all*.

For many, personal and functional interactions are very similar—they say nothing. Why? Mostly, it is because of *fear*: fear of saying too much, fear of saying something clever that others may think is stupid, or fear of saying something relevant that some might find offensive. In an effort not to exclude anyone, we often succeed at boring everyone. The *hey* phenomenon is so prevalent in the corporate world that it is turning brands, which one could argue are a company's personal ad, into something very similar to the Match.com headlines that say nothing at all. In our world of "sound bites," in the context of building lasting relationships, there simply must be more.

Executives with the fiduciary responsibility to lead an organization have become so bland that you wonder: Who exactly, as a company, are they trying to date? In an effort to please everyone, they often succeed at engaging no one. Executives and their companies believe that with enough clout, scale, and arrogance, they can simply survive by being generically likeable. And for some, it may work—at least in the short term. But for the rest of us, almost everyone has to be ready to turn some people off.

If everyone refuses to discuss the elephant in the room, if mediocrity is not only tolerated but accepted as the norm, and if the status quo is encouraged as not rocking the boat, isn't that just another version of *hey*? The fear of being disliked afflicts many because of the greater perceived risk. Most executives fear that if they make a bold statement, they risk alienating customers, their bosses, and their bosses bosses. That fear ultimately takes the edge off the candor—the authenticity—and the core of that executive and the company.

Lack of Candor in Business Relationships

This same lack of candor resides in business relationships as well. Business leaders must commit to such transparency that a multitude of constituents will be empowered to make informed judgments beyond an acceptable level of scrutiny. Unfortunately, openly candid and honest dialogue seems to elude many in our current business environment. Leaders have little incentive to make their operations more transparent because of an elongated but reasonable belief that they will be judged unfairly. Business relationships with the media point to great recent examples of companies fighting back when they believe their stories have been misrepresented or compromised.

I recall stories of Mobil Oil cutting all contact with the *Wall Street Journal* and withdrawing its advertising out of anger about news stories about the company. The Bechtel Group had ABC run a report disputing a *20/20* episode that wrongly accused the company. Illinois Power responded to a segment on CBS's *60 Minutes* by disseminating a video of their own that showed edited interviews with company executives. Yet, for some reason, this effort to fight back when you think you have been wronged doesn't manifest itself with intracompany or other externally focused business relationships.

Relationship-Centric Best Practice: Courage to Fail

Tom Darrow, principal and founder of Talent Connections, LLC—a member of the coveted *Inc.* 500—and past president of the Society of Human Resource Management (SHRM) in Atlanta, shared with me a great reaffirming insight about candor and encouraging the courage to fail: As John Wayne once said, "Courage is being scared to death, but saddling up anyway." In many ways, candor also requires a built-in belief—not simply one of courage (how you overcome barriers), but specifically the courage to *fail*—that allows us to push the envelope to overcome critical limitations in our daily lives.

Tom referenced his efforts while playing tennis. When he plays opponents of equal or lesser abilities, he said, his game seldom improves. But when he is matched against quicker, more agile players with crisper returns, particularly down the line, he plays a much stronger game—even though he may never reach their level (and yes, even sometimes loses 6–1, 6–0).

Getting people in an environment of candor must begin with upper management. Their commitment to openness and transparency goes a long way in helping the rest of the organization feel the same. With a plethora of regulations from HIPAA to Sarbanes-Oxley, as well as competitive intelligence, upper management tends to believe that intracompany information sharing should, in many ways, remain on a need-to-know basis.

The fear of employee reactions or, worse yet, market reaction to potentially bad news often keeps leadership from sharing anything. And in the absence of information, it is human nature to create imaginative stories in an effort to fill the void.

> Despite popular belief, most employees can hear and see through a positive spin. More detrimental could be their perception and a subsequent rippling effect that says, in Tom's words, "Maybe I should start buttering up the truth, too."

We meet seemingly nice people, and despite a genuine initial interest, there just doesn't seem to be a viable mutual benefit in investing in or nurturing the relationship. Yet, in an effort to be nice and avoid hurting feelings, we are sheepish in our candor. We drag on unnecessary dialogues, personal exchanges, and discussions of projects and opportunities with the exchange of pleasantries to avoid difficult conversations. For many, it is easier to simply ignore and procrastinate than it is to systematically address the elephant in the room.

When it comes to candor and accountability, I believe the number one accountability is still to yourself. There is a common misbelief that 21 days of repetition creates a habit. I'm not convinced it ever will. If you exercise for 253 consecutive days, and on day 254 you decide that you will not exercise that day, shouldn't the 21-day rule get you back in the saddle? Accountability and commitment are core behavioral changes versus one of finite time.

Not letting others down is a personal value. By telling others that they can count on you and trust you, you must make the commitment to follow through. With accountability, focus, and commitment, you fulfill that obligation to self, which permeates in fulfilling your obligation to others. In essence, my candor and accountability to others sprout from that committed seed of candor and accountability to myself.

Most would agree that—particularly as a leader—your actions speak far louder than your words. If subordinates repeatedly see or experience a conflict-avoidance mentality in your business relationships, would you not agree that it will eventually dilute your credibility in their eyes?

100-Day Action Plan for Large-Scale Change or Mergers and Acquisitions

Why do you think most New Year's resolutions don't stick? In one of my keynote speeches, someone suggested that it is because you are drunk when you make them. Beyond that theory, would you agree that they often include no accountability, realistic expectations, or systematic *plan*?

It has been said, "Teach and everyone will learn. Manage and no one will learn." One hundred days is simply too short a time frame to correct any mistakes. As such, it is critical to start with three to five realistic goals with high-impact potentials rather than try to hit an immediate home run.

In many ways, a 100-day plan is really a five-year plan compressed into 100 days. In any large-scale change or merger and acquisition event, orchestrating critical and timely information flow to the right people at the right time is key and it would serve well to execute from a centralized program management office (PMO).

As described earlier, a succinct and quantifiable understanding of the impetus for change, whether a process, an organization, or even change of control coupled with a strong change in the management team, is empowered by relationships of the change agents with the front line. A solid strategy will require a solidified plan for execution. In many cases, change fails not because someone miscalculated the math but because of the underestimation of the human element and cultural attributes. Line executives who initiate change campaigns or put deals together, although astute in their business propositions, often miss the relationship ramifications.

In considering a 100-day action plan for large-scale change or merger and acquisition events, there are three important phases. Each is discussed next.

Phase 1: Pretransaction Due Diligence

The organization must go into any proposed large-scale change or transaction with its eyes wide open and ask itself, "What are we changing? What are we buying? Is this a good fit for the strategies of the business? Are we doing this for the right reasons? Are we running toward something or away from something else?"

As mentioned earlier, I believe that a *premortem* evaluation would save many teams and organizations unlimited levels of frustration and wasted resources. Peel back the organizational levels in search of fundamentally problematic areas such as redundant roles and responsibilities, inappropriate compensation structures, or perhaps dormant litigation issues. Even in our small firm, our team spent an entire day at an offsite session contemplating whether a recent merger was congruent with our mission, vision, and beliefs—not just compatible with where our organization has been, but with where we are headed. Are their products and services consistent with our growth and sales strategies? Do we like their people, and will our respective cultures thrive together under one roof? Are their synergies not only real but also quantifiable? Will our coming together enhance a systematic approach for a greater return for our broad-based stakeholders?

Change will demand a deeper and broader leveraging of existing infrastructures. Identify where the weakest links are in those infrastructures and consider how you will retain them to protect the structural integrity of the organization.

It is also a very good idea to really think through how much this change or merger and acquisition is going to cost. Not just the obvious costs, but costs in potential areas such as relocation or enhancements of key assets (financial as well as human capital), severance for redundant resources, or closing of unnecessary facilities. And let us also not forget the opportunity costs and the focus that any kind of change will detract from one's normal course of business.

Phase 2: The First 100 Days

The first 100 days after a change or acquisition is announced significantly and unequivocally set the tone for what is to follow. It is critical that the organization leave the gate running. From that first minute, everyone wants to see action. Change isn't the decisions you've made up until this point; the organization wants to see them implemented.

The AlliedSignal-Honeywell merger is a good example of using the first 100 days to execute a great number of critical decisions. On day one, the companies announced which facilities around the world would need to change or be shut down. Specific, often painful decisions—many of which will require 50 to 60 subsequent decisions—must be made before that initial announcement. A half-baked plan will raise unnecessary alarms.

Specific programs to modify processes, relocate resources, and add or displace employees are all examples of decisiveness. When coupled with speed and communication, this will help people understand future direction. The faster you move, the more you'll build confidence for success in the organization.

It is critical to get everyone on the same page, including senior leadership and one or two levels below. Get key issues on the table quickly, and leverage a blueprint of a high-performing organization to execute key processes and ensure traction with the execution of a multitude of simultaneous initiatives. If the senior team operates in a dysfunctional manner, it is not realistic to think that the cascading effect to the rest of the organization will somehow supersede it. This highly destabilizing time naturally makes people nervous. And relationships among peers, subordinates, and superiors will help maintain morale, keep the focus on the actual business, and nurture the foundational trust on which it is critical to build.

If you ignore the externally-facing parts of the organization, performance in the business will dramatically deteriorate. If the sales force either checks out or begins to leave, pending orders will be delayed and critical marketing and analyst relation campaigns for an upcoming major trade show may misstep, creating an unflattering or ambiguous buzz in the market.

We saw this firsthand in working with Scitex Vision, an Israeli-based global manufacturer of wide-format digital printers. Approximately six to nine months in advance of the announced acquisition by Hewlett-Packard (HP), a number of critical clients with active deals on the table were reluctant to execute those much-needed purchase orders. This was primarily due to an uncertainty or doubt about impending changes. Not knowing whether Kodak, Agfa, HP, Xerox, or countless others were going to acquire Scitex kept many suitors at bay and a sales force left scrambling to deliver on quota commitments.

People must focus on making decisions quickly, and when a decision has not been made, senior leadership must tell people *when* it will be made. A simple approach to creating certainty in any relationship, and in particular during a time of highly disruptive transformation, is consistent communication as to when you can expect to know a prioritized set of real expectations. Leading by example includes reaching out to understand the new organization, producing concrete deliverables, and setting conservative/realistic time frames for completing difficult work. More than ever, taking the time to meet, talk, and listen with key people will solidify respective expectations and build confidence and their buy-in as to the importance and direction of the pending changes.

The first 100 days also represent an incredible development opportunity, giving key people in one's relationship bank the positive experiences they will remember throughout their careers—not to mention publish on their resumes. For many, large change or merger and acquisition events are the Super Bowl, the World Series, the NBA Finals, and the Stanley Cup all merged into one. The right people on the bus will uncover new talents that they never knew they possessed. Only tough questions and real-time radar tracking the essential moving parts will ensure both sequential and parallel execution of significant milestones. Keep in mind that most people will prioritize requests for those they know, like, trust, and respect.

Phase 3: The Longer Term

After the initial 100 days, it is critical to devise a soul-searching litmus test for the entire organization. Beyond the initial shock and disbelief of the actual change, is the resulting organization their cup of tea? It's okay to come to the conclusion that the new people, processes, procedures, structure, attitude, or simply just the way things are done now isn't what they signed up for. It is not okay, however, to check out and forget to tell others.

Next, it is critical to review the organization's competency map after the dust has settled. Do we have the human capital needed to deliver long-term value? If the answer is anything but a resounding "yes," it is imperative to leverage critical intra-company relationships to extend your reach in the market and fill those gaps as diligently as you can.

In many cases, a post-100-day organization will continue to face a multitude of challenges. Only by being the positive force and continuing to bring people together will you uncover answers to unresolved questions. A Socratic leadership style of engaging the audience for their most pressing issues and openly, directly, and transparently addressing those concerns will further solidify in people's minds that this really is a worthwhile home for their professional endeavors. Use town hall meetings, "Ask the CEO" campaigns, forums, intracompany blogs, and anonymous "call the CEO with an idea" as tools to embrace the far reaches of the business, remembering that it is incredibly difficult to be a remote employee.

10

Social Media and Business Relationships

In the first edition of this book, I introduced a number of new social networking applications and wrote about the impact of LinkedIn, Spoke, Ryze, Jigsaw, and YouTube on our daily lives. Since social media has become so ubiquitous in the past couple of years and now there is a plethora of books available on social networking and social media, this updated edition has provided me with the opportunity to take a different path—one of asking how social media is affecting our relationships. What are some best practices for organizations to craft a compelling social media policy? How will social media create new roles and realms of responsibilities within and external to the enterprise? And as evidenced by one of my most popular blog posts, what will tomorrow's social leaders look like?

Let me preface this section by saying that the worst thing you can do on social media is to *sell*; doing so unequivocally turns everybody off. Most people will disengage when confronted with overt and covert sales pitches—personal or professional. If you want to promote your brand, you must add value, create intrigue, or provide a contrarian perspective. If you want to sell your product or services, use social media to solve customer service issues, provide additional ideas on how your consumers (business-to-business [B2B] or business-to-consumer [B2C]) can get even more value from your products or services they've already purchased.

The best thing you can do on social media is *listen, engage, and influence*. Attend any social media conference, and countless examples—from @comcastcares on Twitter, to State Farm's Get an Agent campaign on YouTube, to Chase Community Giving on Facebook, to Coke's and Starbucks's masterful loyalty marketing online—all point to a real-time medium to get a candid finger on the pulse of your target audience. What they're thinking, what they find of value, and what information they put to use can all dramatically affect how you do business in the decade ahead.

So, by now you have a LinkedIn profile, a Twitter account, a YouTube channel, and a Facebook fan page—how's that working out for you? Getting any business from your social media efforts? If the past couple of years have been all about this shiny, sexy new toy called social networking, the next few years have to be about return on investment (ROI) from your online efforts.

"Social" Defined

Let's get clear on several definitions first:

- **Social networking** (LinkedIn, Facebook, Twitter, You-Tube, etc.) is about *presence*; you having a (hopefully) professional presence on these sites to create awareness and marketing gravity for your unique brand and quantifiable value-added services.
- **Social media** is the *platform*, or the vehicle to get you there, and it encompasses more than social networks. It includes being more searchable, paying for unique positions online, and using conversion strategies to take buyers from interested to engaged.
- **Social market leadership** is about *purpose*. It's a fundamental shift in buying behavior that business professionals must understand and master. To succeed, you'll have to have a very real purpose of why you're online, whom you're trying to "date," and what will influence their thinking and call to action.

This past year, I had the opportunity to work closely with Matt Rosenhaft and team at Social Gastronomy on several engagements. One of the best explanations of the evolution of social networking is his fishing analogy, shown in Figure 10.1.

Use of the public social networks—LinkedIn, Facebook, YouTube, and so on—is similar to you going ocean fishing: you're throwing a huge net out there for anything that you may catch.

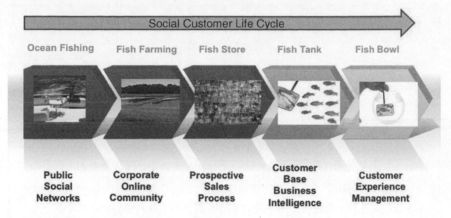

FIGURE 10.1 Evolution of the Social Customer Life Cycle
Source: Social Gastronomy, LLC.

It could be a marlin or a car tire! As your value to a community matures, your value-added proposition evolves with corporate online communities (fish farming). These are more controlled environments with private access, profile-based interactions, and a very real business purpose of why these users are there.

When you share content, engage and influence others, and in the process create an opt-in scenario where they want to buy from you, you've created a fish store. As you learn key insights about not just their demographics but also their psychographics (preferences, tastes, digital habits), you've created a fish tank. When you apply those insights to enhance their unique experiences with you and your brand, online and offline, you've created a fish bowl. Each scenario is more intimate and much more focused on the clients' interests, preferences, and habits than on your products and services.

Relationship-Centric Best Practice: LinkedIn Etiquette, Please

Having used a number of social networking technologies over the past several years, I continue to be mesmerized by

(continued)

Relationship-Centric Best Practice: LinkedIn Etiquette, Please
(Continued)

the sheer lack of professional etiquette when it comes to utilizing these tools and sites.

By far, the most prevalent one is LinkedIn, and a great deal of market buzz surrounding this platform has reinvigorated the following top 10 etiquette requests of everyone who sees a direct and relevant benefit to achieving their personal and professional objectives from this environment.

The Top 10 LinkedIn Etiquette Requests

1. *Connect to those you truly know.* I don't know you. We just met. What makes you think I know you well enough (or know anything about you, for that matter) to expose or recommend you to my portfolio of relationships, which I have worked a lifetime to build? Please, don't send invites to people you don't know or have anything in common with other than what you perceive is in it for you.

2. *Please don't bluff.* This is not the place to pretend we have a mutual friend or that so-and-so referred you to me, because the fastest way to dilute if not completely lose your credibility is for me to pick up the phone, call the referring party, and be told that he or she has no idea who you are. If you drop a name, make sure it's a legitimate one.

3. *Find a way to become interesting.* LinkedIn provides a number of generic requests for connections, forwards, and recommendations. If you want to elevate yourself above the noise, let that really interesting person within you out! Most people choose whether or not to open your e-mail based on the subject line, so you should come up with something more clever than

simply, "Let's connect." Make the subject line engaging. Give me a reason to not only open it, but act upon it! Similarly, make the content of the request relevant, pertinent, and actionable. And last, don't add to my plate by asking me to make up how I should introduce you to my contacts. Instead, arm me with the ammunition I need to help put your best foot forward.

4. *Be contextually relevant.* What I did for a living 20 years ago has little or no bearing on what I do for a living now. Don't send me a request for something that has no bearing on what's of interest or value to me. It's amazing how many people simply forget that, although powerful, practical, and useful, tools like LinkedIn are just that—tools.

5. *Me and 10,000 other people.* Although one of LinkedIn's core strengths is to reconnect past colleagues, *colleague* is the operative word here. When I was with Silicon Graphics (SGI) in the mid-1990s, SGI had 10,000 employees. Just because we worked for the same company in the same decade, you are making a huge assumption that we were colleagues or that I know someone who used to work at the same company at the same time. Remember, relationships are between individuals.

6. *Don't be guilty by association.* I am amazed to read recommendations for individuals who apparently everyone else in the world (other than the recommender) thinks is an absolute incompetent buffoon. Do not recommend people based on a popularity contest or out of guilt because they did the same for you, because whether you like it or not, your connection to them and association through LinkedIn recommendations aligns your credibility with theirs.

(continued)

Relationship-Centric Best Practice: LinkedIn Etiquette, Please (Continued)

7. *Trust continuum.* Draw a line with a tick mark at each end and one in the middle. This represents what we call the trust continuum. The center is neutral. To the left is −1; to the right, +1. Most people start out in the center. I don't know you, so you have two opportunities. You can either choose to enhance your position with a consistent level of predictability and move to the right, or choose to dilute your credibility—my faith in your word and deeds—and move yourself to the left. If others won't say it, let me: I seldom invest time and effort in those hanging out on the left.

8. ***Don't abuse the connection.*** If you do, you'll be removed. Nobody likes to get egg on his or her face. If I connect with you online and the very next day you send me five requests to recommend you without us ever having worked together, or even worse, you suddenly barrage me with requests from others, you have clearly abused our connection. Some people I connect with based on the nature of their work, intellectually stimulating conversations we've had, or the perception of greater mutual opportunities ahead. Make me regret this and you are three clicks away from being completely removed from my LinkedIn network.

9. *So what?* In this day and age, companies use titles like you and I change underclothes. You are an assistant senior vice president of global pencil pushing at Company XYZ. So what? (1) I have never heard of that company and have no idea what it does. (2) What is your realm of responsibilities? What results did you deliver? What impact did you have on the viability and growth

of the organization? Profiles with little to no content under a title are the digital version of an empty suit.

10. *Use good judgment.* The good Lord gave us all discretion. I am amazed at how few people actually use it. LinkedIn is a social networking tool for business professionals. It is not Match.com, eHarmony, or Facebook for college dropouts. Use spell check. Use correct grammar. This is a forum for business professionals, so keep requests on the business side. Make sure your comments and recommendations are professional, polished, and exemplary of your style, thought process, and how you want to be perceived. Last, remember to include a current photo! Your college yearbook picture from 1982 is not the best way to get your professional image across.

Make no mistake about it—there is a lot of noise in all of our respective markets. Every client evaluates a multitude of options that are competing for mind share; every industry expert recommends a plethora of options, all of which can solve that particular problem. Those in many professions are unsure where to turn when competitors can't delineate and differentiate themselves from the next 10 similar options, or worst yet, they try to compete on price alone—which is often a losing proposition.

Following are a handful of strategies you need to understand to become successful in leveraging social media to engage your relationships. See the Relationship-Centric Best Practice box on pages 267 and 268 for a list of tactical recommendations.

A Core Shift in Buyer Behavior

Social media has empowered buyers in a way that we have not seen previously. For the past two decades, I've worked with a

Customer *Buying* Process

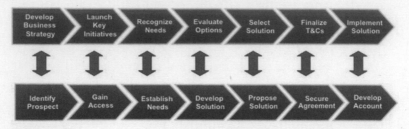

Your *Selling* Process

FIGURE 10.2 Traditional Selling and Buying Processes

multitude of companies focused on selling their products and services in a B2B environment. Countless sales processes I've seen and many I've helped build constantly aimed to align the way an organization engaged and sold its products and services to the manner in which its target buyers evaluated and selected such products and services (Figure 10.2).

The search engine in the new norm of the buying cycle has enabled buyers to extensively research potential providers of products and services prior to ever engaging them (Figure 10.3). Social media has the power to enable buyers to check your references, build their own lineup of experts, and make a buying

Customer *Buying* Process

| Develop Business Strategy | Launch Key Initiatives | Recognize Needs | Evaluate Options | Select Solution | Finalize T&Cs | Implement Solution |

Google — David Nour

FIGURE 10.3 New Norm of Socially Enabled Buying Process

decision without even letting the business professional know they are in the market, let alone engaging them in a sales process.

So, how do you sell to a buyer that you don't even know is in the market for your services? How do you influence the market to make sure you are credentialed and considered for an engagement? Organizations and individuals alike who cannot manage the transition to the new "buyer norm" will face considerable headwinds in building or retaining relationships and thus market share.

When I first began my consulting practice, every so-called expert I met recommended that I create a hard-copy media kit to send out to prospective buyers. It had to contain my resume, extensive copies of my articles and position papers, a detailed description of my services, and a list of clients along with reference letters from each. They suggested that I get a list of association and corporate executives and start dialing for dollars! We all reached out to our markets and educated the prospective clients, and they logically evaluated their options. We then diligently followed up until we got an engagement; if not, we planted a seed for the next opportunity.

Social media has helped buyers become a lot more educated about the consultants and speakers they engage, including the perceived value we can bring, from a lot of other places than just our web sites. They're reading blog posts and watching video clips of us on a multitude of social media sites (did you know there are 50+ video distribution sites? YouTube is just one!) where we're engaging the audience, and past clients independently, freely, and candidly discuss the results they were able to achieve with our help. They're reading our LinkedIn recommendations and are independently reaching out to those existing clients to check our references—before they ever engage us!

By the way, if your business caters to end consumers, you need to understand that consumers don't care about your corporate structure or how many copiers you own! What they do care about is how to get the item they want, when and where they want it, at a competitive price (notice I didn't say the cheapest!). My former chief executive officer (CEO), Bruce Kasanoff of NowPossible.com, has captured what he refers to as "1toEverything: A Customer's View of the Connected World," shown in Figure 10.4.

When consumers have a bad experience, they won't tell 10 friends; they'll tell 10,000 friends online. It takes years to develop a reputation and only a handful of instances to destroy it! If you have both a bricks-and-mortar presence and a strong online presence, you have an incredible leadership opportunity: to provide an unparalleled experience with an integrated convenience factor—not price *or* convenience, but a competitive price *and* local relationships.

How can your business integrate a stronger convenience/ higher perceived experience each and every time it engages its most valuable relationships?

Greater Impact of Influencers on the Decision Process

Social media represents the rise of indirect, influencer-dominated channels of communication, and it requires a new approach to developing and maintaining critical relationships. Business professionals who can leverage market influence can dynamically disrupt the current market status quo.

So how do you build a relationship with someone you don't know is considering your unique value?

You have to change your mind-set from revenue to influence. Internal and external influencers now have a greater impact on the decision process. First, they must see you as the definitive expert in your chosen field to recommend you when they hear that buyers are having a challenge you can solve. Second, you must arm them with ammunition to make that connection; leaving this part to chance is futile. And third, you

Identify	Differentiate	Interact	Customize
anything in the world via a digital device	options based on my current status and preferences	with objects, people, experiences, insights	my next interaction based on this one
• Restaurant	• Which will I like best?	• Intuitive interfaces	• Remember my choices
• Home for sale	• Is it fairly priced?	• 3D views	• Remember where my favorites are located
• People	• Is it the highest quality?	• Demos	• Observe how my choices relate to others
• Hotel	• What is its proximity?	• Data overlays	• Save me time, money, and effort
• Flight	• Is it compatible with other components?	• Personal interactions	• Reduce complexity
• Event	• What are friends' or experts' opinions?	• Add pictures to words or vice versa	
• Part number	• What are delivery options?	• New games	
• Health risk	• What is my physical condition (vital signs, alcohol usage, weight . . .)?	• Deeper insights	
• Item for sale		• Immersive entertainment	
• Plant or flower		• Relevant news	
• Bird		• Interesting patterns	
• Artwork			
• Song			

Original IDIC framework created by Don Peppers and Martha Rogers. Exhibit adapted by Bruce Kasanoff of NowPossible.com.

FIGURE 10.4 1toEverything: A Customer's View of the Connected World

have to identify a very succinct path for the buyers to take—lead them down the path to engage you.

Start by getting very succinct about who you're trying to "date." Personally or professionally, you cannot date everyone. So, the more succinct you become about the profile of your target buyer, the more fruitful your social media efforts will be. Next, identify what will influence their thinking. What will move their needle, get them intrigued, push a button, or create a sense of curiosity to further research the topic? I recently wrote an article titled "If You're Not at the Table, You're on the Menu!" Do you think it raised a few eyebrows and got some attention? Sure, it also created a half-dozen speaking inquiries from business unit leaders who wanted their teams to hear how to enhance their performance through strategic relationships.

When I asked these executives how they found me, consistently they mentioned an internal lieutenant or an outside adviser who had handed them an article I had written or forwarded them one of my video blogs. That's influencer marketing.

Social Search Addresses Key Challenges with Traditional Search Engines

In my social media strategy consulting engagements, I'm recommending a fundamental shift in the manner in which people distribute information via the Web, moving from a traditional direct distribution model to an indirect version in which you need a value-based network to reach and influence the right audience. These distributors (influencers) are critical to getting the word out. As a business professional, you will need something compelling, interesting, and relevant to access that distribution. They pay for the privilege of distributing your content with real currency: their prioritized attention and market reach.

ComScore, which is the Nielsen of the Web, reports that 70 percent of people who search will not go to the bottom of the first page; 90+ percent will not go to the second page! If I'm a buyer and you're not coming up in my search results, you're not on my short list. If you're not on my short list, you're not on my radar for the upcoming engagement.

Guess what? Buyers are not calling consultants anymore asking for media kits. They get online and they search! Only an estimated 20 percent of people who search know exactly what they're looking for: "change management expert." The other 80 percent are searching long-tail keywords, descriptors of their challenge: "engaging speaker for senior executive audience on getting change right."

The challenge is that they're searching for an emotional pain, not your buzzword methodology (Figure 10.5). They're searching for a challenge they're trying to solve, and most corporate web sites aren't talking about challenges or problems. Google searches will deliver intellectual results, that is, keywords. Social searches deliver emotional results, that is, another buyer who had a very similar challenge and you, an expert in that subject, who happened to have solved it for that client. They're reading LinkedIn discussion groups for "nightmare consultants" or forums where what a consultant promised was anything but what was delivered!

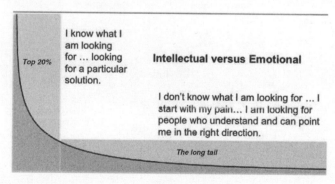

FIGURE 10.5 Social Search
Source: Social Gastronomy, LLC.

Reinventing Relationships in a Postdigital World

If everything is becoming digital, how will digital matter? The buyers don't really care if the expert interaction is on the Web; they just want to get what they need, when they need it. A lot of organizations still segment their online and offline marketing, creating an artificial barrier to developing a seamless and consistent client experience. Social media is changing buyer behavior to be more agile and fluid, and growth strategies must adjust the model to support the reflected changes.

So, you need to reorient your traditional growth strategies to reflect the new postdigital, relationship-oriented, and influencer-driven social interactions. You must start by thinking of your clients in a more holistic five-phase life cycle (Figure 10.6):

1. Where are they most likely to hear about you, and how can you educate the market with a unique value-added proposition?
2. How can you give buyers an opportunity to self-select/opt in as intrigued by your perspective?
3. By helping them along a buying cycle, how can they engage you as a prospect when you've influenced their thinking?

FIGURE 10.6 Holistic Customer Life Cycle

4. When they become clients, how can you empower them to share their experiences?

5. How can you help them educate the market on your behalf—independently and candidly?

Social market leadership leverages a multichannel, multidirectional approach toward building relationships around enabling the key interactions that support the awareness, influence, interest, buying, and referral processes. By the way, you can't apply a traditional marketing approach to the social networks and collaborative technologies. You can't just broadcast your advertising or public relations (PR) message on social networks and expect your target audience to engage.

Social market leadership is about building value-based relationships with communities of like-minded buyers. As described by Joseph L. Pine II and James H. Gilmore in their book *The Experience Economy*, professionals who aim to consistently develop exceptional experiences for all who engage them will deliberately elevate themselves above the market noise. Exceptional experience will then bleed through into marketing and sales, with the ability to mass distribute client delights.

Business professionals who will be able to effectively and efficiently "socially enable" their client relationships will be able to increase the growth in net-new client acquisition, reduce the cost of client retention, and enhance their market leadership position as thought leaders in their industry.

Relationship-Centric Best Practice: Social Market Leadership Tactics

So, how do you tactically develop social market leadership before, during, and after you begin a business relationship? Here are 10 tips:

(continued)

Relationship-Centric Best Practice: Social Market Leadership Tactics (Continued)

1. Develop a profile of your target buyer. Research them on LinkedIn, and create a profile of what they find of interest/value.
2. Don't think of your interactions as a single event; instead think of them as a campaign with a focused social media effort to create awareness for the client organization.
3. In advance of each interaction, research top industry trade publications; for corporate clients, identify internal and external communication channels, such as newsletters, SharePoint sites, intranets, and private social networks.
4. Submit focused and relevant content (articles, videos, blog posts) often, driving awareness and traffic to your personal or corporate brand.
5. Leverage social networks, blogs, and your broader influence footprint to create dialogue—ask questions, post comments, and stir the pot to provide a contrarian perspective; always include links for them to learn more.
6. At every interaction, cut your input (methodology, features/benefits, etc.) in half and find a way to interact with and engage the audience in a dialogue; get them engaged with compelling online and offline questions.
7. Before you wrap up any interactions, invite them to a community you've developed exclusively for clients to continue the conversation.
8. After an interaction, share insights and your unique perspective with a broad audience.
9. Look for partnership opportunities to extend your reach—both within and external to your organization.
10. Get and give digital references/recommendations, focused on the mutual positive experience.

Meet Our Content Curators

The rapid expansion of social media as a fundamental value-added service of a team or the organization in the market has created a plethora of new enterprise roles and responsibilities—from community managers to directors of social media and to chief content officers. Although their backgrounds vary greatly, I've found the best ones to be very well grounded in traditional marketing expertise, to have a solid understanding of the power and promise of this new medium, and to have a genuine desire to create dialogue and candid interactions with their respective constituents. One such example is a content curator.

When executing a social market leadership strategy, you have to develop digital relationships that become evangelists of your brand and quantifiable value. To do this successfully, if you're trying to sell more than your products and services and share unique intellectual property (IP) as part of your personal or organization's brand as well, you'll need to post compelling content online; this includes new videos, blog posts, tweets, and LinkedIn and Facebook status updates. The challenge is that other than a handful of exceptions, such as Butterfly Publisher, there are relatively few tools with the ability to disseminate content and help you proactively manage this deluge.

To strengthen your brand with social media, you must create new and compelling content—*consistently*. The challenge is who has time, the bandwidth, and the wherewithal to make sense of it all? Who has time to sift through content, pick the best and most trustworthy ones, and craft an appropriate response or counterpoint? It's a unique corporate communication role, not commonly defined or omnipresent in many organizations. And respectfully, many traditional media people are really bad at translating what they've done for the past 100 years to this new medium in an effective manner.

So, I'd like to introduce you to Jennifer and Chris, the Relationship Economics Content Curators. Let me describe what they do:

Content Curators Get Their Brands. Jennifer and Chris have invested significant time, effort, and resources to truly understand the types of clients we work with, the types of market challenges and opportunities we address, and the value we add. Not only can they articulate our unique value proposition in relationship economics—"helping clients create unprecedented growth through a unique return on their strategic relationships"—but they understand it well enough to defend it. As content curators, they understand a succinct profile of our buyers and how to influence their thinking, perspective, and call to action. This is the foundation of their role, without which the rest wouldn't be nearly as successful.

Content Curators Get You! Your name is your biggest brand, and if you're going to have an online voice, the content that is researched and provided for your review, and the comments made on your behalf, actually have to sound like you! We all have a voice, and consistency in articulating a unique perspective or an independent insight through that same voice is critical in building and nurturing digital relationships. As content curators, Jennifer and Chris send me sample paragraphs of "something you'd say!"

Content Curators Invest Focus and Bandwidth. To constantly find, group, organize, and share the best and the most relevant content on specific issues online requires unparalleled focus and dedicated bandwidth. The key is "constantly" because of the instantaneous nature of digital conversations. If you're going to tweet once a month, save time and effort—don't! It would be similar to you exchanging e-mails with people once a month! As content curators, Jennifer and Chris approach me several times each week with key questions, discussion points, or results of our most recent campaigns.

Content Curators Nurture Digital Dialogues. Social media is not a personal billboard. If you focus on educating first and marketing/selling second, you'll create marketing gravity and pull through demand. Digital conversations are just that—an exchange of ideas, perspectives, and points of view. Can you imagine walking through a museum and having the curator consistently tell you the price and the delivery time frame of every piece you passed? There may be beautiful paintings and sculptures there, but most people would leave in about five minutes! The same thing happens online. You may not always agree with a particular point of view, but a dose of dissent is actually intellectually stimulating. As content curators, that's what Jennifer and Chris do—they engage our profile of economic buyers and market influencers in a dialogue on key points such as strategic relationships, innovation, and lasting change.

Content Curators Are Citizen Editors. They comb through a vast sea of content, taking it upon themselves to collect and share the best and most relevant content online for others to consume. As content curators, Jennifer and Chris publish highly valuable content created by both our team and other thought leaders in the market. They are methodical, often bringing utility and order to our social market leadership efforts.

Content Curators Are Learning Teams. The social media landscape simply changes too fast for any one individual to try to keep up with it all. Although Jennifer and Chris bring unique experiences to this role, they also are constantly learning, attend multiple webinars each week, attend social media conferences, read position papers, and quickly discern social media experts who are contenders versus the sea of pretenders—it suddenly seems that every unemployed businessperson now is a LinkedIn expert!

Content Curators Track and Analyze. They have hunches for what works, but they verify, validate, or void their critical assumptions with key campaign tests. Instead of posting the same message on 100 sites, they create four compelling, yet unique, dialogue tracks and test them on various sites. Each dialogue has a unique call to action, which allows us to analyze what message resonated with various stakeholders we're trying to engage. During our monthly calls, we review both the previous month's campaigns and key action items on the road map ahead. In short, as content curators, they understand and track our progress along a continuum of digital relationships.

Content Curators Are Steadfast but Agile. The previously mentioned tracking and analytics provide timely insights as to the required changes in course correction. Content curators are not large oil tankers requiring cost-benefit analysis to make changes in tactical execution; rather, they are speedboats able to turn on a dime. As content curators, Jennifer and Chris succinctly understand our overarching strategy and are steadfast in following our compass, yet agile enough to know what's not working and when the same effort would yield little or no results. On the contrary, even too much of a good thing is still too much!

Content Curators Go Beyond "Not Invented Here." They extend their reach to "invented everywhere." The fundamental value of Jennifer and Chris as our content curators is their understanding and ability to participate in an open dialogue regarding insightful information. Although they understand and protect our intellectual capital and property, they also understand that the currency of the realm in digital relationships is the free exchange of great ideas. As such, they reach out for permission to quote other sources, and they freely give others permission to use our content with appropriate credit. This effort enhances our research and development (R&D) and helps raise the bar in constantly manufacturing, not just republishing, compelling content.

Content Curators Drive Results. There are two types of social media resources: those who are cost centers and those who are revenue producers. In early conversations with Jennifer and Chris, we discussed the results that I cared about—influencing conversations, which influences relationships and influences our desired outcomes. As content curators, they are creating marketing gravity, which translates into revenue results.

How are you establishing your social market leadership with a similar role?

What's Your Social Media Policy?

In several client meetings this past year, the conversation often centered on the need for a social media policy—what the organization was going to give its employees access to, what personal accounts/social networking sites were permitted, and what the employees could or could not do, say, or be online. Whether you work for a progressive organization or a conservative, risk-averse one, it seems that everyone has an opinion on the best approach. Here are four prevailing camps:

1. *Ostrich Look-Alikes.* "I'm on Facebook to keep up with my teenage daughter; it has no relevance to our business, and it's going to go away soon enough. Besides, bandwidth, viruses, and time-wasting are all good reasons for us to block complete access to any and all of it from our company." Seriously? You don't think employees are getting online with their smart phones or personal laptops, or around the corner at the coffee shop? Here is one of my favorites: A local, well-recognized brand that promotes on Facebook a payment application it developed that blocks access to Facebook for its employees!

   If you are locking it down because you don't want your employees to participate and adversely affect your brand marketing, you're right to do so. It is working, but probably not in the manner you intend. Your biggest competitor may allow its employees to engage with the market using social media, thereby lowering its cost of customer acquisition and retention in the process.

2. *Generic Find and Replacers.* "Just give me someone else's social media policy, and I'll replace their company name with mine." How's that working for you on human resources (HR) forms, supplier contracts, and other documents that clearly define your unique organization, culture, and relationships critical to your success? If you search online, you can actually find a web site that has 120+ different social media policies from a broad array of organizations to choose from.

3. *Bureaucratic Wordsmithers.* "We need to wordsmith this document as it is part of our policy." The only thing I think about when I hear this one is the mid-1990s version of the company mission statement, where it took the entire organization countless 12-hour debates in 15 conference rooms over a six-month time frame to replace "a" with "the"! Power doesn't corrupt—powerlessness corrupts! Focus on a plain English version that succinctly captures intent and direction, and work with social media law experts to legalize it.

4. *Agile Landscapers.* "We understand that social media opens a whole new can of worms for our organization. We really need a strategic approach to developing our social media engagement program, as the very 'squishy' nature of social engagement lends itself to potential judgment calls on behalf of our organization." These leaders are really smart, because they get that the 20-somethings (and, yes, even sometimes the 30-somethings) in the organization need to understand that personal actions online reflect on the corporate image. What you say and do online will either enhance or dilute your reputation and thus people's perception of you!

If you fall in to any of the first three camps, sorry, I can't help you. But if you're savvy enough to understand that this is the Wild West and that a track-and-trust culture will get you a lot further than the prevailing command-and-control version, here are 10 questions our team has devised to help start a dialogue in your organization:

1. *What level of corporate transparency do we want to have?* It is a spectrum, and you need to figure out how open you really want to be.

2. *What is our definition of intellectual property (IP)?* Your corporate IP is a corporate asset—think copyrights, patents, trademarks. But IP also includes corporate proprietary information, customer information, and so on. How do you define what is yours, your employees', your partners', and your customers', and what do you share with the market?

3. *What are customers expecting in terms of the customer experience?* Do they expect to be engaged? Do they expect real-time feedback and response? Do they expect your people to be empowered to participate in social engagement? Knowing how much will also drive the organization's view of how you should participate.

4. *What do our employees expect in terms of employee engagement?* Do they expect a wide-open policy for everyone? Are there industry regulations regarding participation? How is management participating?

5. *Are there internal vehicles employees can use to vent?* Are you giving employees an outlet for voicing feedback? How is morale? Most who say, "I hate . . . web sites" are actually ex-employees. Did you just go through a round of layoffs? You may want to think about how your employee base will react.

6. *How do we describe our corporate culture?* Do you or your employees have a clear idea of your culture? It will come

out, so be prepared. If your management team is more paranoid than North Korea, don't expect to see a rosy picture put forth to potential customers. Corporate culture is one area that definitely shows up on social media.

7. *What is the line between personal and professional branding?* If an employee posts information concerning his or her company on a personal page, who owns the content? Can you influence what someone posts in his or her spare time about himself or herself? The short answer is that if the person shares with the world that he or she is an employee of the company, then that person is responsible to the company for protecting the brand.

8. *What do we want the world to know about us as a company?* Your employees are ambassadors for your company, for better or worse. For many prospective buyers, their first point of introduction may be through the social interactions of an employee, whether professional or personal. If you don't have a clear message, what do you think will happen in the market?

9. *What are our expectations around professionalism for our employees?* If you have a dress code, code of conduct, and so forth, then it would be logical to have a more restrictive code for social media conduct. If you have loose expectations around how employees are expected to engage, then you probably don't expect to have a corporate image projected from your employees.

10. *Who owns the relationship/account?* If your junior account team person connects to one of your customer's employees, what happens when that employee leaves your company? Who owns the customer when a sales rep leaves who is directly connected to the customer on LinkedIn? How about when they have built their pipeline over social media? What happens when your customer service people build a following on Twitter with a personally branded account? What if your employee starts an account on behalf of the company?

Certainly not easy questions, but then again, social media is a disruptive force, which I believe will evolve many industries.

Social Market Leadership—What's Your Next Move?

I'm convinced that the longer you stay in the consulting business, the more you tend to see it all. I actually had an executive tell me that he saw no value in social media, other than a waste of his already limited resources, and that he had been there for more than 30 years, so he must have done something right! Needless to say, it was a very short meeting.

What he and many other executives underestimate is the need for both a defensive strategy (to protect their brands) and an offensive approach (to take their message to the market) toward driving growth opportunities. By the way, the last time I checked, you cannot score and therefore win playing defense alone.

So, why did the executive fear exploring this new medium? I refer to it as the "cozy complacent syndrome," and it's more of a mind-set challenge than anything else. No one ever gets fired if they hire IBM, execute a strategy McKinsey recommends, or become a "fast follower." The comfort in cozy complacent syndrome is that people with this affliction allow others to take the innovation risk and think that they can swoop in, copy their ideas, and still end up winning the race!

Here are five reasons a fast follower strategy is a losing proposition when it comes to social market leadership:

1. **You start by taking a reactive posture!** As a fast follower, you're intentionally sitting back to see what the rest of the market does. Your ideas, processes, and operation are trained to react. You have abdicated any real vision to uncover new opportunities. How's that working out for you so far? And by the way, how will you ever attract world-class A-players when you're positioning yourself as always letting

others explore innovative ideas? Without forward-thinking people, processes, and operations, when the disruption comes—and make no mistake about it, social media is disruptive—you won't have the internal capabilities to respond!

2. **You need highly optimized decision making and new product development and launch practice in the world!** As a fast follower, given the incredibly fast-paced nature of social media (I'm humbled by what I learn in this space on a *daily* basis), you'll need the infrastructure to decide exactly when to enter the market with a social media campaign or reengineer or rearchitect a competitor's campaign in a way that the target customers view them as indistinguishable. And you still need to drive the marketing gravity/pull from your efforts. In the digital relationship maturity model, to go from doing nothing and being reactive to crossing the proverbial chasm to becoming proactive, predictive, and visionary requires pioneers, slow followers, and laggards. Note that not included in this list were fast followers; I've yet to meet a successful fast follower.

3. **You'll need a lengthy social market leadership strategy cycle.** As a fast follower, you'll need time to gear up, copy the innovators, and get a strategy, a road map, and a campaign put together before the onslaught of competition does the same. Not to mention the work you need to do to actually build, nurture, and turn digital relationships into revenues and profits before the window of opportunity deteriorates. Although this kind of thinking may have been successful in the past, the pace of change and speed of doing business directly (online) has increased to the point where product and service cycles are much shorter, and influencer marketing today wins market share tomorrow.

4. **You'll need the right people to follow!** As a fast follower, you'll need to listen to the right people online, follow their every move, and hope like mad that the firm

has good insights. And revenues/results today are actually lagging indicators of past sales and marketing success, so the results you see today may in fact be dramatically different than what lies ahead. Imagine following Wang or DEC computers in the 1980s, or even the mighty Apple in the 1990s, before the iPod. These market leaders suffered great losses; Wang and DEC never recovered, and Apple did so only due to consumer electronics, not computers. So, for everyone following Sony with the Walkman and the Discman, how did that fast follower strategy work for you? Social market leadership requires the same agility to move quickly and to learn from it for the next campaign if a particular approach doesn't yield the desired results.

5. **You'll need to change the view.** I remember seeing a poster of a dog sled team years ago when I was at SGI (another market leader that went off the cliff). The poster read, "If you're not the lead dog, the view never changes." Innovators are constantly in the front, exploring new views of uncharted market opportunities. I often ask prospective clients what's the "iPod" of their industry, and when they struggle to respond, it's a telltale sign that innovation, although a desired trait, may not be part of the organization's DNA. Becoming the next anything is really boring—even Google, a market innovator, was just the next Yahoo!

When it comes to social market leadership, it's time to leave the cozy complacent mind-set and become the "first something."

Tomorrow's Social CEO

I recently presented social market leadership to a group of executives, and the consensus was that senior executives, and CEOs in particular, are not social today. A recent Forrester Research study confirms that very few of the CEOs or board members at top global companies have any material presence on the popular social media sites.

I submit they should, and here's why. Social media continues to play an ever-growing part in our lives. As the next generation of leaders rise to become CEOs, consumer trends, consumption, and preferences will change and social media will continue its ubiquitous trend. CEOs who have a firm grasp of social media will speak the new language of their stakeholders and can leverage this medium when recruiting, scouting market opportunities, engaging and nurturing relationships with their end consumers (think B2B2C strategies), and empowering social customer relationship management (CRM).

Unfortunately, in our current research of *Fortune* 500 CEOs, we've found very few who have a social profile. This abstinence, fueled by the more vulnerable publicly traded companies, even extends to CEOs of technology companies. For example, Eric Schmidt of Google is an infrequent Twitterer and is not a blogger; Steve Ballmer of Microsoft has no blog and no Twitter account; Michael Dell is on Twitter but is not an external blogger. Steve Jobs of Apple and Larry Ellison of Oracle have no Twitter, Facebook, LinkedIn, or blog presence that we could find.

I believe in the coming years there will be a changing of the guard that favors social media over silence. Online users spend an estimated 23 percent of their time on social networking sites— twice as much time as we spend on any other online activity. Consider where many of us get our news: less from the direct sources such as the *Wall Street Journal*, the *New York Times*, or television broadcasts, and much more through social networks.

But it is not just end consumers. Enterprises are increasingly becoming more social; regardless of their size, internally and externally, they continue to be influenced and affected by social media. Social media has the potential to significantly increase the live television viewing audience and alter public perceptions of a political candidate, a nonprofit cause, or an organization's ethical and responsible behaviors.

Look around and ask yourself, can a CEO remain relevant if he or she is not versed in the new language of the broad constituents being served?

The next generation of CEOs will possess drastically different attitudes when it comes to content and information sharing with public and private domains. We see definitive examples today of the companies that actively monitor, react to, and engage with what business and consumers are saying about them, outpacing their competitive peers. The immediacy of social media is making long, drawn-out research campaigns or focus groups cumbersome and outdated by the time the results are published.

A number of our clients are using Twitter to test new product or service ideas; they're getting immediate feedback from a broad base of distribution channels, alliance partners, and end consumers of their ultimate value-added services. They're learning firsthand unique applications of their products or services and are building and nurturing powerful communities of like-minded individuals. It's a robust combination of scale with the granularity to make a substantive change—quickly and in a much more responsive manner than previously possible.

The next generation of business leaders will be versed in social media. I don't need a crystal ball to predict how CEOs in the future will use social media. Here are five best practices that many of the socially engaged CEOs of today are implementing:

1. They're targeting a defined audience. They have a clear reason to be social and have something valuable and distinctive to say. They have established succinct social expectations, and they're choosing the right platforms.
2. They're enhancing their paid and earned media strategies with social market leadership—which is about both a

defensive and an offensive presence. Defensively, they're protecting their brand, while offensively they're articulating a vision.

3. They're using social media to become talent scouts, attracting and retaining the brightest minds—both within and external to the organization.

4. They're using social media to become signal scouts via their competitors, the thought leadership community, and potential merger and acquisition targets.

5. Visionary CEOs are implementing social CRM dashboards within their enterprises. Customer support is using social media tools such as CoTweet to answer questions; sales organizations are using social media to identify more real-time, self-opted prospects and read what's really happening with their customers; and savvy marketing teams are using social media to identify new channels to connect with new or existing customers.

Final Thoughts

I know you had a lot of reading choices, and whether you purchased this book or it was given to you, I'm grateful for the gift of your time. I hope you found the content of interest and value, whether as a reminder of the critical importance of relationships you already possess or as a source of some new insights on how to more intentionally, strategically, and thus quantifiably transform your most valuable business contacts into personal and professional success. Keep in mind several of the key concepts:

- There is a Grand Canyon–sized difference between knowing relationships are important and doing the right things and doing them now.

- You may know that relationships are critical, but is that knowledge cascading down to your respective teams?

- As a society, we're becoming increasingly disconnected, and in many ways, we're losing our ability to engage people—those who will make decisions to work with us, support us, help us, work for us, and go above and beyond the call of duty on our behalf. They do this not simply because of our authority, but because they know, like, trust, and respect us.

- People can't trust you unless you give them an opportunity to get to know you. Give them the chance to do just that, and get to know who they are, not simply what they do.

- Relationships are an investment. Read the prospectus, aim to enhance your portfolio of relationships, and diversify and build for quality, not just quantity. Throw away the stopwatch and get a compass!

- Influence the conversations and you'll influence the relationships. Influence the relationships and you'll influence the outcomes you desire.

- You don't have the bandwidth to invest in everyone equally, so how will you prioritize your most valuable relationships?

- It's never about the coffee or the meal. It's about an opportunity to engage others and not only strengthen your existing relationship bank but expand your portfolio of pivotal contacts.

- You can't possibly improve anything you don't measure. Create a value pyramid of your current relationships and identify those critical and most instrumental to your success—both today and in the future.

- Your 2 A.M.s and Joans will help you think big and constantly raise the bar on your personal and professional development.

Finally, do justice, love kindness, walk humbly—sometimes they come together in a single encounter. The late Thurgood Marshall, Supreme Court Justice, was one of the young lawyers who argued the *Brown v. Board of Education* case, which ended the injustice of legal school segregation. He once said:

> People are people; strike them and they will cry out; cut them and they will bleed; starve them, and they wither away and die. But treat them with respect and decency; give them equal access to the levers of power, attend to their aspirations and grievances, and they will flourish and grow and join together to form a more perfect union.

Here's to your strategic relationship success!

—David
www.RelationshipEconomics.net

About the Author

David Nour is *the* thought leader on Relationship Economics®—the quantifiable value of business relationships. In a global economy that is becoming increasingly disconnected, The Nour Group, Inc., has attracted *Fortune* 100 consulting clients and driven unprecedented growth through a unique return on their strategic relationships. David has pioneered the phenomenon that relationships are the greatest off–balance sheet asset of any organization, large or small, public or private.

He annually delivers 50 keynote speeches at leading industry association conferences, corporate meetings, and academic forums. He is often a guest lecturer at the Goizueta Business School at Emory University and Georgia Tech's College of Management. He is an active member of several professional organizations, including the Association for Corporate Growth (ACG), American Management Association (AMA), Institute of Management Consultants (IMC), and the Society of International Business Fellows (SIBF).

David's unique perspective and independent insights on relationship economics have been featured in a variety of prominent blogs and publications, including the *Wall Street Journal*, the *New York Times*, the *Atlanta Journal and Constitution*, *Association Now*, *Entrepreneur*, and *Success* magazine. He is the author of several books, including *ConnectAbility* (McGraw-Hill), *The Entrepreneur's Guide to Raising Capital* (Praeger), and the *Social Networking Best Practices* series.

An Eagle Scout himself, David is passionate about youth with his foundation's support of the Centennial Scouting movement, Junior Achievement, One Voice (aiming to create peace in the Middle East), and the High Tech Ministries.

A native of Iran, David came to the United States with a suitcase, $100, limited family ties, and no fluency in English. He earned an executive MBA degree from the Goizueta Business School at Emory University and a BA degree in management from Georgia State University.

For more information:
The Nour Group, Inc.
888-339-1333 | 404-419-2115
info@relationshipeconomics.net

David Nour Speaking Topics

Relationship Economics®:
The Art and Science of Relationships

This 2010–2011 cornerstone keynote speech has been delivered to more than 50 corporate, association, and academic forums; it is based on the best-selling book *Relationship Economics* and is focused on the quantifiable value of business relationships and a systematic process to identify, build, nurture, and leverage personal, functional, and strategic relationships. Socially enabling individuals and institutions to drive results is also covered in this session.

Customer Economics™: Fueling Enterprise Growth Through a Holistic Social Customer Life Cycle

Based on a new book, *customer economics* encompasses the vision and the discipline to reorient organizations from their current functional structures and line of business go-to-market strategies to adopt a more holistic view of their customers. Social media has helped swing the power pendulum to the customer while many industries con-tinue to get disintermediated. Customer economics isn't about Facebook, Twit-ter, or YouTube. It's about socially enabling organizations to listen louder and think faster, so they can respond in real time to changing market dynamics, and in the process, adapt their revenue models, reinvent themselves, and grow their top lines, top talent, and top relationships.

Adaptive Innovation™: Adaptable Business Models for Changing Market Demands

How do you create greater market value than your competitors? How do you help your distributors differentiate your products or services? Simple. Disrupt your value chain! *Adaptive innova-tion*, by definition, is destructive in its character, is open to a broad base of business models, and must be driven by high-performing teams—teams that are focused on maximizing the current and future capabilities of their respective organizations. To create sustainable competitive advantage, companies must develop a relationship-centric culture with the courage to fail and learn from those failures.

ConnectAbility™: Eight Keys to Building Strong Partnerships with Your Colleagues and Your Customers

Driven by the newly released *ConnectAbility* book (McGraw-Hill), this discussion focuses on a systematic approach for developing superior partnerships (manufacturer/distributor, wholesaler/reseller) by applying powerful lessons learned from emotional awareness, personal authenticity, humor, and servant leadership.

Inner Circle™: Who Are You Listening To?

Global chief executive officers (CEOs), politicians, professional athletes, and award-winning entertainers all rely on an inner circle of trusted advisers. How about you? Who is in your inner circle, how did they get there, and what makes them so valuable? Whose inner circle do you belong to, how did you get in, and what are the rules for confidentiality and self-interest? If you're not in, what will it take to become the voice others listen to and rely on?

The Immigrant Success DNA: What Immigrants Do That Americans Have Forgotten!

First-generation immigrants are four times more likely to become millionaires in this country than those who were born here. Why? This compelling presentation uses a series of immigrant success stories to convey their inherent drive, commitment, work ethic, and dedication to personal and professional development.

Flight Risk™: Why Most High Potentials Leave!

All of those A-players you've spent time, effort, and resources on are walking out the door—maybe not physically, but certainly mentally. Learn why they leave and how to keep four generations of a diverse workforce wanting to stay.

Delivery Options

- *Keynote speech*—60 to 90 minutes in duration, including copies the book of *Relationship Economics*
- *Keynote speech and breakout session(s)*—preceding option, plus a two- to three-hour mini-workshop and a town hall–format discussion to further help the attendees internalize the key messages
- *Keynote speech, breakout session(s), and follow-through*—preceding option, plus a series of webinars, digital or field town hall meetings, or 10 × 10 × 10 Strategic Relationship Planning™ (SRP) advisory, coaching, and mentoring

Index

ABC (television network), 241

Accelerated access, 172

Access level, 173

Access spectrum, 185

Accountability, 229

Accountants, 22, 153, 156

Achieving Success Through Social Capital: Tapping Hidden Resources in Your Personal and Business Networks (Wayne), 14

Acquisitions, 149

Acquisitions vs. mergers, 139

Action plan for large-scale change or mergers and acquisitions
  about, 244–245
  pretransaction due diligence, 245–246
  first 100 days, 246–248
  longer term, 248–249

Adams, Stephen, 225

Adaptive innovation, 138–139, 221, 222–223

Adaptive innovation value chain, 224

Addition strategy, 152–153

Ad-hoc relationships, 148

Affiliate relationships, 148

Ahmad, Sameena, 210

Albrecht, Karl, 97

Alexander, Greg, 58–61

Ali Reza, Fasil, 38

AlliedSignal-Honeywell merger, 246

Al-Saie, Basim, 38

Alston + Bird, 158

The Anatomy of Buzz: How to Create Word of Mouth Marketing (Rosen), 15

Anderson, Jonathan, 210

Apple, 130, 221

Approvers, 174–175

Association for Corporate Growth (ACG) Thompson survey, 55

A-Team development
  hard asset focus of, 237–238
  profiling potential leaders, 66
  relationship development, 67
  relationship development challenges and opportunities, 68
  relationship development learning environment, 69–70
  relationship-centric assessments, 70
  relationship-centric goals, 68–69
  relationship-centric on-boarding, 67
  relationship-centric role models, 67–68

Attorneys, 22, 153, 156, 179–180

Axelrod, Beth, 58

B2B environment, 260

Bain study, 229

Baker, Chloe, 182

Baker, Wayne, 14

Bakosh, Rick, 60–61

Ballmer, Steve, 280

Barnes, Jay, 122

Bates, Adam, 124

Bechtel Group, 241

Beckstrom, Rod, 14, 75, 125–127

Behavioral assessment tools, 123

Behavioral assessments, 70

Beyond Budgeting (Hope and Fraser), 93

Big Four accounting firms, 147

Blank, Arthur, 70

Blink: The Power of Thinking Without Thinking (Gladwell), 15, 212

Blue Ocean Strategy (Kim and Mauborgne), 211

Blueprint for high-performing teams, 55–57

Blueprint for strategic relationship planning (SRP)
  historical perspectives, 107–108
  looking forward, 108–114
  return on involvement, 114–118

Bluffing, 256

Board-level social network, 32

Boone, Jim, 82

Bossidy, Larry, 79

Bowling Alone: The Collapse and Revival of American Community (Putnam), 3, 15

Bowtie effect, 111–112

Brafman, Ori, 14, 125–127

Brand awareness vs. business development
  about, 145–146
  before being customers, 146–151
  after being customers, 151–153

"The Brand Called You" (FirstCompany), 134

Brand equity, 210

Brand identification, 270

Branding and sales vs. strategic business relationships, 147

Breadth and depth, 183–184

Bricks-and-mortar advantage, 262

Broad-based generalists, 184

Brokerage and Closure (Burt), 14

Brown, Dan, 22–24, 102, 166

Buckets, 203

Bureaucratic wordsmithers, 274

Burt, Ron, 14

Business development, 147, 155

Business ethics vs. ethics, 229

Business process engineering (BPR), 235

Business relationships, 241

Business-relationship "don'ts," 25, 35

Buyer behavior, core shift in, 259–262

Buying cycle, 266

Buzz: Accelerating Natural Contagion (Rosen), 15

Campaigns for change vs. governing change, 141–142

Candor
  lack of, 229
  lack of, in corporate America, 239–244
  and responsibility, 243
  as way to retain and develop talent, 102

CBS (television network), 241

Centers of influence, 48–49

Centralized planning, 92

Chaet, Bob, 35

Challenges of relationship-centric goals, 161–162

Change agents
  competencies of, 232
  nature of, 231
  recruitment and development of, 233
  relationships of, 189
  social networks of, 235

Change management
  about, 229–230
  action plan for large-scale change or mergers and acquisitions, 244–249
  change through merger and acquisitions, 237–239
  influencers and the influenced, 236–237
  lack of candor and stand in corporate America, 239–244
  networkers of influence as strategic asset in, 234–236
  strategic relationships of key agents in navigating change, 230–234

Change through merger and acquisitions, 237–239

Channel partners, 149

Churchill, Winston, 117

Cialdini, Robert, 15

Citizen editors, 271

Client-centric teams, 158

Cognitive process, 191

Cohen, Don, 15

Collaboration, 234

Colleague status, 257

Command-and-control culture, 131, 275

Commitment, 243

Commodity town path, 26

Competencies, individual, 56–57

Competency, elements of, 157–158

Competency gaps, 248

Competitive differentiation, 97, 105

ComScore, 264

Configuration process, 192

Conley, Keith, 25

ConnectAbility (Nour and Ryback), 118

Connection abuse, 258

Connections map, 138

Consortiums, 148

Consultants, 22, 153, 180

Contact and context, 212

Contacts vs. relationships, 43, 196

Content curators, role of and activities
    of, 269–273

Content reputation, 211–214

Continuous opportunity, 10–11

Convenience factor, 262

Co-opetition, 224

Core values statement, 192

Corporate brand vs. personal brand, 276

Corporate culture, 275–276

Corporate image, 276

Corporate reputation, 105–107

Corporate transparency, 275

Cost centers and revenue producers,
    272–273

Costs, 99–100

Courage to fail, 242–243

Covey, Stephen M. R., 15

Coyle, James, 236

Cozy compliant syndrome, 277

Credibility, 232

Cross, Rob, 125, 128

"Cross Border Investigations" (KPMG),
    124

Cubic growth, 46

Cultural impacts and change, 244

Cultural influences, 210

Cultural process, 191

Currency exchange
    content reputation, 211–214
    meeting overlaps, 215
    out-of-office contacts, 214–215
    personal brand construction, 211
    relationship deposits, 215–216
    relationship knowledge, 214
    travel and horizon growth, 209–211

Current relationship bank, 108–110

Customer life cycle, 266

Customer preferences, 147

Customer support, 282

Dailey, Pat, 19, 28–30

Daily view of goals, 162

Daniels, Charles, 150

Danzig, Bob, 103

Darrow, Tom, 242–243

Decentralized organizations, 127

Decentralized relationship network, 103

Decision makers, 173–174

Decision process, 262

Decision role, formal, 173

Decision timelines, 247

Dell (company), 146

Dell, Michael, 280

Design process, 189–190

Destiny shapers, 103

Dialog tracks, 272

Dig Your Well Before You're Thirsty
    (Mackay), 15

Digital dialogs, 270–271

Direct goals, 160

Distribution partners, 149

Diversification difficulties, 171

Diversity

    quality, and required investments, 201–206

    role of, 169

    of social networks, 123

Diversity characteristics, 195

Division barrier, 194

Driving Results through Social Networks: How Top Organizations Leverage Networks for Performance and Growth (Cross), 125

Dodds, Peter Sheridan, 236–237

Due diligence of relationships, 238

Ebbert, Stephen, 26–28

Eisenhower, Dwight, 117

Ellison, Larry, 280

Enabling Positive Social Capital in Organizations (Wayne), 14

Engineers, 153

Entrepreneurial process, 191

Environmental process, 191–192

Equity goals, 161

Execution (Bossidy), 79, 211

Execution skills, 176–177

Expansion strategy, 152–153

Experience Economy (Pine and Gilmore), 267

Exponential growth, 47

Facebook, 3, 4, 121, 253–254, 259, 269, 273, 280

Fast follower strategy, 277–279

Favor economy, 16, 216

Fear of reactions, 239–240, 242

Fear of standing out, 240

Feedback sources, 281

First 100 days action plan, 246–248

FirstCompany (magazine), 134

Florcruz, Jamie, 210

Focus and bandwidth, 270

Follow the money approach, 154

Following through system, 113–114

Ford Motor Company, 93

Forrester Research, 279–280

Fraser, Robin, 93

Freakonomics (Levitt and Dubner), 212

Frustrations, 192–195

Fuel efficiency, 52

Fuel efficiency of growth, 53

Functional areas appropriate for social network analysis (SNA)

    adaptive innovation, 138–139

    large-scale change and mergers and acquisitions, 139–141

    leadership development, 131–136

    revenue growth, 129–131

    strategy execution, 136–138

Fundamental flaws in strategic relationship planning (SRP), 91–94

Future builders, 103

Future-proofed strategy, 95, 96

Fuzzy goals, 7–8

Gatekeepers, 177

Generalists, 183, 184

Givers, 102

Giving, 36

Gladwell, Malcolm, 15, 121

Goals. *See also* relationship-centric goals; relationship-centric goals for revenue growth

    quantifiable, 217

    and realism, 161–162

Goals, strategies, objectives, and tactics (GSOT), 165

Godin, Seth, 237

Goldsmith, David, 148

Good to Great (Collins), 61, 211

Google, 12, 31, 172, 204, 225, 265

Gossip and Reputation (Burt), 14

Growth, attributes of, 4

Growth probability, 52–54

Growth slope, 46–50

Growth speed, 50–51

Guilt by association, 257
Gupta, Marty, 189

Handfield-Jones, Helen, 58
Hanifan, L. J., 3
Haphazard and reactive efforts, 9–16
Hard assets, 46, 238
Harvesting conversations, 17
Hayzlett, James, 4
Heath, Chip, 239
Heath, Dale, 239
Heavy Hitter Selling: How Successful Salespeople Use Language and Intuition to Persuade Customers to Buy. (Martin), 4
Heavy hitters, 23
Hey phenomenon, 240
High-value generalists, 184
Historical perspectives, 107–108
Home Depot, 70–71, 158
Hope, Jeremy, 93
Human resources (HR) strategic relationships, 65

Illinois Power, 241
In Good Company: How Social Capital Makes Organizations Work (Cohen and Prusak), 15
In Search of Excellence (Peters), 211
Inc. (magazine), 172
Inclusion as strategic asset, 168–169
Incrementalism, 98
Incrementalism vs. innovation, 138
Industry image, 105
Influence, 94
Influence goals, 160
Influence: The Psychology of Persuasion (Cialdini), 15
Influencer marketing, 264
Influencers and the influenced, 236–237
Influencer's impact on decision process, 262–264
Influential hubs, 22

Information distribution model, 264
Information technology, 140
Innovation, 98, 153
Innovation strategy, 152
Innovation vs. advertising, 220–222
Innovation vs. incrementalism, 138
Innovators and uncharted market opportunities, 279
Intellectual capital, 116
Intellectual property (IP), 269, 275
Interaction phase, 9–24
Interim leadership, 132
Intracompany relationships, 37
Investment effort required, 186
Investment focus vs. transaction-centric focus, 60
Investment relationship, 198–199
Investors, 36–37
Invitations, 256

Jarrett, Kenneth, 210
Jigsaw, 30, 253
Jobs, Steve, 130, 221, 280
Johnson, Stuart, 181
Joint ventures, 149
Journal of Applied Psychology, 55

Kasanoff, Bruce, 262
Kennedy, J. F., 90
Key enablers, 195–201
Keywords, 265
Kraft Foods Canada, 240

Lack of candor and stand in corporate America, 239–244
Lack of purpose, 6–9
Large-scale change and mergers and acquisitions, 139–141
Leadership, interim, 132
Leadership development
    about, 165
    inclusion as strategic asset, 168–169
    mentoring program for, 131–136

Leadership development (*Continued*)
  myopia in, 165–168
  pivotal contact relationship investment
    matrix, 182–186
  pivotal contacts, 172–176
  pivotal contacts, sources of, 176–182
  portfolio diversification, 169–171
Leadership development program
    failures, 165
Leadership focus, 166
Learning foundation, 64
Learning process, 191
Lessons learned, 44
Level of influence relationship, 200–201
Lever arm, 51
*Light the Night Walk for Leukemia and
    Lymphoma Society*, 182
Linear growth, 46
LinkedIn, 30, 121, 253–259, 261, 265,
    269, 271, 276, 280
LinkedIn etiquette, 255–259
Longer term action plan, 248–249
Looking forward
  current relationship bank, 108–110
  following through system, 113–114
  most valuable relationships, 110–113
  relationship currency exchange,
    113–114
  relationship resource allocation,
    109–110
Luminaries, 184

Mackay, Harvey, 15
Made to Stick (Heath and Heath), 239
Management barrier, 194
Mapping the water cooler, 104
Marcus, Bernie, 70
Marginville path, 26
Marketing
  vs. business development, 155
  online vs. offline, 266
Marshall, Thurgood, 283–284
Martin, Steve W., 3

Matrix effectiveness, 103–105
McClelland, Mac, 73–74
McGaw, Steve, 78
McIntosh, Bob, 20
McKinsey Quarterly, 31
Media kits, 261, 265
Mediocrity as norm, 241
Meeting overlaps, 215
Mentors, 45, 64, 135, 199
Mentzberg, Henry, 189
Mercer/Business Week study, 229
Merger and acquisition advisors, 180
Mergers, 149
Mergers and acquisitions. *See also* action
    plan for large-scale change or
    mergers and acquisitions
  change through, 237–239
  failures of, 229
  large-scale change and, 139–141
  losses through, 239
Mergers vs. acquisitions, 139–141
Message and delivery of speakers, 83–86
Michaels, Ed, 58
The Mirror Test (Hayzlett), 4
Mission statement, 192
Mobil Oil, 241
Money Tree Report (Pricewaterhouse
    Coopers), 225
Monitoring programs, 135–136
Mother Teresa (Agnes Gonxha Bojaxhi),
    34, 35
Moye, John, 182
Moye, Pam, 182
Munson, Elizabeth, 182
Munson, Jim, 182
Mutual trust, 125
Mutual trust, respect and value, 177
Myopia in leadership development,
    165–168

Nardelli, Bob, 70–71
Network Duality of Social Capital (Burt),
    14

Networkers of influence as strategic
asset, 234–236
Networking, phases of
corporate relationship deficit disorder,
37
cultural divide, 38–39
follow-through phase, 23–37
interaction phase, 9–24
preparation phase, 5–9
Networking failure, reasons for
engagement of wrong people, 21–24
failure to arm others with right
ammunition, 24–30
fuzzy goals, 7–8
givers, takers, and investors, 34–37
haphazard and reactive efforts, 9–16
lack of purpose, 6–9
premia, 5–39
relationship development plan
absence, 8–9
Niche specialists, 184
No access personnel, 178–179
Not invented here (NIH) culture, 232, 272
Nour, David, 30

"1toEverything: A Customer's View of
the Connected World" (Kasanoff),
262, 263
Online efforts, return on investment of,
253
Opportunity costs
of change, 246
in relationship building, 218
of status quo, 232
Organization chart, traditional, 104
Organizational application and impact
of social network analysis (SNA),
128–129
Organizational growth
about, 45–46
growth probability, 52–54
growth slope, 46–50
growth speed, 50–51

Oster, Shai, 210
Ostrich look-a-like approach, 273
Ostwalt, Phil, 123–124
Out-of-office contacts, 214–215
Outsiders as leaders, 133

Paparelli, Charlie, 23
Parayre, Roch, 95–97
Parker, Andrew, 128
Patches vs. dyes concept, 10–11
Peer influence, 166
Peer-level relationship mentors, 64
People barrier, 194
Performance evaluations, 102–103, 133
Personal action plans, 91
Personal brand, 216
Personal brand attributes and
development, 134–135
Personal brand construction, 211
Personal brand equity, 210
Personal brand vs. corporate brand,
276
Personal evaluations, 167
Personal relationship plan, 217–220
Personal SWOT profiles, 134
Peters, Tom, 134
Pillars of strategic relationship planning
(SRP)
competitive differentiation, 105
corporate reputation, 105–107
cost, 99–100
matrix effectiveness, 103–105
process optimization, 100
revenue growth, 98
strategic focus, 95, 97–98
talent development, 100–103
Pivotal contact relationship investment
matrix
about, 182–183
access spectrum, 185
breadth and depth, 183–184
investment effort required, 186
relevancy, 184–185

Pivotal contact sources
  no access personnel, 178–179
  restricted access personnel, 178
  unrestricted access personnel, 178
Pivotal contacts
  about, 172–173
  approvers, 174–175
  decision makers, 173–174
  decision role unknown, 176
  described, 166
  exclusive and memorable experiences
    for, 182
  and philanthropic causes, 181–182
  prioritized matrix, 183
  return on involvement, 114–115
  sources of leadership development,
    176–182
  in strategic relationship plan, 91
  user-evaluator, 175–176
Planning process, 91, 190
Planning vs. strategy, 89
Platform, social media as, 254
Plato, 168
Political savvy, 167–168
Porter, Michael, 190
Portfolio diversification, 169–171
Portfolio of relationships as
    differentiating asset, 224–226
Portfolio relationship, 199
Positioning process, 190
*Positive Organizational Network Analysis
    and Energizing Relationships*
    (Wayne), 14
Power process, 191
*The Practice of Social Influence in Multiple
    Cultures* (Cialdini), 15
Premortem evaluation, 245
Preparation phase, 5–9
Presence through social networking, 254
Pretransaction due diligence, 245–246
PricewaterhouseCoopers, 158, 225
Private equity advisors, 180
Private individuals, 177

Process optimization, 100
Productive relationships, 75
Professional certification process flaws,
    156–157
Professionals struggling with
    relationship-centric goals for
    revenue growth, 153–156
Profitability of growth, 53
Project joint ventures, 148–149
Protecting unique cultures, 240
Prusak, Laurence, 15
Psychological assessment tools,
    123
Public social networks, 254
Purcell, Kevin, 99–100
Purpose, 6–7, 254
Putnam, Robert, 15

Quality as mind-set, 229
Quality characteristics, 195
Quantifiable relationships
  organizational growth, 45–54
  relationship-centric culture, 54–59
  ROI reinvented, 71–86
  Rolodex value perception, 59–62
  strategic relationships on-boarding,
    62–71
  success map, 43–44
Quantifiable value, 20
Quantity characteristics, 195
Qubein, Nido, 213

Rainmakers, 155, 157
Reading and development, 82–83
Real change management, 230–232
Realism, goals for, 161
Reciprocity, 215, 216
Relationship advisory board, 65
Relationship assessments, 118
Relationship bank, 37, 91
Relationship bank attributes, 200
Relationship bank for strategy execution
  about, 189

diversity, quality and required
investments, 201–206
frustrations of, 192–195
investment relationship, 198–199
as key enabler, 195–201
level of influence relationship, 200–201
portfolio relationship, 199
relationship value pyramid, 196–197
schools of thought about, 189–192
situation relationship, 197–198
time and effort invested, 201
2 a.m. relationship, 199–200
Relationship building, 22
Relationship capitalization vs.
relationship creation, 4, 154
Relationship coaching, 65–66
Relationship competencies, 71
Relationship compliance training, 65
Relationship creation vs. relationship
capitalization, 4, 154
Relationship currency
defined, 113, 209
deposits of, 16, 209, 216–217
value promised and value delivered
through, 226
Relationship currency exchange, 91,
113–114
Relationship currency for adaptive
innovation
adaptive innovation, 222–223
exchanging currency, 209–217
innovation vs. advertising, 220–222
personal relationship plan, 217–220
portfolio of relationships as
differentiating asset, 224–226
relationship-centric innovation value
disruption, 223–224
Relationship deposits, 213, 215 216
Relationship development plan absence,
8–9
Relationship development training, 65
Relationship development vs.
transactional networks, 89

Relationship diversity, 108
Relationship DNA, 118
Relationship Dynamic Chart, 103,
125–126
Relationship dynamics, 125–127
Relationship economics
as art and science of relationships, 4–5
becoming an asset and arming with
information, 28–30
campaigns for change vs. governing
change, 141–142
heavy hitters at functions, 22–24
monitoring programs, 135–136
organizational paths, 26–27
performance and relationships, 20
relationship dynamics, 125–127
relationship-centric problem solving,
78
ROI reinvention, 89
sales transformation, 99–100
shared leadership, 132–133
super hubs, 73–74
transformation business development,
60–61
Relationship economics online tools
relationship assessments, 118
relationship value pyramid template,
206
Relationship economics retreat, 77
Relationship giving, 36
Relationship integration process, 66
Relationship investors, 36–37
Relationship knowledge, 214
Relationship quality, 108
Relationship resource allocation,
109–110
Relationship Signature DNA, 70
Relationship Signature Index (RSI), 70,
117–118
Relationship value pyramid, 196–197,
203–204
Relationship value pyramid template, 206
Relationship webs, 49

Relationship-centric best practices
  asking better questions, 17–18
  blueprint for high-performing teams, 55–57
  centers of influence, 48–49
  client-centric teams, 158
  continuous opportunity, 10–11
  courage to fail, 242–243
  daily view of goals, 162
  feet on the street, 150–151
  follow the money approach, 154
  LinkedIn etiquette, 255–259
  most influential, 172–173
  personal relationship plan, 219–220
  pivotal contacts, 172–176
  pivotal contacts and philanthropic causes, 181–182
  political savvy, 167–168
  protecting unique cultures, 240
  purpose, 6–7
  relationship currency deposits, 216–217
  relationship value pyramid, 203–204
  relevant contacts and reciprocity, 180–181
  self-evaluation, 80–82
  social market leadership tactics, 267–268
  A-Team development, 61–68
  value-based relationships, 13–15
  welcoming more than just the employee, 39
Relationship-centric culture, 54–59, 223
Relationship-centric goals
  challenges of, 161–162
  direct goals, 160
  equity goals, 161
  functional area benefits from, 129
  influence goals, 160
  in strategic relationship plan, 91
Relationship-centric goals for revenue growth
  about, 145

brand awareness vs. business development, 145–153
professional certification process flaws, 156–157
professionals struggling with, 153–156
relationship-centric goals, 159–162
reputational capital, elements of, 157–159
Relationship-centric innovation value disruption, 223–224
Relationship-centric innovators, 221
Relationship-centric organizations, 56–57
Relationship-centric problem solving, 78
Relationship-centric readiness, 79
Relationship-centric reading, 66
Relationship-centric values, 71
Relationships
  categorization of, 203–205
  vs. contacts, 43, 196
  most valuable, 110–113
  in postdigital world, 266–267
  social media directing, 253
Relevance, 257
Relevancy, 22, 184–185
Relevant contacts and reciprocity, 180–181
Replacement, 153
Reputation
  and market share, 146
  time to develop, 262
  of trust, 72
Reputation Perception Assessment (RPA), 118
Reputational capital, 114–118, 157–159
Reputational capital, elements of
  competency, 157–158
  trust, 158–159
Research, 83
Resources barrier, 195
Responsibility spreading, 133
Restricted access personnel, 178
Retained search executives, 180

Return on human capital, 62
Return on impact, 79–82
Return on impact matrix, 80
Return on influence, 72
Return on integration, 75
Return on investment, 71
Return on involvement
  focus and leadership role, 76–78
  pivotal contacts, 116–117
  relationship currency deposits, 217
  relationship signature index, 117–118
  reputational capital, 114–118
Return on objective, 116
Revenue growth, 98, 129–131
Revere, Paul, 121
Risk taking and innovation, 232
ROI reinvented
  about, 71
  becoming an object of interest, 82–86
  return on impact, 79–82
  return on influence, 72
  return on integration, 75
  return on involvement, 76–78
ROI reinvented tool, 86
ROI reinvention, 71–86, 89
Rolodex value perception, 59–62
Romer, Paul, 225
Root causes, 234, 235
Rosen, Edmund, 15
Rosenhaft, Matt, 254
Rotational leadership, 133
Rumelt, Richard, 91–92
Ryback, David, 118
Ryze, 253

Sales, 154
Sales transformation, 99–100
Sales turnover, 58
Scanning the periphery, 95
Schmidt, Eric, 280
Schools of thought about relationship
  bank for strategy execution, 189–192
Science News Online, 236

Scitex Vision, 247
Seidl, Randy, 99–100
Self-evaluation, 80–82
Selling after the sale, 151
Selling and buying processes, 260
The 7 Habits of Highly Effective People
  (Covey), 211–212
Shared leadership, 132–133
Shoestring model, 112
Signal scouts, 139
Silicon Graphics (SGI), 150, 235, 257
Silicon Valley, 225–226
Silo mentality, 232, 234
Silos, 138
Silvia, Dale, 135–136
Situation relationship, 197–198
Six Degrees: The Science of a Connected Age
  (Duncan), 15
60 Minutes (program), 241
Small business, 253
Smart, Brad, 55, 58, 59
Smith, Rick, 29–31
Smith, Will, 156
Social, definition, 254–255
Social capital, 3
Social CEO of tomorrow, 279–282
Social Gastronomy, 254
Social market leadership
  fast follower strategy, 277–279
  and media strategies, 281
  and purpose, 254
  strategy cycle, 278
  tactics, 267–268
Social media
  interaction steps throughout, 268
  as platform, 254
  with private access, 255
  target audience, 281
  uses of, 253
Social media and business relationships
  about, 253–254
  buyer behavior, core shift in, 259–262
  content curators, 269–273

Social media and business relationships
 (*Continued*)
  influencer's impact on decision
   process, 262–264
  relationships in postdigital world,
   266–267
  social market leadership, 277–279
  social media policy, 273–277
  social search vs. traditional search
   engines, 264–266
  tomorrow's social CEO, 279–282
  conclusions, 282–284
Social media conference, 253
Social media policies, 273–277
Social network analysis (SNA)
  about, 121–127
  diagram of, 122
  functional areas appropriate for,
   129–142
  organizational application and impact
   of, 128–129
  origins of, 121
  schools of thought about, 4
Social networking and presence,
  254
Social networking applications, 253
Social networking tools, 30–31
Social networks
  board level, 32
  of change agents, 235
  diversity of, 123
  power of, 128
  quality of, 124
  shape of, 123
Social Networks and Loss of Capital
  (Wayne), 14
Social search vs. traditional search
  engines, 264–266
Socially enabled buying process, 260
Soft assets, 46, 71, 238
Sony, 221
Speaking, message and delivery
  techniques, 83–86

Specialists, 183, 184
The Speed of Trust: The One Thing That
  Changes Everything (Covey), 15
Spin, 243
Spoke, 30, 253
Stand, 239
The Starfish and the Spider (Beckstrom),
  14, 75, 125
Status quo, 241
Strategic business relationships vs.
  branding and sales, 147
Strategic dashboard, 192
Strategic focus, 95, 97–98
Strategic Management Journal, 92
Strategic relationship on-boarding, 63
Strategic relationship planning (SRP)
  about, 89–91
  blueprint for, 107–108
  fundamental flaws in, 91–94
  pillars of, 95–107
Strategic relationship triangulation, 31, 33
Strategic relationships, 4, 45
Strategic relationships of key agents in
  navigating change, 230–234
Strategic relationships on-boarding
  about, 62–64
  best practices for, 64–66
Strategic service providers, 180
Strategy execution, 136–138
Strategy execution barriers to, 193–194
Strategy execution pyramid, 193
Strategy execution, schools of thought
  about
  cognitive process, 191
  configuration process, 192
  cultural process, 191
  design process, 189–190
  entrepreneurial process, 191
  environmental process, 191–192
  learning process, 191
  planning process, 190
  positioning process, 190
  power process, 191